COMPULSORY INCOME MANAGEMENT IN AUSTRALIA AND NEW ZEALAND

Also available in the Research in Comparative and Global Social Policy series

Welfare Reform and Social Investment Policy in Europe and East Asia

International Lessons and Policy Implications
Edited by **Young Jun Choi**, **Timo Fleckenstein** and **Soohyun Lee**

"A powerful, illuminating analysis of social investment policies across the lifecycle – this timely and useful volume is a must-read for those interested in a balanced perspective on recent developments in social policy."
Neil Gilbert, University of California, Berkeley

HB £75.00 ISBN 9781447352730
384 pages February 2021

Welfare, Populism and Welfare Chauvinism

By **Bent Greve**

"This important book sets out to tackle the welfare–populism nexus and convincingly shows that the new divisions in our societies instigate welfare chauvinism."
Steffen Mau, Humboldt University of Berlin

PB £26.99 ISBN 9781447350446
HB £75.00 ISBN 9781447350439
168 pages December 2020

Minimum Income Standards and Reference Budgets

International and Comparative Policy Perspectives
Edited by **Christopher Deeming**

"The volume offers a rich, historically and culturally grounded international menu of perspectives on an important social policy approach, with lessons for both research and policy at a time of growing economic insecurity."
Baroness Ruth Lister, Loughborough University

HB £75.00 ISBN 9781447352952
272 pages May 2020

Local Policies and the European Social Fund

Employment Policies Across Europe
By **Katharina Zimmermann**

"Moving beyond the methodological nationalism that has characterised most of the existing literature, this innovative study offers a fresh perspective on the variegated influence of European integration on social policy."
Daniel Clegg, University of Edinburgh

HB £75.00 ISBN 9781447346517
224 pages October 2019

For more information about the series visit
bristoluniversitypress.co.uk/research-in-comparative-and-global-social-policy

COMPULSORY INCOME MANAGEMENT IN AUSTRALIA AND NEW ZEALAND

More Harm than Good?

Greg Marston, Louise Humpage, Michelle Peterie, Philip Mendes, Shelley Bielefeld and Zoe Staines

First published in Great Britain in 2022 by

Policy Press, an imprint of
Bristol University Press
University of Bristol
1-9 Old Park Hill
Bristol
BS2 8BB
UK
t: +44 (0)117 374 6645
e: bup-info@bristol.ac.uk

Details of international sales and distribution partners are available at
policy.bristoluniversitypress.co.uk

British Library Cataloguing in Publication Data
A catalogue record for this book is available from the British Library

ISBN 978-1-4473-6149-7 hardcover
ISBN 978-1-4473-6150-3 ePub
ISBN 978-1-4473-6151-0 ePdf

Cover design: Andrew Corbett
Bristol University Press and Policy Press use environmentally responsible print partners.
Printed and bound in Great Britain by CPI Group (UK) Ltd, Croydon, CR0 4YY

FSC
www.fsc.org
MIX
Paper from responsible sources
FSC® C013604

Contents

List of abbreviations

ALRC	Australian Law Reform Commission
CDC	Cashless Debit Card
CIM	Compulsory Income Management
CCT	Conditional Cash Transfer
EFTPOS	electronic funds transfer at point of sale
IM	Income Management
MSD	Ministry of Social Development
NTER	Northern Territory Emergency Response
UBI	universal basic income
UBS	universal basic services

About the authors

Greg Marston is Professor in the School of Social Science at The University of Queensland, Australia. His research programme concerns poverty and unemployment, social security and social justice, work and emerging technologies. Prior to entering academia Greg worked in a range of peak bodies in the non-profit community services sector at state and national level. His publications include *The Australian Welfare State: Who Benefits Now?* (Palgrave Macmillan, 2013), *Half a Citizen: Reflections on Work and Welfare in Contemporary Australia* (Allen and Unwin, 2011) and *Social Policy and Discourse Analysis: Policy Change in Public Housing* (Ashgate Publishing, 2004).

Louise Humpage is Honorary Associate Professor in the School of Social Sciences at the University of Auckland, New Zealand. She has published widely on social policy, welfare reform, government policy for Indigenous peoples, refugee policy and resettlement, citizenship and public attitudes to the welfare state. Her sole-authored monograph, *Policy Change, Public Attitudes and Social Citizenship: Does Neoliberalism Matter?* was published by Policy Press in 2015. Louise left academia to work for Kāinga Ora, New Zealand's housing agency, in 2021.

Michelle Peterie is Research Fellow in the Sydney Centre for Healthy Societies at The University of Sydney, Australia, where she co-leads the Sydney Centre for Healthy Societies' research theme on Work, Education and Welfare. Michelle has published widely on lived experiences of un(der) employment, poverty and social security receipt, as well as the reverberating impacts of immigration detention. Michelle is the author of *Visiting Immigration Detention* (Bristol University Press, 2022) and the co-editor of *Emotions in Late Modernity* (Routledge, 2019). She is Associate Editor of *The Australian Journal of Social Issues* and a recent co-convener of The Australian Sociological Association's Sociology of Emotions and Affect thematic group.

Philip Mendes is Professor in the Department of Social Work at Monash University, Australia. His research interests include young people transitioning from out-of-home care, social security payments and welfare conditionality, supervised injecting facilities, and social workers and policy practice. He is the author or co-author of 12 books including *Young People Transitioning from Out-of-home Care: International Research, Policy and Practice* co-edited with Pamela Snow (Palgrave Macmillan, 2016), the third edition of *Australia's Welfare Wars* (UNSW Press, 2017) and *Empowerment and Control in the Australian Welfare State: A Critical Analysis of Australian Social Policy Since 1972* (Routledge, 2019).

Shelley Bielefeld is ARC DECRA Fellow and Senior Lecturer in the Griffith Law School and the Law Futures Centre at Griffith University, Australia. Shelley was the Inaugural Braithwaite Research Fellow at the School of Regulation and Global Governance (RegNet) at the Australian National University. Dr Bielefeld's interests include Indigenous law and policy, welfare law and policy, discrimination, intersectionality, racial states, regulation and governance and poverty surveillance. Her Australian Research Council funded projects are *Regulation and Governance for Indigenous Welfare: Poverty Surveillance and its Alternatives* (DE180100599) and *Conditional Welfare: A Comparative Case Study of Income Management Policies* (DP180101252).

Zoe Staines is ARC DECRA Senior Research Fellow in the School of Social Science at The University of Queensland, Australia. Her research interests include welfare conditionality, neoliberal subjectivities and decoloniality. She is particularly interested in exploring how social and penal policies combine to regulate, discipline, and punish those socially constructed as 'deviant', especially in settler colonial contexts. Zoe has published in top-tier national and international sociology, social policy, and criminology journals, is co-author of *Island Criminology* (Bristol University Press, forthcoming 2023), and is also Associate Editor of the *Australian Journal of Social Issues*.

Acknowledgements

The authors would like to thank all the participants who gave up their time to share their perspectives on income management in Australia and New Zealand. These firsthand accounts, from a diverse range of citizens, cut through the political spin and policy gloss that surrounds income management policies. Listening well, even when the words that are shared might make some policymakers and politicians feel uncomfortable or challenged, is a quality that is in short supply in many policy communities. We hope we have done justice to the powerful stories we gathered as we sought to understand and interpret the everyday experience of income management. In the words of the title of Dvora Yanow's classic book on interpretative policy analysis, we trust we have provided a sufficiently compelling answer to the question 'how does a policy mean?'.

We would also like to thank community stakeholders and advocates, academic researchers, policy advisers and politicians for sharing their perspectives on how income management operates at different levels; from the ground level to the ideational level of normative policy prescriptions, and the intermediary level of service delivery organisations in the different regions and capital cities across Australia and New Zealand. Finally, we would like to thank Dr Steven Roche and Dr Elfriede Sangkhul who provided invaluable research support at critical stages of the research project, a project that we are grateful was funded by the Australian Research Council.

Series preface

Heejung Chung (University of Kent, UK)
Alexandra Kaasch (University of Bielefeld, Germany)
Stefan Kühner (Lingnan University, Hong Kong)

In a world that is rapidly changing, increasingly connected and uncertain, there is a need to develop a shared applied policy analysis of welfare regimes around the globe. Research in Comparative and Global Social Policy is a series of books that addresses broad questions around how nation states and transnational policy actors manage globally shared challenges. In so doing, the book series includes a wide array of contributions, which discuss comparative social policy history, development and reform within a broad international context. Initially conceived during a meeting of the UK Social Policy Association Executive Committee in 2016, the book series invites innovative research by leading experts on all world-regions and global social policy actors and aims to fulfil the following objectives: it encourages cross-disciplinary approaches that develop theoretical frameworks reaching across individual world-regions and global actors; it seeks to provide evidence-based good practice examples that cross the bridge between academic research and practice; not least, it aims to provide a platform in which a wide range of innovative methodological approaches, may it be national case studies, larger-N comparative studies, or global social policy studies can be introduced to aid the evaluation, design, and implementation of future social policies.

Although social security remains one of the primary vehicles to alleviate poverty and enhance individuals' wellbeing, there is still fierce debate regarding the 'deservingness' and 'undeservingness' of cash welfare benefits worldwide. Across the political spectrum, the discourse on 'welfare conditionality' has embraced the notions of activation, reciprocity, communal responsibility, and even punitivism. In this latest contribution to the book series, Marston, Humpage, Peterie, Mendes, Bielefeld, and Staines offer a fascinating and timely account of the lived experiences of welfare conditionality based on a large number of interviews with income management participants and community stakeholders in Australia and New Zealand. Income management or, in the authors' words, the "widespread quarantining of social security payments" has been a unique feature of the Australian and New Zealand conditionality experience. Still, it carries much broader implications for philosophical and applied debates on social citizenship in other welfare geographies. By taking a critical approach that emphasises the value of bottom-up policy making, personal autonomy, relational and procedural justice, the authors demonstrate the practical fallacies of an ideological reliance on ever 'thinning' social rights in rapidly changing and digitising labour markets. By successfully giving voice to those directly affected by income management, the authors reimagine the relationship between government, individuals, and the communities they inhabit in a way that is of critical significance beyond the empirical cases of Australia and New Zealand and makes for captivating reading to all those searching for a new welfare settlement fit for the coming post-COVID-19 era.

1

Framing welfare conditionality

Introduction

The focus of this book is on social security and the lived effects of welfare conditionality in Australia and New Zealand. Our choice of terminology is deliberate. In normative terms, social security systems should facilitate a basic level of economic security by providing a source of income for individual citizens, regardless of their labour market status. In this sense, a social security system is a collective means of risk pooling and an expression of social citizenship in a modern welfare state. It is important to outline the normative basis for social security up front, particularly when public discourse about those who at some point in their lives depend on state income support is frequently derogatory. Terms like 'dole bludger' or 'scrounger' give contemporary expression to much older moral divisions between 'deserving' and 'undeserving' poor. These labels also have deep and lasting effects for those who are subject to them. Stigma, shame and the internalisation of negative messages about so-called 'welfare dependency' damage social security recipients' sense of self and contribute to feelings of exclusion from society (Patrick, 2017). Discourses about social security and welfare reflect various changes in social security policy goals.

One of the key changes in social security systems in the Anglophone world has been a shift away from poverty relief and towards labour force participation as a central policy aim. Related to this shift, work activation requirements and associated welfare conditionality (behavioural conditions attached to the receipt of payment) have increased in many countries over the past two to three decades (Clasen and Siegel, 2007; Patrick, 2017). Understanding this change entails acknowledging that the means and the ends of social security systems serve competing constituents and interests. Increased behavioural conditionality attached to the receipt of payments, for example, can receive popular support from the broader public, who have come to accept the conventional wisdom that 'getting tough' on social security recipients is both morally justifiable and ultimately beneficial for recipients. This belief persists despite a lack of research evidence to support or substantiate it. As is outlined in the chapters of this book, evidence about the costs and benefits of conditionality has had very little bearing on social security policy settings in Australia and New Zealand. George Lakoff (2004) argues that when the facts do not fit the mental frame of policymakers it is all too frequently the facts that get rejected, rather than the frame. This process is similar to confirmation bias, which is the tendency to interpret new evidence as confirmatory of one's existing beliefs or theories.

Populist views about welfare and social security recipients have become a powerful legitimising discourse for ramping up welfare conditionality. Embracing a paternalistic ethos, politicians of various ideological persuasions proclaim that they are going to 'end welfare as we know it' (Clinton, cited in Carcasson, 2006) or end 'the age of entitlement' (Hockey, 2012) as they reform social security systems with a view to 'providing a hand-up, not a hand-out'. What is implied by these political slogans is that low-income households and unemployed individuals need both 'sticks and carrots' in order to join society and to remain connected to mainstream values that centre on the virtues of paid employment, home ownership and the heteronormative family form. The emphasis on pre-determined means and ends in social policy alerts us to the continuing faith in the logic of the phrase 'help and hassle', coined in the mid-1990s by Lawrence Mead (1997, p 24) in his book *The New Paternalism: Supervisory Approaches to Poverty*. Mead's book and others like it became the inspiration for a range of conditional welfare schemes in Western Europe and in the US, Canada and Australia. Mead (1997, p 133) argues that, 'in the absence of prohibitive barriers to employment' and other market-based goods and services, 'the question of the personality of the poor emerges as the key to understanding and overcoming poverty'. In this policy paradigm, psychology and behavioural economics become the key forms of knowledge deployed to address poverty. One effect of a dominant behaviouralist discourse is that it de-politicises the problem of poverty by making the social problem of unemployment the problem of the unemployed. In turn, this ethos legitimises the disciplinary efforts of state authorities to change people's attitudes and behaviours through a mix of sanctions and incentives. Individualising discourses take the relations between work and welfare outside the collective realm of social interactions and institutional forces. Another effect of these discourses is to downplay precarity in the work–welfare nexus to the point where social insecurity becomes normalised (Wacquant, 2009).

The distribution of burdens and benefits across social security systems has become decidedly uneven. In many countries, for example, the receipt of an aged or invalidity pension consists of a relatively straightforward assets and income test to determine eligibility, whereas social security payments for citizens of workforce age tend to have additional participation requirements, which can range from workfare type schemes, applying for a certain number of jobs, or signing up to an employment service provider to participate in compulsory training. These conditions are not simply technical; they reflect cultural values around appropriate citizen–state relations and competing ideas about how to diagnose and address unemployment. The incremental design of social security systems involves a series of moral and political choices about redistribution of material resources and symbolic recognition of what counts as a valued social or economic activity, which is connected to social identity and status hierarchies. Acknowledging the broader social, political and cultural context of social security policy and practice matters if we want to fully comprehend the *why* and the *how* of policy change, as well as the contradictions between care and control that are inherent in welfare state dynamics.

A key test of the public accountability of governments is determining whether policies are effective in addressing stated objectives. It is also important to examine the unintended effects of policies, as the disjuncture between what is intended and the experience of what is implemented can be significant. As Ruth Patrick (2017, p 13) argues in her study of welfare reform in the UK: 'The mismatch between the policy narrative and approach on the one hand, and the lived experience of benefit claimants on the other, undermines the overarching welfare reform project and its posited rationale.' In a similar fashion, the aim of this book is to explore this disjuncture by asking critical questions about contractual constraints and behavioural expectations attached to the receipt of social security payments in the context of conditional welfare programmes in Australia and New Zealand. Both these countries have significantly ramped up the conditions attached to the receipt of cash transfers, particularly for Indigenous peoples and people of workforce age. Extending the use of conditional welfare has been central to successive governments in both countries. Similar to other nations, such as the US and many countries in Western Europe, the duration and severity of sanctions has increased. The coverage of these sanctions has also extended to groups that were previously exempt, such as sole parents and people with disabilities. What is unique to the Australian and New Zealand experience of conditionality, and which is the key empirical focus of this book, is the widespread quarantining of social security payments. This practice is referred to as Income Management (IM).

IM quarantines a proportion of social security payments. Money cannot be withdrawn as cash and cannot be used to purchase prohibited goods and services, such as alcohol, illicit drugs, gambling products and pornography. Policy specifics vary, but the proportion of social security payments quarantined is generally 50 to 80 per cent, and even up to 90 per cent (Bray et al, 2014). In Australia, IM was officially introduced to help protect children from abuse and neglect, and women from financial and physical violence (hence the limitations of purchases to food and essential household and personal items, and the exclusion of alcohol, gambling and pornography). IM represents a radical experiment in poverty governance, conditional welfare and social policy administration (Mendes, 2013). The aim of this book is to investigate the design and implementation effects of this experiment, following a form of research ethics that is dedicated to uncovering inconvenient facts. This book seeks to highlight the ramifications of government actions, to interrogate the disjuncture between the political representation of IM programmes and their on-the-ground effects, so that the taken-for-granted character of these practices is removed (Dean, 2009).

Conditionality and Compulsory Income Management

Conditionality in social security can take many forms. In some cases, such as Conditional Cash Transfers (CCTs) which were rolled out across Latin America and other developing countries during the 1990s, low-income households are offered financial incentives for participating in a range of activities, including school attendance, health checks and training. These programmes are offered in an effort to reduce poverty. While there were some short-term gains in reducing poverty, the long-term effects of CCTs have been more mixed. Most studies of CCTs find positive long-term effects on schooling, but fewer find positive impacts on cognitive skills, learning, employment, earnings or socio-emotional skills (Millan et al, 2019). In countries such as the UK, the US and across Western Europe, conditional social security payments tend to operate in terms of applying penalties and sanctions for non-compliance with activation requirements, many of which take the form of job-search or training. In effect, this means payments can be reduced or withdrawn altogether for a designated period, which drives people further into financial hardship and puts their housing and food security at greater risk. When they were first introduced, sanctions were generally only applied to unemployed people who were held to be responsible for losing their jobs, but they are now more likely to be attached to the job-seeking behaviour of all claimants (Adler, 2016). It is important to note that there are very few mechanisms available for citizens who wish to question a sanction decision. In fact, one of the striking aspects of welfare reform over the past two decades is that administrative appeal and redress options have become weaker as sanctions and penalties have incrementally increased (Adler, 2013).

Income Management in Australia and New Zealand takes welfare conditionality to a new level. As a form of conditionality, IM in Australia and New Zealand relies on a rationale of 'hard paternalism' in an effort to induce behavioural change among socially disadvantaged populations in specific locations (Bielefeld, 2014a; Mendes et al, 2014). 'Soft paternalism' assumes that individuals lack the knowledge and/or information to make appropriate choices, whereas 'hard paternalism' assumes the right to directly intervene in what is perceived to be 'poor' decision-making on the part of individuals (Thomas and Buckmaster, 2010). The most marginalised in the community are those most often those subjected to 'hard paternalism' (Spies-Butcher and Chester, 2014). Richard Sennett's (2003) work on respect and inequality is also informative here, as he argues that one of the consequences of recent welfare reforms has been a scarcity of respect, particularly when citizens are infantilised and rendered mere spectators to the definition of their own needs and the means of meeting them. For some groups in society, a lack of respect, self-determination and autonomy is an all too familiar pattern. In Australia, for example, Indigenous peoples were the first to be targeted by IM, which supports the view that the welfare regime in Australia frequently oppresses rather than empowers Indigenous Australians (Bryson and Verity, 2009).

Income quarantining was introduced in Australia in 2007 as part of the then Liberal–National Commonwealth Government's Northern Territory Emergency Response (NTER), which involved suspending the *Racial Discrimination Act 1975* (Cth). IM was legislated in an effort to help protect children from abuse and neglect, and women from financial and physical violence in the Northern Territory. However, these official claims were highly contested. In 2010, James Anaya, the United Nations Special Rapporteur, found the NTER to be racially discriminatory, infringing the human rights of Indigenous peoples. Anaya (2010) argued that measures such as banning alcohol and pornography and quarantining a percentage of essential income represented a significant limitation on 'individual autonomy'. Some Indigenous leaders offered qualified support for the intervention, while also raising concerns about the blanket approach. Following the NTER, Cape York Indigenous Leader Noel Pearson told ABC Radio National on 22 June 2007:

> 'I'm in agreement with the emphasis on grog [alcohol] and policing. I'm in agreement with attaching conditions to welfare payments. But the difference between what we've put forward to the Government and the proposals announced by Minister Brough, there is a difference in that we would be concerned that those people who are acting responsibly in relation to the payments they receive should continue to exercise their freedoms and their decisions, we should only target cases of responsibility failure.'

Since the introduction of IM in Australia, decreasing so-called 'welfare dependence' and increasing employment participation have also often been cited as social and economic goals of IM (Mendes, 2013; Deloitte Access Economics, 2015). While successive federal governments in Australia have claimed success in meeting these varied goals, it is difficult to determine from existing evaluations whether reported social benefits have been due to IM or other programmes and factors. Further, official evaluations have raised significant concerns regarding the capacity of IM policies to meet their stated objectives, and a range of issues have been identified with regard to implementation and the material and non-material effects of the policy (Department of Social Services, 2017; Mavromaras et al, 2019). The Australian National Audit Office (2018) conducted its own investigation into the adequacy of the 2017 government-funded evaluation of the IM trials, finding that the methodology used by the contracted evaluation agency (ORIMA Research) was inadequate and that relevant data were excluded from the analysis. Despite these concerns being put on the public record, IM was expanded to additional geographical areas across Australia. Since 2007, IM has also been expanded in Australia to include young people and other groups considered 'welfare dependent'. Approximately 39,000 Australians participate in IM programmes at the time of writing.

In New Zealand, from 2012, all 16- and 17-year-old benefit recipients (Youth Payment) and 18-year-old parents on a benefit (Young Parent Payment) became subject to IM as a means to inhibit future 'welfare dependency'. The majority of a young person's benefit is redirected towards board/rent and other utilities by a contracted, non-government Youth Service provider. Given high rental prices in many New Zealand cities, some young people (particularly those on YP) have little or no income after rent is paid. For those with some income remaining after such redirections, up to $50 is paid directly to the young person's bank account to spend as they wish, while the remainder goes on a Payment Card to be used at a limited number of suppliers (mostly supermarkets). There is no way to avoid IM unless young people meet their educational obligation to be in education or training for six months or longer and have achieved all the incentive payments ($10 per week each) associated with this educational obligation, as well as budgeting and, where relevant, parenting education obligations. This means some young people could be on IM for months, if not years, and only come off it when they 'age-out' of the YP or YPP benefits, or exit the benefit for some other reason (Humpage, 2018).

There are some clear similarities between the IM policies adopted by Australia and New Zealand. Both policies quarantine part of a benefit income to ensure it is spent on basic essentials such as housing and food, while restricting the purchase of alcohol in both countries, plus pornography and gambling in Australia and electronic goods in New Zealand. This is achieved via a debit card that prohibits such spending and can only be used at selected outlets. In both countries, there is an assumption that such purchases are financially inappropriate for benefit recipients on low incomes as they divert spending away from healthy foods/habits and meeting the needs of dependent children (Humpage, 2018). How IM is administered also differs between the two countries. In Australia, multiple versions of IM have developed since 2007, which means operational guidelines are varied. Income is managed through the BasicsCard or Cashless Debit Card (CDC). In New Zealand, the Ministry of Social Development (MSD) administers the Payment Card, which is not part of any commercial banking debit card system. Balances can be checked through an online system available to all benefit recipients. This is somewhat similar to the BasicsCard, which was used for phase one and phase two of IM in Australia, administered by Centrelink, Australia's social security agency. In contrast, later phases of IM in Australia contracted a for-profit financial services provider called Indue Ltd to build and implement an IT infrastructure to administer IM through a Visa-based system that can involve penalty fees and other financial costs not associated with the New Zealand system (Bray et al, 2014; Humpage, 2018). The privatisation of IM administration in Australia reflects a longer history of contracting non-government providers to deliver the activation elements of the social security system in what can be referred to as an acceleration of the 'poverty industry' (Hatcher, 2015). In contrast, New Zealand's Youth Service, which mentors and manages the income of YP/YPP recipients, represents the first time that any organisation other than the government social security agency, Work and Income, has been involved in the administration of benefit entitlements (Humpage, 2018).

Documenting first-hand accounts of IM in Australia and New Zealand is critical, as the voices of those directly impacted by these strict forms of conditionality have frequently been lost or ignored in the political debate about the costs and benefits of these policies. The pages that follow are intended to draw critical attention to the material and cultural effects of these policies, including how the maligned identities of social security recipients feature prominently in narratives about the justification for the disciplinary hand of the state. How social problems are framed matters, because it can make radical policy change appear (un)necessary or at least more (un)palatable, particularly when representations of issues tap into values that resonate with the public. Concepts such as 'reciprocity and obligation' or 'freedom and democracy', for example, are heavily institutionalised in liberal societies and as such they have a powerful symbolic purchase on the public imagination when it comes to legitimising policy action. These universal themes can be woven into competing storylines about why government action is needed. As Stone (2001, p 138) argues: 'definitions of policy problems have a narrative structure; that is they are stories with a beginning, a middle and an end, involving some change or transformation'. Analysis of the discursive and material elements of IM policies in the book draws on the work of Bacchi (2009), who has made a major contribution to understanding the significance of dominant political ideas and discourses in shaping concrete policy directions. One of the values of Bacchi's framework is an acknowledgement of the importance of understanding the effects of social problem representation. Bacchi's approach draws attention to three types of effects: 'discursive effects' (problem representation), 'subjectification effects' (how people are constituted in laws and policies) and 'lived effects' (identity effects and social relations between professionals and citizens). Mapping policy discourses over time and between Australia and New Zealand helps to clarify how value debates are influencing individual and collective action in social policy domains where there are high levels of contestation.

We have sought to ensure that agency and the affective dimension of policy change are captured, including a fuller and richer account of the capability and complexity of people on the receiving end of policies and those tasked with policy implementation. Attention to power, agency and social identity has been influential in critical social policy, as has giving attention to the relationship between policy, citizen and practitioner in order to theorise agency and the enactment of social policies in and through the state (Dobson, 2015). Hunter's (2015) work on political action understands that the state does not exist as a thing in itself, but rather comes into being through processes of relational contestation, everyday actions and the wide variety of people and material and symbolic objects that make up the state. Lea's (2008) anthropological study of health interventions in Australia's Northern Territory, for example, has uncovered the way that human actors 'become' institutional actors through ritualised processes of providing services with varying degrees of personal investment, hope and despair.

The level of analysis, here, is principally concerned with the interactions between people and policies, and how people 'speak back' to policy as they express their hopes and frustrations. Everyday interactions between citizens, the state and associated third parties reveal that people are not simply passive victims of disciplinary state policy. Citizens are also courageous, capable and creative in how they negotiate everyday interactions with the state as they seek to maintain a sense of dignity and control. In his ethnographic study of poverty in Australia in the early 2000s, Mark Peel (2003) ensured that his research subjects were represented as being much more than one-dimensional victims of inequality and injustice. Listening carefully to stories of hardship reveals how people are both capable and vulnerable in the face of material disadvantage, as well as defiant and angry about the policy assumptions made regarding their abilities and their situation. The authors hope they have managed to capture these capabilities and vulnerabilities in how they have illustrated the diverse ways in which ordinary citizens wrestle with extraordinary demands on their material resources and time. In order to do justice to these accounts, the starting point is to reject the fantasy that poverty is deserved. In short, thinking about justice means listening to those who know about injustice (Peel, 2003).

The aim of the interviews with IM participants in both countries was to add depth and detail to an understanding of IM by inviting people who had been subject to the policy to speak at length about their experiences, perceptions and values. During the interviews, themes around financial capability, practical issues with the cards and perceptions about IM policy were explored, and any forms of individual or collective resistance that had been expressed were identified. Examples of dominant discourses about IM were also presented to determine how much of a distance there is between the different policy storylines (social identities/stereotypes) and the lived effects of the policies (experiences, ontological identity). One of the key aspects of recent research on identity and poverty suggests that when low-income citizens accept the idea that there are people who fit the stereotype of the 'welfare dependent' they are doing so in one sense to reject a stigmatising 'categorical identity', thereby preserving their 'ontological identity', their sense of self-worth (Lister, 2004). Humanising the 'othered' subjects of welfare reform and thinking well about poverty and disadvantage requires carefully connecting first-hand accounts with wider structures and processes that generate good fortune and wealth for some while generating misfortune and disadvantage for others. Sometimes these structures are deliberately obscured, hidden behind an enduring mythology about how self-responsibility, independence and hard work explain differences in economic security and wealth. In other cases, it is a narrow conception of welfare in the public sphere that obscures the redistribution of government expenditures through the tax system – expenditures that overwhelmingly advantage middle- and high-income households (Marston et al, 2014).

Context and concepts

A dual focus on the symbolic (knowledge representation and identity recognition) and the material (economic redistribution) provides the conceptual framework for the comparative analysis of IM in Australia and New Zealand contained in this book. A comparative social policy analysis between two countries allows for a more in-depth focus on the institutional and historical factors that shape policy transfer and convergence between these social security systems. We need to understand more than just whether the policy of IM is achieving its stated objectives. There is a need to understand the effects of the policy on social identity and autonomy, particularly with regard to identity intersections between class, age and race (Williams, 1999), and to ask legal, ethical and moral questions about what is at stake in the individual–state relationship when autonomy and basic freedoms are constrained in ways that have hitherto been considered a step too far in social policy.

Specific social policies are implemented within nation states, but their origins stretch back in time and across space. In an interconnected world, policy ideas travel across shores and borders. As has already been noted in these introductory pages, the idea and practice of welfare conditionality is not unique to Australia and New Zealand, and there is a common language about the purpose and intent of conditionality across different national contexts.

However, the shape and contours of conditionality are also mediated by a nation's cultural and political values and its social and economic fabric. As such, it is important to briefly outline some of the similarities and differences between the welfare states in these two countries. In welfare state typologies, Australia and New Zealand are generally put beside each other in the category of 'liberal welfare states'; characterised by a selective and residual social safety net, which allows market mechanisms a greater capacity to determine the distribution of income and life opportunities (Ramia, 2020). In this sense they are highly commodified welfare regimes. This type stands in contrast to other categories of welfare state, including the 'social democratic' regimes of the Scandinavian countries, which are more universal and less commodified, and the 'conservative–corporatist' regimes of countries such as France, Spain, Italy and Germany, which have more pronounced status differentials preserved by traditional family values (Esping-Andersen, 1990).

While useful in a heuristic and theoretical sense, large number country comparisons can miss the differences between countries that are within a welfare state category. Australia and New Zealand have much in common in terms of their welfare state design (Castles et al, 2006), but there are also important differences between these two island nations and other countries in the liberal welfare state category, such as the US, Canada or the UK. Some of the differences between Australia and New Zealand's social protection systems are more apparent at a particular period in history, while at other times there is a high degree of convergence. An appreciation of these historical differences is highly relevant to the study presented in this book, because it helps to explain some of the unique aspects of IM in each country, including the different approaches to implementation taken by their respective governments.

In terms of similarities, Castles' oft-cited book *The Working Class and Welfare* (1985) constructed New Zealand and Australia as belonging to one model, the 'wage earner's welfare state'. Castles makes the case that the two welfare regimes developed earlier than and were different from Europe. In terms of substance, the central difference lay in the exceptional role of minimum labour standards in Australia and New Zealand when compared with their Western European counterparts (Ramia, 2020). Another feature of the Australian and New Zealand wage earner's model was high levels of industry protection in the form of tariffs, used as a policy tool to compel employers to provide comparatively high minimum wages, which were determined by industrial arbitration tribunals (Ramia, 2020). However, wages were generally differentiated according to the gender of the worker, such that men were accorded higher rates than women based on the assumption that men were more often financially responsible for the family. For Indigenous Australians, equal pay was not awarded until

1965 and restrictions on the receipt of social security benefits remained in place until 1966. Even where Indigenous peoples secured wage or social security incomes, they were often 'managed' (and in many cases, stolen) by government-appointed 'protectors' until as late as the mid-1970s (Parliament of Australia, 2016; Sanders, 2012). Thus, gender inequality and racial discrimination were legally institutionalised features of the system, which led Australian sociologist Lois Bryson (1992) to remark that, in effect, what was institutionalised during the course of the twentieth century in the Antipodes was a 'white, male wage earner's welfare state'.

These labour market inequalities have continued into the twenty-first century. The overall gender pay gap (which includes work-related bonuses and fringe benefits) in Australia and New Zealand stands at around 14 and 18 per cent respectively (ABS, 2020; Strategic Pay, 2020). The gender pay gap has flow-on effects for retirement income. The income differential between Indigenous Australians and non-Indigenous Australians is even more dramatic. In 2019, the median weekly household income among all Indigenous Australians aged 15 and over was $623 compared with $935 for non-Indigenous Australians (ABS, 2019). This indicates that the Indigenous median weekly income was 33 per cent lower. Selective and restrictive immigration policies in the second half of the twentieth century were also utilised as a method to exclude workers from countries where labour was relatively poorly paid, thereby theoretically disallowing the wages of Australian and New Zealand workers from being undercut. The final element of the wage-centred welfare regimes in Australia and New Zealand was the design of the social security system, which was 'residual', meaning that it was mainly designed to protect only those who could not find paid work (Marston and Zhang, 2019).

Despite effectively capturing the similarities, Castles (1985) underplays the differences between Australia and New Zealand across time, particularly with regard to the treatment of arbitration and conciliation. Castles's model assumes that the systems of arbitration, once created, remained virtually unchanged (Ramia, 2020). Whereas, in reality the arbitration systems in both countries have undergone significant changes in terms of governance and scope. In the Australian case, competitive federalism between state governments and the national government led to a centralisation of industrial powers during the course of the twentieth century. Labour market deregulation through enterprise bargaining is the more recent trend in both Australia and New Zealand. The trend towards relative wage flexibility between skilled and unskilled workers, and also within occupational groups between higher and lower paid workers, has contributed to an overall decline in wage growth and an increase in labour market inequalities in Australia since the 1990s (Briggs and Buchanan, 2000). In New Zealand, the labour market also remains relatively weak, with a decline in entry-level jobs and an increase in casualisation. A sober analysis of these trends suggests that the wage earner's welfare state model has been faltering for some time, unable to deliver economic security for all.

What is striking about this sober analysis is the extent to which the labour market reality in Australia and New Zealand has become disconnected from the political rhetoric of the major political parties. Rather than acknowledging the reduced capacity of the labour market to deliver income security and rights, political leaders continue to espouse hollow sounding statements, such as 'the best form of welfare is a job' (Gregoire, 2019). In Australia, this statement has been deployed to resist growing calls from the business and social services sectors to lift the rate of JobSeeker Payment (the unemployment benefit formerly called the Newstart Allowance) from being one of the lowest in the OECD (Mendes, 2020a). The rate paid to those on working age social security payments in Australia is also lower than the rate paid to aged or disability pensioners, an anomaly that has its origins in the outdated assumption that unemployment is a temporary condition. In this respect, the social security system in Australia is not fit for purpose to meet twenty-first century economic and social conditions (Marston and Zhang, 2019). Setting a path to refurbish and positively transform the social security system is a theme returned to in the final pages of the book.

An historical perspective helps explain some of the differences and similarities between Australia and New Zealand. It is also important to situate these two countries within a global context. The broader literature on welfare state design and expenditure includes an analysis of a range of historical continuities and discontinuities with an overall theme of strong convergence among OECD countries in terms of social expenditure patterns and a greater emphasis on targeting in poverty management (Henman, 2004; Schmitt and Starke, 2011). One of the main areas of continuity in poverty management among Anglophone countries has been a deep suspicion of 'the poor', particularly the able-bodied, which dates back to the Elizabethan poor laws in England, which were primarily concerned with notions of containment and confinement. The best expression of this containment logic and moral assessment of worth was the development of the poorhouse across countries such as the UK, the US and Australia between the seventeenth and nineteenth centuries. Poorhouses were established in the name of merging material assistance with thrift and humanity. This dual logic of care and control has been a persistent feature of governing the poor and the unemployed. What has changed over time has been the dovetailing of human and digital methods of assessment and surveillance. In her analysis of the trajectory from physical poorhouse to 'digital poorhouse', Virginia Eubanks (2018, p 16) makes the following argument: 'For all their high-tech polish, our modern systems of poverty management – automated decision-making, data mining and predictive analytics – retain a remarkable kinship with the poorhouses of the past. Our new digital tools spring from punitive, moralistic views of poverty and create a system of high-tech containment and investigation.'

The growth of the digital welfare state and improved ability to capture and harness 'big data' have reinvigorated debates about the prioritisation of quantitative data in policy making, while other forms of evidence, such as the life stories of those impacted by policies, are consigned to the lower rungs of evidence hierarchies (Marston and Watts, 2003, p 145). Rose (1991, p 674) described this partiality towards numericising social phenomena as 'governing by numbers', an example being the reductive reconceptualisation of poverty 'into a matter of the numbers claiming social benefits'. As a consequence, the dominant logic of welfare reform becomes narrowly focused on reducing the numbers of people 'dependent on welfare', giving rise to 'workfare' and 'work-first' programmes that deploy state authority to compel workers into training and jobs while frequently ignoring their needs and material resource deficits (Soss et al, 2011, p 14). The strong paternalism inherent within work-first poverty management policies and programmes means that those who fail to comply with the programme logic face a range of sanctions and penalties.

Indeed, one of the convergence trends in liberal welfare states has been a stronger intersection between the penal state and the welfare state. Wacquant (2009, p 43) makes the following point in his analysis of the convergence between the logic of 'workfare' and 'prisonfare' in contemporary poverty management and welfare conditionality: 'The down-sizing of the social-welfare sector of the state and the concurrent upsizing of its penal arm are functionally linked, forming two sides of the same coin of state restructuring in the nether regions of social and urban space in the age of ascending neoliberalism.'

One of the enduring storylines about poverty and the poor is the idea that market discipline, reinforced by state surveillance and control, is a necessary antidote to economic disadvantage. The digitisation of social security monitoring and compliance can further reinforce this market logic. In a recent report, the UN Special Rapporteur on Extreme Poverty, Philip Alston (2019), raised a concern that 'digital welfare states risk becoming Trojan Horses for neoliberal hostility towards social protection and regulation'. The significant role played by the private sector in automating social security assessment and in social security compliance is just one of the concerns linked to a new mixed economy of welfare. Over the past two decades there has been a significant 'risk shift' where corporate interests have superseded the role played by public benefits, all in the name of choice and consumer empowerment (Hacker, 2006).

This contemporary expression of market discipline combined with state control accentuates a longer trend in political rationalities. Although neoliberalism can be enacted through a hollowing out and rolling back of the state, it also frequently involves an intensification of state-led disciplinary practices as a means of actively advancing market mechanisms and forms of citizen surveillance (Schram et al, 2003; Wacquant, 2009). IM policies, for example, construct adults as failed subjects who must be governed by the discipline of a strong state (Bielefeld, 2014a). Better understanding how people experience new forms of disciplinary social security programmes involves a commitment to listening and interpreting first-hand accounts. The broad aims of the empirical study, outlined below, were to consider the impact of the IM policy paradigm on people's autonomy and agency in the context of their material circumstances.

The comparative Income Management study

The research reported here has been guided by the following research questions:

- What are the similarities and differences between the New Zealand and Australian cases of IM?
- How have social security recipients individually or collectively responded to the IM policy agenda?
- How have procedural rights and administrative justice been impacted by IM?
- How have front-line professionals and other community stakeholders responded to the compulsory IM policy agenda?

In addressing these questions there were three interlocking stages to the mixed methods research design. Stage one mapped and compared the policy development of IM in Australia and New Zealand, including a document analysis of the discourse around compulsory IM in print news media and online social media during this period. Stage two examined the administrative and wider sociolegal implications of compulsory IM since its introduction in Australia and New Zealand. Stage three involved a national online survey and a series of individual and group interviews with income support recipients across Australia and New Zealand who were subject to IM. Politicians and community stakeholders were also interviewed for their views on policy development and implementation.

The corpus for the document analysis consisted of political discourse (parliamentary speeches, Hansard, parliamentary committee reports), media discourse (print news in the form of national broadsheet stories on IM) and an analysis of public discourse via social media (Facebook/comment threads) where IM participants came together online to share their experiences and views. The time period for the corpus was 2007 to 2020 in Australia and 2012 to 2020 in New Zealand. In the process of analysing the textual data, comparisons were made between the two countries in terms of representations of state–citizen relations and the degree of contestation regarding popular support for the policies. The focus on administrative aspects of the policy and sociolegal issues examined the application of social security law and whether social security recipients are worthy of being accorded the same citizenship rights as others (Bielefeld, 2014a, 2015). The forms of redress available to citizens affected by compulsory IM were also explored. This aspect of the study included an examination of any available review rights under administrative law and any access to justice issues affecting such rights in both Australia and New Zealand. In 2013, the Commonwealth Ombudsman's office in Australia identified 'systemic problems in the administration of Income Management, which include the lack of timely reimbursement of money wrongly taken out of Income Management accounts of Indigenous welfare recipients' (Bielefeld, 2015, p 1074). The sociolegal analysis also examined citizens' complaints relating to compulsory IM policies made to statutory authorities. Such complaints are a clear way of highlighting the unintended effects of IM implementation, as well as whether this form of feedback is resulting in changes to the policy settings.

In capturing experiences of IM, both breadth and depth were sought through the use of an online survey and semi-structured interviews. The online survey was conducted in 2019, only in Australia. The survey consisted of a total of 45 questions, though respondents were directed to different parts of the survey based on their responses. A total of 199 eligible responses to the online survey were received from across Australia. Responses were sought from individuals who were 18 years of age or older and who had either:

- experienced IM in Australia (either at the time of doing the survey, or in the past); or
- not directly experienced IM, but currently lived in an area where IM had been implemented in Australia.

The rationale for accessing both groups was to explore whether those with direct experience of IM had different perceptions and experiences of the policy when compared to those without direct experience. Respondents who had direct experience of IM were asked about the nature of their experiences with IM (including type of IM, challenges prior to IM, reason for being placed on IM, length of time on IM, impacts of IM, advantages/disadvantages of IM, being exempted from IM and/or circumventing IM). All respondents were also asked to give a self-report indication of their financial behaviour and locus of control, and they were asked general questions to gauge their level of endorsement of IM policy in their local area.

In addition to the national survey – which sought to provide a general overview of IM as experienced by affected individuals and communities – semi-structured interviews were conducted at four IM locations in Australia:

- Greater Shepparton, Victoria
- Playford, South Australia
- Ceduna, South Australia
- Federal Division of Hinkler, Queensland, which includes the cities of Hervey Bay and Bundaberg and a number of regional towns.

A total of 114 interviews were conducted across the four trial sites – 75 with IM participants, and 39 with local stakeholders. Two of the trial site locations, Shepparton and Playford, are longstanding IM sites where the BasicsCard was introduced in 2012. The other two geographical areas, Ceduna and Hinkler, are trial sites for the more recent CDC. The CDC was introduced to Ceduna in 2016 and to Hinkler in 2019. These four sites were chosen for the Australian component of the study because they reflect both the evolution of IM in Australia and its recent broadening to target not only predominantly Indigenous communities, but also sites that have comparatively few Indigenous residents (though it is noteworthy that even in these locations, Indigenous populations are still disproportionately subject to IM). Interviews were conducted in person and over the phone in late 2018 and throughout 2019, with some follow-up interviews on IM exemption requests conducted in 2020. Research participants were assured that, while their stories would be shared and their voices amplified, their identities would remain confidential. Most interviews occurred one-on-one to ensure maximum confidentiality and comfort, but several group interviews also took place to accommodate participants – usually with partnered couples or small groups of kith and kin – who requested to be interviewed together.

A similar process of data collection was used in New Zealand. To allow for representation across New Zealand, interviews were conducted in both the North and South Islands across both regional and city areas. Interviews were conducted with 20 young people. Twelve were YPP recipients (all female, eight of whom identified as Māori, three as European/Pākehā and one as Pasifika), five were YP recipients (all female, three of whom identified as Māori, one as European/Pākehā and one as both Māori and Pākehā), and three had transitioned to Student Allowance or Sole Parent Support (two female, one male, two of whom identified as Māori and one as both Māori and European/Pākehā). Sixteen employees of youth service providers were interviewed and eight representatives from advocacy and welfare groups were also interviewed. Three face-to-face semi-structured interviews were conducted with representatives from the MSD in New Zealand, and three politicians from different New Zealand political parties were interviewed.

What follows

The beginning chapters of the book provide a narrative of the relationship between policy and politics in welfare governance in Australia and New Zealand, highlighting the contested evidence base for conditional welfare and the continuation of IM. Chapter 1 provides a policy analysis of compulsory IM in Australia and New Zealand. While the policy logic of hard paternalism and punitive approaches to poverty management will be familiar to many social policy scholars and practitioners, the unique characteristics of compulsory IM in these two countries are presented in an historical and comparative overview. Chapter 2 outlines the policy developments and the nature of the political discourse in Australia and New Zealand that rationalised this new form of hyper-conditionality. The basic question this chapter seeks to answer is how these two countries arrived at a moment where they felt it was necessary to introduce policy changes that are quite unique compared with other countries with high levels of welfare conditionality. The focus of the discussion is on notions of welfare and income support recipient subjectivities, noting the differences and similarities between the two countries in relation to narratives around race and nationalism in settler colonial societies, and the construction of families and children in the justifications for introducing compulsory IM.

Chapters 3 to 6 present the empirical findings from the comparative study. The discussion in these chapters draws on qualitative and quantitative data to examine practical and administrative issues associated with the implementation of IM, emotional and identity-related effects, and sociolegal issues. In the final chapter of this section, individual and collective resistance to the policies on the part of beneficiaries and advocates are discussed. Although the empirical data are specific to Australia and New Zealand, the analytical themes are internationally relevant, as the varying impacts of conditionality are analysed and questions of identity, agency and autonomy are addressed.

Chapter 3 examines the policy implementation of compulsory IM, with consideration given to the limits of the consultation approaches used by the Australian and New Zealand governments, the mixed economy of welfare in the delivery of compulsory IM, and the role of intermediaries such as front-line social services and for-profit companies that provide the cashless welfare technologies. The chapter details the range of practical and administrative issues that have been identified by research participants living on compulsory IM in Australia and New Zealand. The chapter also considers the perspectives of community stakeholders on IM. These interviews provide a rich source of data concerning the degree of contestation within government and between the state and civil society over IM policy and practice.

Chapter 4 explores the impact of compulsory IM on participants' wellbeing and sense of self. It illustrates that, while financial stress and reduced financial control are key concerns for many participants, the infantilisation and stigmatisation that compulsory IM involves are also powerful stressors. Together, these factors can contribute to significant reductions in participant wellbeing, negatively impacting cardholders, their families and their communities.

Chapter 5 examines social policy and the law, both in terms of social security law that facilitates IM and administrative law as it pertains to citizen redress and review. Analysis of the legal restrictions imposed through compulsory IM in Australia and New Zealand is needed to ascertain the extent to which the autonomy of welfare recipients is impacted and how this affects consumer choices. An under-examined aspect of compulsory IM is the constraints it places on the contractual capacity of welfare recipients subject to it, and how this relates to structural equity barriers. This chapter explores how law can impact the relationships between citizens and what factors are considered by lawmakers in determining whether some people are worthy of being accorded the same citizenship rights as others, thereby drawing attention to the distribution of burdens and benefits in administrative justice.

Chapter 6 moves from a discussion about rights to highlight individual and collective resistance to the material restrictions associated with 'being on the card' and the socio-emotional impacts of constrained autonomy and misrepresentation discussed earlier in the book. For the purposes of this chapter, resistance is understood as the refusal to accept the material conditions of IM and/or the devalued social status attached to being arbitrarily categorised as 'irresponsible'. Resistance can occur through formal and informal channels, and it can be overt or covert, as the participant interviews highlight.

The final chapters of the book draw together conclusions from the cross-national empirical study and outline incremental alternatives to compulsory IM as well as more radical alternatives to conditional welfare.

Chapter 7 discusses the possible value of voluntary IM, which was given qualified support by some research participants. It then focuses on financial capability, drawing on educational and development models, as well as exploring the role that NGOs might play in a mixed economy of welfare that is less concerned with surveillance and control. In considering alternatives to punitive forms of welfare conditionality, this chapter highlights some of the differences between New Zealand and Australia, as there are lessons Australia could learn from the use of mentors and more empowering forms of budget support as is done in New Zealand. The links between economic security and wellbeing are drawn out, using public health research that demonstrates that economic insecurity is a strong determinant of mental health among the population.

Chapter 8 takes a global perspective on economic and social security and considers new and emerging risks that income support systems must respond to in the twenty-first century, including shifting age and household formation demographics, increased geographical mobility, new forms of precarious labour associated with changes in technology, and environmental risks resulting from climate change. There is an urgent need to revisit first principles when determining the primary policy goals of a social security system. The case is made that addressing the inadequacy of income support payments, ensuring decent employment and training opportunities, and providing accessible social services is a better starting point for creating healthy, economically secure and inclusive communities compared to continuing with policies that are not achieving desired results for governments or citizens.

Conclusion

Ultimately, this book seeks to make a contribution to understanding the lived experience of new forms of conditionality in social security policy that have developed in two countries that have many similarities and some key differences. Clearly, the conclusions drawn from this analysis are not generalisable to the whole population subject to IM in either Australia or New Zealand. Nor are the conclusions generalisable to all forms of conditionality that exist in other parts of the world, many of which have very different design features. What is offered is a level of analytical generality about the importance of voice and citizen agency in policy design and implementation. Like any other citizen, people who rely on social security for some or all of their income are trying to make their way in the world, in many cases with fewer resources. Grounded perspectives on new and emerging forms of conditionality provide the basis for both a critique of existing arrangements and for making the positive case for a social security system that provides genuine security and 'real freedom for all' (Van Parijs, 1997). What this book points to across the following chapters is that imposing stringent conditions and constraints on the receipt of social security not only interferes with agency and autonomy, but it can also introduce a host of new risks and unintended consequences that may ultimately generate more harm for people and their communities.

2

Why Income Management?

Introduction

This chapter explains how the Australian and New Zealand governments both arrived at a moment where IM was considered a viable policy idea, then implemented and extended it over time. Drawing on parliamentary debates, policy documents and interviews with politicians and policymakers, the policy process in both countries is traced, drawing particular attention to the political discourses used to frame IM. This reveals what political 'problem' each government identified. In Australia, where discourse was highly racialised, existing tropes around the need to 'save the children' and reduce 'criminality' within Indigenous communities were dominant. In New Zealand, a broader welfare conditionality discourse aimed to 'save' the young people subject to CIM, largely from their parents but sometimes from the state; but this was less explicitly racialised, even though Indigenous peoples – along with sole parents and disabled persons – are disproportionately more likely to receive social security payments and thus be under IM administration. Distorted representations of community crime and crime reduction were also not a prominent feature of the policy justification for IM, as in Australia. To explain these differences, the chapter indicates how international trends in welfare conditionality intersected with and were mediated by existing political discourses, interests and institutions to embed CIM policy into both countries' social security systems.

Analysing Income Management within the broader policy field

As Chapter 1 highlighted, IM emerged from an international context in which forms of welfare conditionality are increasingly framed as not only appropriate but necessary to address the 'welfare dependency' associated with social security recipients. The ideational dimension of policy change and social problem framing is always political because to evoke the origin of a social problem is to assign blame and praise (Edelman, 1988; Bacchi, 2009). 'Welfare dependency' situates dependency on the state for income support as negative and corrosive (Fraser and Gordon, 1994; Jensen, 2014) while other forms, such as dependency on markets, are regarded as natural and virtuous. The valorisation of a (paid) 'work ethic' as *the* solution in Anglophone countries thus both narrows understandings of welfare to a form of cash transfers and suggests solutions located in both market participation and individualism. Blaming some individuals or groups for a social cleavage while hiding the benefits of those who profit from misery and misfortune is central to representation, and such framings have long been used to justify paternalistic social security policies, particularly for Indigenous peoples, sole parents and people with disabilities (Fraser and Gordon, 1994; Bielefeld and Beauport, 2019).

For these reasons, the interpretative policy analysis offered in this chapter is centrally focused on the 'ideas' – that is, 'claims about descriptions of the world, causal relationships, or the normative legitimacy of certain actions' (Parsons, 2002, p 48) – that framed and justified IM. Paying explicit attention to the values, discourse and subjectivities used to construct the social problem helps us understand how governments rationalised and gained political support for IM (Bacchi, 2009). We argue that Australian and New Zealand policymakers drew from this broader, international policy lexicon about welfare conditionality when making decisions about what policies might be implemented in their respective countries.

This is not surprising, since in today's 'fast policy' context (Peck and Theodore, 2015), policy making is thought to be increasingly marked by short development cycles, rapid rollout of programmes and continuing policy experimentation, where policymakers often turn to other jurisdictions for 'ideas'. However, while some evidence was found that indicates that Australia and New Zealand looked to international experiments with behavioural economics aiming to reduce the cost of social security and improve social outcomes via *discretionary or additional* payments (Buckmaster and Ey, 2012; Fletcher et al, 2013), they do not appear to have directly copied these countries; instead they adopted *compulsory* IM programmes to limit the freedom on social security recipients to spend 'core' entitlements (Mendes, 2013).

Moreover, considerable interchange of policy knowledge between Australia and New Zealand might be expected. These are neighbouring countries, have many institutional similarities as former British colonies, and have a history of sharing public policy ideas (Castles and Mitchell, 1992; Goldfinch and Roberts, 2013). Yet there is little evidence of direct transfer of knowledge about conditional social security policies between these countries (Dolowitz and Marsh, 2000). The present analysis instead supports claims that policies are 'assemblages' rather than discrete 'things' because they are not simply 'transferred' but reinterpreted as they travel across cultural/political boundaries and are mediated by local settings (Peck and Theodore, 2015; Stone, 2017).

One key aspect of these local settings is their 'institutions': the policy-making structures and the practices embedded in formal organisational arrangements, electoral systems, division of powers within a particular federal or unicameral state (John, 2003). These institutions both mediated the adoption of new policy ideas in each country and, once established, made the abolition of CIM more difficult. Although CIM itself was new to both countries, each had a long history of welfare conditionality, having encouraged the unemployed to adopt the 'right' behaviours through work activity obligations since the 1990s and having extended this expectation to a wider group of social security claimants (notably sole parents and people with disabilities) in the 1990s and 2000s (Marston and McDonald, 2007; Mendes, 2013; Humpage, 2015). IM is thus an extension of existing behavioural tools through which individuals are envisaged as being enabled to become responsible and, simultaneously, through which 'welfare' is cost-effectively and justly targeted (Patrick, 2017).

The chapter also demonstrates how the transfer of policy ideas was mediated by 'interests': policy and political actors such as politicians and policymakers, interest and lobby or consumer groups, as well 'policy entrepreneurs' (individual or collective actors in the policymaking process), who promote certain policy solutions to pursue their own preferences, electoral objectives and political agendas (Béland and Cox, 2016). IM was introduced by conservative governments who favoured forms of welfare conditionality in both countries, but centre-left governments maintained (and in Australia extended) the policy. This tells us something about how 'path dependency' can emerge once key interests have been embedded into institutions and have been rationalised through policy discourses that are difficult to oppose (such as 'saving' children). The authors of this book suggest that worrying about public opinion (and how this might shape electoral outcomes) may have diminished any differences between centre-left and centre-right parties on these issues.

While this chapter notes the key role that policy entrepreneurs, both politicians and other actors, played in promoting CIM, it also considers what interests were *not* being fully represented in both countries (Bacchi, 2009). The greater racialisation of political discourse in Australia may explain why governments selectively used some Indigenous people's ideas or support to promote IM, even though those subject to the policy had few opportunities to influence its design or implementation. In New Zealand, institutions and interests representing Indigenous peoples were conspicuously absent from the debate about IM, despite this policy's similarly disproportionate impact on Māoris and despite an Indigenous political party being part of the government. Further, although sole parents and people with disabilities are more likely than other citizens to receive a social security benefit and thus be disproportionately impacted by IM, they, too, feature little in policy debate. These problems become evident as the policy trajectory of IM is examined, first in Australia and then in New Zealand.

The emergence of Compulsory Income Management in Australia, 2006 to 2007

In Australia, IM is usually regarded as emerging from a 'critical juncture' whereby choices were made that set in motion a new form of path dependency in policy (Collier and Collier, 1991). This critical juncture was the Liberal–National government's 2007 Northern Territory Emergency Response (NTER) to the *Little Children are Sacred* report by the Northern Territory Board of Inquiry into the Protection of Aboriginal Children from Sexual Abuse (NTBIPACSA, 2007). This report largely focused on sexual violence, but highlighted a range of associated problems facing Indigenous communities in the Northern Territory, a large self-governing territory within the Commonwealth of Australia containing one per cent of the total Australian population but over a quarter of the Indigenous population, living mostly in remote locations (Bray et al, 2014). The problems the report addressed stem from deep and continuing structural and racial injustices, including colonisation based on the fallacy of '*terra nullius*', the forced removal of Indigenous children from their parents, and high numbers of Indigenous peoples living in remote locations which are culturally and genealogically meaningful but to which provision of government services is consistently poor. These inequities contribute to Indigenous Australians being overwhelmingly and disproportionately represented in Australia's most socio-economically disadvantaged groups (Moreton-Robinson, 2015; Humpage, 2016; Staines et al, 2020a). Reflecting this broader historical–political context, the NTBIPACSA (2007) recommendations were broad, including land reforms and alcohol prohibitions, but importantly not IM. The report did note that some people it had consulted thought that providing at least 50 per cent of payments in the form of food vouchers would reduce alcohol consumption, but that others criticised this as paternalistic and encouraging of dependency.

Although Federal Minister for Families, Community Services and Indigenous Affairs, Mal Brough, and others had highlighted dramatic allegations and investigations of child sexual abuse in Indigenous communities to lobby for the NTBIPACSA (2007), the Liberal–National government dismissed most of the Inquiry's recommendations (Arthur and Ayoub, 2020; Anderson, 2011). Co-chair of the NTBIPACSA and Alyawarre woman, Pat Anderson (2011: 26) later remarked, 'Critically … our [first] recommendation about working *with* Aboriginal communities was ignored' and instead, a series of 'deeply problematic … "get tough"' interventions were announced. The government instead mobilised the Australian Army to take control of Aboriginal lands and introduced a number of 'emergency' measures, including alcohol and pornography restrictions in some jurisdictions, and the provision of additional powers to law enforcement agencies, ostensibly to protect Indigenous children from abuse and neglect (Arthur and Ayoub, 2020).

As part of the NTER, then Prime Minister John Howard (2007, np) said his government would be "quarantining … 50 per cent of welfare payments to stem the flow of cash going towards alcohol and other substance abuse and to ensure that funds meant to be used for children's welfare are actually used for that purpose". CIM was to be applied universally to "stabilise and protect communities in the crisis area" (Brough, 2007, np) and overcome the "unique" and significant forms of dysfunction said to be found there. However, contradicting this claimed uniqueness, Howard (2007, np) also indicated that Cabinet would consider extending IM "in certain circumstances to the wider community where individuals are abusing their children or failing to fulfil their parental responsibilities". This supports academic researcher Jon Altman's claim during an interview as part of this study that the NTER "was just really using the [Northern] Territory as a bit of a greenfields for practising punitive welfare measures on the most vulnerable, politically marginalised Australians". In the 12-month initial phase, however, CIM was imposed for all people who had been, or became, in receipt of payment for two years or longer and lived in 73 prescribed communities or their associated outstations, and in the ten town camp regions of the Northern Territory, with application to those outside these communities decided on a case-by-case basis by Centrelink (Buckmaster et al, 2012). In 2008, more than 70 per cent of the Northern Territory's Indigenous peoples lived within these prescribed areas (Arthur and Ayoub, 2020).

To justify the NTER (and CIM), Indigenous disadvantage was framed as a problem of Indigenous *culture* rather than of structural inequalities (Altman, 2008). This was achieved by centring public discourse around the NTER on two key tropes: the need to save children and, relatedly, to address Indigenous criminality. For instance, Brough (2007, p 6) spoke about high rates of child abuse in the Northern Territory, 'where normal community standards, social norms and parenting behaviours have broken down'. This was selective use of evidence, since Bailey et al's (2017) investigation of official child safety data shows higher rates of child safety notifications for those *outside* the Northern Territory, and higher rates for *non-Indigenous* children than Indigenous children between 2003–4 and 2006–7. According to the government, CIM was also intended to reduce the amount of income spent on substance abuse and gambling, to ensure funds provided for the welfare of children were spent as intended, and to protect vulnerable people from financial exploitation, usually in the form of a practice known as 'humbugging' (Arthur and Ayoub, 2020). This involves directly asking someone to share their income or material goods with you, which is a component of demand resource sharing common among many Indigenous Australians (Altman, 2011). In an interview for this study, academic researcher Jon Altman said that demand-sharing is a response to scarcity:

> 'like a form of social insurance. When it works well it's like – it's like bonding social capital. It's like, 'okay, you've got $20 today. I've got nothing'. People say, 'Give me $10'. You've got $20, you give them $10. It's great. You've got $10, they've got $10. Next time you say it to them. So, it can work very well.' (Altman, 2011)

However, as Altman went on to say: 'on the negative side, its operation can result in excessive demands generating hardship'. The government's focus only on the negative effects justified taking control of a proportion of a recipient's income support payment to pay for necessities such as food, clothing, housing and utilities, which can either be accessed using a PIN-protected debit card using an electronic funds transfer at point of sale (EFTPOS) system developed specifically for IM, known as the BasicsCard, or by arranging for Centrelink to make payments on their behalf (for example, recurring rent and utilities payments). Individuals can transfer funds between their IM account and their BasicsCard but cannot receive cash or otherwise share income with family or other community members (Arthur and Ayoub, 2020).

Although now strongly associated with the NTER, policy tracing contradicts the common view that the NTER was the 'critical juncture', since CIM policies were already under development before the intervention was rolled out in September 2007 – in the lead up to a Federal election. Reflecting the government's growing interest in using the social security system to apply behavioural economics principles to alter individual behaviour and social norms and thus address wider forms of social disadvantage (Buckmaster et al, 2012; Klein, 2020), Brough (2006a, p 2) first publicly discussed the idea of quarantining social security income in 2006. He said that some children do not receive sufficient nutrition, education and life skills because:

> 'these children are often in homes where alcohol and drug abuse is common. Irresponsible gambling strips the family of the cash to maintain a functioning household and domestic violence is a regular occurrence. There are a myriad [sic] of essential support programs provided by State and Federal governments as well as the community sector. However, these programs don't address a fundamental issue for the dysfunctional families I have described, where the greatest temptations are created by available cash. … It is, in fact, the payments that are provided by society to uplift these families, and in particular the children, that provide the substances to fuel the violence and destruction. Society then picks up the pieces at the hospitals, prisons and morgues.' (Brough, 2006a)

This statement framing 'welfare' as the problem shows that the 'saving the children' and 'criminality' tropes that dominate IM discourse in Australia were in play well before the NTER (Staines et al, 2020; Peterie et al, 2021). Although the government likely intended to implement CIM more widely, the earliest iteration of CIM announced in September 2006 proposed using IM for:

> cases where there is an identified and substantiated risk to the child's welfare, but not one that is sufficient to warrant that child's removal from the family. Let me emphasise – because the practical issue of identifying these families is often cited in opposition to my proposal – *these children are already known to State systems.* (Brough, 2006b, np, emphasis in original)

Discursively constructing these parents as 'criminals' suggested it was justified to remove their agency over their income. This perspective was reinforced by Brough's (2006b) claim that an existing Centrepay tool – which had allowed social security recipients to voluntarily ask Centrelink to pay housing and utility bills directly from benefits or to purchase food vouchers since 1999 (Buckmaster et al, 2012) – did not go far enough. Similarly, Prime Minister John Howard (in Howard and Brough, 2007, p 2) argued that quarantining benefit incomes would 'stem the flow of cash going toward alcohol abuse', which was said to be associated with criminal and other problematic social behaviours. This comment suggests that large numbers of social security recipients abuse alcohol, despite multiple international and Australian studies finding that welfare populations are typically not overrepresented in terms of their alcohol consumption (see Staines et al, 2020a). Chapter 3 also highlights that little attention was paid to existing research evidence or to genuinely evaluating CIM once it had been implemented.

This use of deviance narratives in the context of social security supports Wilcock's (2017, p 7) claim that social security recipients in Anglophone countries are now the frequent 'object[s] of criminal suspicion, not because of any putative criminal behaviour, but simply by virtue of their recipient status'. There is also convergence of the welfare and criminal justice systems, with both employing increasingly similar technologies of surveillance and control to regulate socially undesirable behaviours (Garland, 2001; Wacquant, 2009; Gustafson, 2011). However, the 'saving the children' and 'criminality' discourses around IM are also built on a long running 'benevolent supervision' narrative, whereby government officials in Australia have attempted to control Indigenous lives purportedly 'for their own good' because they are considered 'incompetent and unworthy of access to rights afforded to others' (Bielefeld and Beauport, 2019, p 338). The notorious Stolen Generation policy saw dual heritage children removed from their families to be adopted into white families or to live in institutions, and often used as unpaid labourers, on the basis that Indigenous mothers in particular were not regarded as meeting the moral standards of motherhood promoted by the government (Moreton-Robinson, 2000). 'Slow worker' clauses in Queensland legislation permitted gross underpayment of wages, while Indigenous workers also went unpaid for their labour in key industries in Western Australia's Kimberley region. Other state and federal policies gave officials control over the bulk of Indigenous people's incomes, or paid them in rations only (Klein, 2020). More recently, Arthur and Ayoub (2020, p 2) note that as Indigenous peoples became eligible for social security entitlements, concerns about potential 'misuse' of income was thought to justify providing only 'rations and clothing' instead of unemployment benefits. Academic Rob Bray said in an interview conducted for this study that CIM follows in this tradition:

> 'If you control how people spend their money, then they can't spend it on alcohol and you've solved the problem. Once people learn that they can have these wonderful lives without spending their money on alcohol, they'll change their method of living and become assimilated, good middle-class people. I honestly think the logic is that simple.' (Arthur and Ayoub, 2020)

Brough (2006a, p 2) initially stressed that 'this is not a problem unique to Aboriginal communities', but:

> 'the inspiration for the approach I have outlined today came from visiting distressed Aboriginal communities and listening to their concerns and fears. One common sentiment expressed to me was that "sit down money" was no good, it is destroying families. Of course, it is not the money that is doing the damage but rather what it is being spent on.' (Brough, 2006a, p 4)

While the authors believe that such references to Indigenous support for CIM were intended to build the legitimacy of a policy that – even prior to the NTER – would disproportionately impact Indigenous peoples, it is true that many communities had experimented with forms of voluntary income quarantining prior to 2007. These examples are discussed further in Chapter 3, which notes that their impact was not formally evaluated. However, when Acting Aboriginal and Torres Strait Islander Commission Chairman, Lionel Quartermaine, suggested paying income support using a smart card that would prevent recipients from buying alcohol and drugs in 2003, this idea was rejected by the then Minister for Indigenous Affairs, Amanda Vanstone (Arthur and Ayoub, 2020). This suggests that Brough's support for IM was critical to its becoming policy, making him one of the key policy entrepreneurs for IM.

Brough (2006a) specifically noted that his thinking was informed by the Family Income Management initiative, which, since 2002, had attempted to assist voluntary participants to improve their budgeting skills and financial literacy in some communities in Cape York, Northern Queensland. This was funded by the Department of Families, Housing, Community Services and Indigenous Affairs (FaHCSIA) but staffed and managed by a group of local Aboriginal organisations, Cape York Partnerships, as well as Westpac Bank (Buckmaster et al, 2012). Brough (2006a, p 3) claimed: 'As the discretionary dollars within these families and communities have reduced so has the violence, drug and alcohol abuse. All of this was achieved without increasing by one dollar the payments received by these families.' However, social policy researcher Ilan Katz noted in an interview for this study that the initiative was a *community-driven* programme, not one imposed by government, which likely contributed to its success.

Building on this experience, federal funds were allocated in 2006 to design the Cape York Welfare Reform Project. While heavily influenced by Cape York leader Noel Pearson, who is highly critical of 'passive welfare' and whose thinking has also been shaped by behavioural economics, the next chapter provides more detail on the Cape York version of IM to argue that there were less punitive, community-led policy options that the government could have chosen to implement if it had had the political will. Instead, it seems that the existence of the Cape York initiatives – and support for IM from some Indigenous leaders and communities in Cape York and elsewhere – helped to legitimate the NTER version of CIM, which explicitly targeted Indigenous communities. Pearson's (2008) support for CIM was particularly prominent in media reporting, making him another important policy entrepreneur – even if he did believe IM should be used only when poor behaviours had already been demonstrated (see Chapters 1 and 3). This message was easily lost when he made comments suggesting that critics of CIM should:

> Ask the terrified kid huddling in the corner, when there's a binge drinking party going on down the hall, ask them if they want a bit of paternalism. … Ask them if they want a bit of intervention, because these people who continue to bleat without looking at the facts, without facing up to the terrible things that are going on in our remote communities, these people are prescribing no intervention, they are prescribing a perpetual hell for our children. (Pearson, 2008, p 1)

The National Congress of Australia's First Peoples (2011), the Australian Indigenous Doctors' Association (2010) and the Secretariat for National Aboriginal and Torres Strait Islander Child Care (2008) all raised significant concerns about CIM, but Pearson was not alone in offering support. Klein (2020) argues that while some Indigenous leaders actually believed in CIM, others supported it because they wanted to get a seat at the negotiating table with government to lobby for other Indigenous development projects, given cuts in social services funding. No matter how mixed Indigenous support was, an Australian Council of Social Services (ACOSS) representative interviewed for this study said that this affected their agency's advocacy: "It became difficult for us as an organisation to just literally stand up and oppose [CIM] where Aboriginal communities themselves decided they wanted that." This type of political manoeuvring helped create a public perception of community legitimacy, making it difficult for any future government to backtrack from IM.

Extending Compulsory Income Management in Australia, 2007 to 2021

In November 2007, a Labor government was elected. While the Labor Party had been critical of the NTER's suspension of the *Racial Discrimination Act*, it had voted in support of this emergency initiative and generally supported IM (Mendes, 2020b). It was thus not a huge surprise that Labor continued IM, arguing that evidence from an independent Review Board report on the NTER and other evaluations justified this. Path dependency was likely one reason for their support; as Jon Altman put it, 'once you put in that multi-million-dollar architecture, and those bloody machines in every community and all the rest of it'. A representative from ACOSS also noted when interviewed that Labor's retention of IM made sense: "Because I think [IM] plays well in the electorate ... not many people are that sympathetic to people who are on income support, particularly if they're unemployed or of working age." However, key stakeholder interviewees uniformly noted the significance of the new Minister for Families, Communities and Indigenous Affairs, Jenny Macklin, who, like her predecessor, was 'absolutely totally committed' to the CIM policy (Bray, interview). In particular, she was influenced by the stories of Indigenous women who had experienced abuse or the effects of alcoholism and drugs in their communities and said that CIM worked for them (Bray, interview; Altman, interview; Katz, interview).

Demonstrating considerable overlap with their Liberal–National predecessors, this vulnerability to violence and victimhood – especially amongst women, children and older people – was framed as a problem of cultural dysfunction and/or obligation associated not only with 'an intergenerational cycle of passive welfare' (Macklin, 2009a, p 127) but also with the cultural norms of Indigenous society (see Anderson, 2011; Peterie, 2021). CIM was said to help 'people to order their lives ... giving them access to the basics of life by reducing the amount of welfare funds available for substance abuse and other risky behaviours' (Macklin, 2009a, p 127). Benefit recipients were thus framed as a moral and physical danger to innocent children, because 'the social security system was said to produce individuals who lacked discipline and purpose and were therefore more likely to succumb in moral vice', abusing and neglecting family members rather than being responsible with benefit funds (Peterie et al, 2021, p 64). However, Labor's discomfort with the suspension of the *Racial Discrimination Act* saw some important modifications and extensions to CIM.

Within this context, CIM was first extended to Western Australia, where a Child Protection IM pilot enabled child protection case workers to refer individuals to CIM, with up to 70 per cent of parents' income support and family payments quarantined to ensure that the essential needs of children at risk were met (Buckmaster et al, 2012; Mendes, 2013). Contending that '[i]ncome management is a key tool in the government's broader welfare reforms to deliver on our commitment to a welfare system based on the principles of engagement, participation and responsibility' (Macklin, 2009a, p 12783), the Labor government then announced New Income Management measures in November 2009. These aimed to 'support' named categories of benefit recipients by reducing immediate hardship, deprivation, and the chances of financial harassment, while encouraging better budgeting and parenting. Those targeted for CIM were: young people aged 15 to 24 in receipt of Youth Allowance, Newstart Allowance, Special Benefit or Parenting Payment for more than 13 of the previous 26 weeks; long-term welfare recipients aged 25 and above (and younger than aged pension age) in long-term receipt of specified payments, including Newstart Allowance and Parenting Payment; vulnerable people assessed by a delegate of the Secretary (in practice, a Centrelink social worker) as requiring IM for reasons including vulnerability to financial crisis, domestic violence or economic abuse; and people referred for IM by child protection authorities (Arthur and Ayoub, 2020). As with the earlier version of CIM, affected social security recipients had 50 per cent of their regular payments and 100 per cent of lump sum payments (such as the Baby Bonus, a payment temporarily made by the Australian Government to parents upon the birth of a child as a means of incentivising population growth) quarantined in a separate account that could only be used for priority goods and services. However, the New Income Management scheme included savings incentives, access to financial counselling and financial incentives ($250 every six months, now discontinued) to participate in IM voluntarily (Buckmaster et al, 2012).

From July 2010, the new scheme was introduced throughout the Northern Territory, including in urban, regional and remote areas, but this was a 'first step in a national roll out of income management in disadvantaged regions' (FaHCSIA, 2009, cited in Arthur and Ayoub 2020, p 15). Thus, while CIM under the Liberal–National government had been focused on one geographical area, Labor combined geographical location with particular categories of social security recipient considered to be 'at risk'. Although more targeted, this new version of CIM was still 'relatively broad in scope to the extent that it subjects all people in the Participation/Parenting measure categories to income management unless they are able to obtain an exemption' (Buckmaster et al, 2012, p 6). Researcher Rob Bray described it like this:

> 'I think their extension was not so much one of seeking to extend Income Management at all, but was merely what device can we use to restore the *Racial Discrimination Act*. The only mechanism they could come up with was [to] target people. So I see them driven by one overwhelming objective, which was to restore the *Racial Discrimination Act*, rather than deliberately extending the policy.' (Interview with Rob Bray)

While including non-Indigenous social security recipients may have been intended to reduce the racialised focus on Indigenous peoples, they were still disproportionately impacted; Bielefeld and Beauport (2019) further note that the measure referring to the 'vulnerable' indirectly discriminates against people with disabilities, who are disproportionately more likely to receive working-age social security entitlements, including the Disability Support Pension. The 'vulnerable' measure also brought many sole parents (the majority of whom are women) under CIM.

From 2012, Place Based Income Management (PBIM) was introduced in five urban and regional communities, selected on the basis of 'unemployment levels, youth unemployment, skills gaps, the numbers of people receiving welfare payments, and the length of time people have been on income support payments', but also in order to target 'people involved in child protection matters and deemed vulnerable to financial hardship' (Buckmaster and Ey, 2012, p 16). Under PBIM, individuals can volunteer to be placed on IM (with similar incentive payments as available under New Income Management until mid-2015) and those considered 'vulnerable' can be referred to the programme by child protection, social or youth workers. Over the following two years, a similar model of IM was implemented in the lands of the A<u>n</u>angu Pitjantjatjara Yankunytjatjara people in Ceduna, South Australia, and also in the Ngaanyatjarra lands, Kiwirrkurra and Laverton in Western Australia (Arthur, 2015). State and territory agencies were further able to refer benefit recipients to CIM regardless of where they lived, preventing benefit recipients escaping IM by changing residence (Bielefeld, 2012; Bray et al, 2014).

Again, the interview data suggest that Labor introduced this place-based element to CIM "to prove that it [CIM] … wasn't just zapping Aboriginal people. It was sort of broader policy aimed at welfare dependency not just Aboriginal [people]" (Katz, interview) and because it was hard to argue that protecting children was not a valid goal. Yet being flagged by child protection or living in a disadvantaged area was still largely viewed as an individual failure that justified restricting individual autonomy – a view in line with the paternalistic behavioural economics of conservative governments – rather than as a problem with structural causes (Staines et al, 2020a).

After the Liberal–National government returned to power in 2013, it ignored a Parliamentary Joint Committee on Human Rights (2013) report noting a number of compatibility issues between human rights instruments and CIM particularly relating to Indigenous peoples (Bielefeld et al, 2020). Instead, the new government commissioned an inquiry into remote Indigenous training and employment. Led by Andrew Forrest, a businessperson handpicked by then Prime Minister and Prime Minister for Indigenous Affairs, Tony Abbott, the review went beyond its initial brief and was heavily shaped by Forrest's (2014) personal views and experiences about how Indigenous policy more generally should be reformed. Although some overseas examples were included, the review did not engage with recent shifts in Indigenous Affairs policy or with relevant reports on the BasicsCard (Klein, 2014; 2020). While Forrest (2014) indicated the government should take an all or nothing approach to his recommendations, only the proposal for 'cashless welfare' was implemented. Forrest (2014, 4) proposed that 80 per cent of all welfare payments, other than age or veterans' pensions, be subject to IM through a 'Healthy Welfare Card' because parity in educational outcomes 'starts with individual responsibility during pregnancy, intensive early childhood preparation and decent schooling. It doesn't mean more money'. Arguing that IM in its current form was too expensive, Forrest (2014, p 104) looked to an example of a cashless debit card where 'the South African Social Services Agency partnered with the private sector to reform the distribution of social security benefits' and where '[c]ollective cost savings have been very large'. However, a representative from the Australian Council of Social Service interviewed for this study noted that these claims ignored that this:

> 'was quite a different environment to what we understood was happening in Australia … because there was a whole lot of people [in South Africa] who weren't banked, they didn't have access to banks and that was the first time through that welfare card that they actually had a card.' (Interview with a representative from the Australian Council of Social Service)

Several of the academic expert interviewees saw Forrest as a key policy entrepreneur who not only advocated for the Healthy Welfare Card but actively brought different groups of people together to persuade them to trial this idea. This not only included some people from some Indigenous communities, but also key supermarket chains and banks:

> 'He's been pretty effective in engaging the banks, like Commonwealth Bank of Australia, and getting them to take an interest in this policy … Andrew Forrest is clearly a very influential individual, and it wouldn't surprise me if the banks saw … undertaking a role in cashless debit as beneficial for them financially.' (Interview with ACOSS representative)

Forrest's (2014) proposal was introduced to Parliament as a Bill in 2015 and enacted as the CDC in 2016. This was a blanket measure for all benefit recipients on certain working-age benefits in new 'trial' geographical areas characterised as having high levels of welfare dependency and drug/alcohol-related social harms. Between 2016 and 2019, the CDC was rolled out incrementally in Ceduna, South Australia, the East Kimberley and Goldfields regions, Western Australia, and the Hinkler region, Queensland. In late 2019, the Northern Territory and Cape York (including Doomadgee) were also established as CDC trial sites, meaning those on BasicsCards in these areas transitioned to the CDC in 2020 (Parliament of Australia, 2019). The criminality trope again came to the fore, with CDC trial site selection in Western Australia justified on the basis of high crime rates:

> Many stakeholders have indicated their desperation to address the very significant harm caused by welfare-fuelled alcohol abuse in the [Goldfields] region. … Western Australian police data indicate that the domestic and non-domestic assault rate in the Goldfields is more than twice the state average. (Turnbull, 2017b)

In late 2020, the Liberal-National government passed the *Social Security (Administration) Amendment (Continuation of Cashless Welfare) Act*, which, in its first draft, tried to establish the CDC as a permanent programme rather than a time-limited trial in the Ceduna, East Kimberley, Goldfields, Bundaberg and Hervey Bay regions, (which represented an increase in the number of people subjected to CIM), to transition CIM in the Northern Territory and the Cape York region to the CDC, and to make a number of other amendments (Arthur and Ayoub, 2020). However, the government did not succeed, and instead managed a two-year CDC trial site extension with an option for voluntary take up of the CDC in the Northern Territory. Thus, the original form of IM continues to operate around Australia, including in the Northern Territory, and PBIM sites Logan and Rockhampton (both in Queensland), Bankstown (in New South Wales), Greater Shepparton (in Victoria) and Playford (in South Australia). There are also child protection sites in Western Australia and South Australia, and the A<u>n</u>angu Pitjantjatjara Yankunytjatjara (South Australia) and Ngaanyatjarra lands and Kiwirrkurra Community, both in Western Australia. Cape York IM participants will be transferred to the CDC in 2021.

Path dependency was well established, given key government institutions and various political/commercial interests now benefited from the continuation of CIM in Australia. However, Mendes (2020b, p 47) notes that, from late 2017, 'Labor began to signify its specific opposition to further extension of IM programs, and indeed its general scepticism concerning the merits of existing IM measures'. It is worth noting, however, that many of its arguments opposing further expansion of CDC trials contradict its earlier claims in support of IM, and mirror long-standing criticisms of IM by the Australian Greens and advocacy groups. Nonetheless, there has been remarkably little difference between centre-right and centre-left governments on CIM to date, and Labor's changes to reinstate the *Racial Discrimination Act* have not eliminated the disproportionate effect of CIM on Indigenous peoples. As of 4 September 2020, 24,718 people were on the BasicsCard across Australia, with 79 per cent identifying as Indigenous (Arthur and Ayoub, 2020, p 4). Discussion now turns to New Zealand to identify the similarities and differences in how Income Management emerged and evolved in that country.

The emergence of Compulsory Income Management in New Zealand, 2012 to 2014

In 2008, New Zealand elected a government led by the National Party in a coalition with three smaller parties who guaranteed supply and confidence. The new government extended forms of welfare conditionality the Nationals had introduced in the 1990s, such as increasing part-time work obligations for sole parents with young children and for Sickness Benefit recipients in 2010 (Humpage, 2015), but chose to conduct a wide-ranging review of New Zealand's welfare system before announcing further reforms. The Welfare Working Group (2010a, p 1) investigated 'how long-term benefit dependence can be reduced and work outcomes improved, including for sole parents … and whether the structure of the benefit system and hardship assistance in particular, is contributing to long-term benefit dependency'. This review brought the concept of IM into the public domain for the first time in New Zealand. However, this section shows that, like its Australian counterpart, the National-led government used the WWG to build support for an already-planned IM policy.

Following a comprehensive public submission process, the WWG (2011) made many radical recommendations, including replacing the social security agency Work and Income with a standalone government entity called the New Zealand Employment Agency, and an extensive range of punitive obligations and sanctions for various types of benefit recipients that were either not widely supported by submissions or had not been discussed at all in earlier papers. Although IM *was* mentioned in the WWG (2010b, p 14) 'Options' paper, this was suggested to apply 'when people with work capacity are on a benefit almost permanently and they demonstrably fail to use the benefit appropriately, for example, failing to provide essentials for children'.

However, the WWG (2011) ultimately recommended IM only for parents on benefits if they did not meet specific 'social obligations' to their children (health checks, enrolments in a primary health organisation, and attendance at preschool or school), parents with drug and alcohol issues, and 16- and 17-year-old sole parents. The WWG (2011) also suggested that 16- and 17-year-olds without children should have their benefits paid to a responsible adult or agent (such as a community organisation) and that both groups would need to meet educational, budgeting and other parenting obligations. Notably, the WWG (2010a) mentioned Australia's trialling of IM but did not provide evidence of the effectiveness of this policy, nor mention its disproportionate impact on Indigenous communities. It also gave the impression that existing supplementary supports (such as food grants provided in the UK, US and New Zealand using payment cards, sometimes restricting spending on alcohol and cigarettes) were forms of IM, although they did not quarantine core entitlements. This review thus engaged in important political work for the National-led government by implying that CIM was already common practice both overseas and in New Zealand.

The WWG's (2011) youth-focused recommendations were reflected in the policy eventually adopted by the National-led government and emerged from actuarial risk modelling used to identify which age groups had the greatest probability of long-term benefit receipt and thus represented the greatest potential cost to the state. The WWG (2010a, p 47) saw insurance-based approaches such as actuarial modelling as 'more likely than welfare-based approaches to give rise to incentives on providers and individuals to reduce the chance of adverse events occurring, the consequences from that event if it does occur, and the broader costs associated with the risk'. The WWG's (2010a) actuarial analysis found that half of all 16- to 18-year-olds entering the social security system spent at least five of the next 10 years on a benefit, and that a third of Domestic Purposes Benefit recipients were teenagers when they had their children. In total, 16- to 24-year-olds were predicted to cost the state $156,000 per person across their lives. Although lower than many other groups (particularly those on the invalid's benefit: $192,000), this was considerably higher than for those on the Unemployment Benefit ($65,000).

The WWG (2010a) framed these young social security recipients as coming from dysfunctional backgrounds, including state care, and as having multiple personal problems such as low educational attainment and disengagement from the workforce, resulting in adverse effects throughout their lives. There was particular concern about the children of those receiving social security:

> Long-term benefit dependency is harmful for children as it leads to prolonged periods of low income and poverty. Children being raised

> in benefit dependent families are at increased risk of joblessness and benefit receipt as adults. Children being raised by teen parents on a benefit are a particular concern from a child development perspective. There is compelling evidence that children of teen parents are at greater risk of a range of poor outcomes. (WWG, 2011, pp 47–8)

As noted earlier in this chapter, similar (tenuous) connections between welfare, dependency and teenage parenting were made in the Australian CIM discourse, and are a common focus for behavioural economics, which the WWG (2010a) explicitly referenced.

Opposition MPs claimed that the National Party in New Zealand had adopted IM because this approach had been explicitly mentioned in the National Party–Association of Consumer and Taxpayers (ACT) Party (2011) confidence and supply agreement. The ACT Party was indeed strongly represented on the WWG, and its leader, David Seymour, said in an interview that the party was happy to take credit for IM. However, the legislative process for CIM began several months *before* this agreement was signed, and policymakers interviewed for this study indicated that the National Party had at least discussed – if it had not already decided to implement – IM in some form before the WWG was established. The National-led government rejected some of the WWG's more radical recommendations, allowing the government to look moderate in comparison and belying the significance of the reforms, including the introduction of CIM as part of a new Youth Service in 2012.

The *Social Security (Criteria for Incentive Payments and Money Management) Regulations 2012* laid out the regulations guiding how a form of CIM, known as 'Money Management' in New Zealand, would be applied. However, only the *Social Security (Youth Support and Work Focus) Amendment Act 2012* was subject to significant parliamentary debate and, interestingly, much of this concerned the way those 'not in employment, education or training' (NEET) or those at risk of becoming NEET would be identified – via actuarial risk modelling – for *voluntary* case management and support services to get them into education, training and work. Much less attention was paid to the Youth Service's role in the *compulsory* application of IM to those on the Youth Payment (YP, for 16- to 17-year-olds who cannot live with their parents due to family breakdown) or the Young Parent Payment (YPP, for 16- to 19-year-old parents).

For those subject to CIM, the majority of their social security payment is redirected towards board/rent and other utilities by a Youth Service provider. If any income remains after this process, up to $50 is then paid directly to the young person's bank account to spend as they wish, while the rest is put on a Payment Card usable at a limited range of suppliers (mostly supermarkets). There is no exemption from CIM unless young people meet their educational obligations to be in education or training for six months and have met all the criteria to receive incentive payments ($10 per week each) associated with this educational obligation, as well as budgeting and (where relevant) parenting education obligations. This means young people are on CIM for at least six months (but in practice often much longer) and only exit when they 'age-out' of the YP or YPP benefits or leave social security for some other reason. If they fail to meet obligations, significant financial sanctions can be imposed YP/YPP recipients must return to CIM (MSD, 2012b; Humpage, 2018). This contrasts with Australia, which offers legislative routes through which individuals who meet certain criteria can be exempted from CIM – though it should be noted that, as described in Chapter 5, these routes are difficult to pursue.

Nonetheless, the paternalistic drivers of New Zealand's CIM policy intersect with a youth development model aiming to empower young people. YP/YPP recipients are allocated a Youth Service mentor who offers hands-on support with budgeting, parenting and educational decision-making. While Chapter 3 highlights tensions between this mentoring role and the surveillance required for the decision-making authority given to Youth Service mentors, this form of case management is arguably more supportive and less punitive than CIM in Australia, although participants who fall into the 'vulnerable' category in Australia are allocated a social worker to act as a case worker. New Zealand's CIM policy also differs from Australia's in its more consistent emphasis on incentive payments for meeting obligations, a form of 'nudge' policy informed by behavioural economics (Thaler and Sunstein, 2008) aiming to promote 'good' behaviours rather than just penalising 'bad' ones. Notably, YP/YPP recipients are also not subject to work obligations, although obtaining part-time work is one of the criteria for demonstrating 'financial competency' when seeking to exit CIM (MSD, 2017). Another nudge policy, the Guaranteed Childcare Assistance Payment is available for those with children under the age of five, to ensure childcare costs are not a barrier to participation in education, training or work-based learning (MSD, 2012b). Aside from obligations under 'family responsibility agreements' in the Cape York model, such as attending financial counselling, Australia has no specific CIM-related obligations (although many social security recipients have work obligations). Apart from the incentive payments noted earlier to attract voluntary IM participants, there are no longer any incentives for CIM participants since the phasing out of Matched Savings Payments (a maximum of $500 to purchase large household items) in 2016.

Interviews with policymakers in New Zealand identified then Minister for Social Development, Paula Bennett – a Māori woman who had received the Domestic Purposes Benefit while sole parenting – as the key policy entrepreneur for CIM in New Zealand. A National Party MP interviewed for the study was aware of what was happening in Australia, stating that:

> 'Preliminary research findings about the effects of income management schemes in Australia are mixed, potentially improving financial stability and increasing spending of food but also making clients dependent on the service and unable to effectively manage their own finances when required (that is, if/when they go off benefit).' (Interview with a National Party MP)

Stone (2017) notes that it is difficult to measure negative policy learning (where policymakers learn what *not* to do from examining the experiences of others), but it is that possible such mixed findings made it politically difficult to explicitly refer to Australia when promoting CIM in New Zealand. However, the notable absence of references to Australia's CIM policy appears to be at least partly explained by the very different way in which New Zealand planned to operationalise CIM, which made the Australian experience less relevant to the policy Bennett wished to design for young people. The present research suggests that her initial inspiration came from a study tour of the UK and US.

More broadly, the performance-based contracts used for the Youth Service reflected an international trend towards governments making incentive payments to non-government agencies that are achieving client outcomes (Moffatt, 2018; Staines et al, 2020b). Although the WWG (2011) noted the success of the Australian Job Network, which contracts non-government organisations to deliver employment services, a National Party MP interviewed for our study said:

> 'I don't know whether Paula [Bennett] was being influenced by international [ideas about non-government providers], but I do know that we had been talking about how you get that local knowledge, and a lot of our work has focused on that devolution of that individual decision making to local people who have that on-the-ground knowledge.' (Interview with a National Party MP)

New Zealand has a long history of contracting out service delivery (Humpage, 2015), but the Youth Service was an important experiment in privatisation, representing the first time MSD had contracted out a case management function. This meant non-government organisations sharing the administration of core entitlements with Work and Income. In 2021, there were 42 contracted Youth Service providers, a mix of tribal/Māori, non-government and private training organisations. Work and Income also ran two Youth Services, because no suitable community organisations could be found (MSD, 2019a). Youth Service employees are responsible for assisting YP/YPP recipients with their entitlement applications, as well as for reporting on and making recommendations regarding incentive payments or sanctions to the MSD's Youth Service Support Unit (MSD, 2012b). In being administered by MSD, the New Zealand Payment Card is somewhat similar to the Australian BasicsCard but contrasts with the CDC, which is run through the commercial banking system by a private, profit-making financial services provider, Indue Ltd (Arthur and Ayoub, 2020; Bray et al, 2014). As a result, operations (and accountability) for CIM are less commercially driven in New Zealand.

In sum, New Zealand's CIM is a far more targeted and potentially more supportive programme than Australia's. However, it is universally applied to all YP/YPP recipients without evidence of problems in their spending habits. New Zealand's then National-led government justified this approach by drawing heavily on the WWG's (2011) framing of unemployment as a cultural deficit whereby benefit recipients lose their work ethic and transmit poor behaviours to their children, perpetuating a cycle of dependence that is costly to the state, as well as morally repugnant. This cognitive filter was in place in claims by Bennett (2012a, p 286) that '[o]f the estimated 14,000 young people Not in Employment Education or Training, we know that up to 90 per cent will go on benefit by the time they are adults'. This was in part blamed on previous policy:

> Today we have teenagers on welfare – teenagers – who are given a weekly sum of money, and then just left to get on with it. Many of these teenagers are parents. It is an abdication of responsibility to simply leave them to fend for themselves and their babies. We have sole parents trapped in welfare with little support, and, quite frankly, little hope. We have women consigned to a life of welfare, because over 30 years ago society said women could not support themselves without a man. But we can make a difference … I will be frank: we want to make welfare a less attractive proposition for many young people. We will not continue to dish out money to young people and teen parents, and just hope that they will be OK. (Bennett, 2012b, p 294)

National Party politicians also echoed the WWG in framing young people as vulnerable children who were victims of their parents' poor behaviour and thus needed 'saving'. For instance, National MP Michael Sabin (2012, p 288) said his government was 'backing those young people, rather than leaving them to sink or swim, because we know that most of them will sink'. Although focusing on young people as victims infantilised them in a similar way to Australia's political discourse, criminality (of young people or their parents) was never a key trope in New Zealand; in fact, the only reference to criminality was in regard to young people being forced to commit crimes to get around CIM rules (Social Services Committee, 2012, p 18). Green Party MP Jan Logie (2012, p 2864) also focused on the role of the state: 'Many of these young people who are in this 16- to 17-year age category have actually come out of Child, Youth and Family Services; they were in care. They are quite vulnerable people. The State, in a sense, has not done very well by some of these kids'.

The political discourse surrounding CIM was also far less racialised in New Zealand, although there was a little more attention paid to the gendered impacts of CIM. In December 2020, there were 1,559 people on YP/YPP Payments, 52 per cent of them Māori and 89 per cent of them female. This compares poorly to benefits in general, where Māori represent 36 per cent and females 54 per cent of all recipients – this latter figure decreased slightly from December 2019 as COVID-19-related forms of unemployment increased (MSD, 2020). Data on levels of disability in this cohort are not recorded. The WWG (2010a) *had* noted that young people on benefits were more likely to be Māori than non-Māori, which was cause for much debate according to a government minister interviewed for this study, but this disproportionate impact on Māori, women or other vulnerable groups (such as people with disabilities) was rarely articulated in policy documents (Office of the Minister of Social Development, OMSD, 2011). The Ministryof Māori Development, the Ministry of Women's Affairs and government organisations were reportedly consulted about the legislation, but if any voiced significant concerns about CIM, these were not made public (OMSD, 2011; Social Services Committee, 2012). Policy documents *do* indicate some concern that treating young social security recipients differently from other young people might be inconsistent with the New Zealand *Bill of Rights Act 1990* and the *Human Rights Act 1993* in relation to the right to freedom from discrimination. However, MSD (2012c, p 6) argued that such treatment was 'justifiable in terms of improved life chances. Increased expectations are balanced with increased support – together these offer young people the opportunity to break from the prospect of long-term benefit receipt and welfare dependency'.

Both the Labour and Green parties raised concerns, particularly about the gendered impact of the Youth Service and CIM, given that 'a young woman with a child will stay on a [Payment] card until she is 19. A male who is, for instance, transitioning from a Youth Payment to an unemployment benefit will move off the card at 18' (Social Services Committee, 2012, p 16). Targeting teen parents, the majority of whom are women, was misguided on numerous levels, according to the Green Party's Jan Logie (2012, p 286):

> The number of young girls having babies is trending down, without Government intervention. The proportion of sole parents with jobs has increased since the 1990s, and has started levelling off only as job growth has slowed. Most people on the DPB are on it for a very limited period of time. Less than 10 percent of current recipients have received the DPB continuously for 10 years or more. We also know

> that there are really significant and valid, actually, reasons for people needing the DPB. A large percentage of women accessing the DPB do so for reasons of domestic violence, and CCS Disability Action told us during submissions that 25.8 percent of people on the DPB have children with disabilities whom they are caring for. There have also been numerous pieces of research in this country that have clearly demonstrated discrimination in the job market, especially based on race, age, and ability.

The Green Party also offered the strongest critique of the racialised nature of CIM and the Youth Service model. While New Zealand has not experienced explicit Stolen Generation or Stolen Wage policies as occurred in Australia, Māori have been subject to similarly paternalistic interventions, including reduced social security entitlements due to questions about their 'deservingness' and cultural norms (Dalley and Tennant, 2004; Stephens, 2015). Logie (2016) highlighted that institutionalised racism saw many Māori ending up in care or having other experiences that might lead them to rely on a benefit at a young age, and that the predictive modelling used to target young people would exacerbate these existing harms. She recalled an MSD official indicating that Māori ethnicity could not be identified as a risk factor because it would be perceived as racist, yet '[a]lmost 60 per cent of those young people in care are Māori', and contact with the child protect system was still considered an appropriate risk factor;'[t]he official said: "Don't worry, we'll get them anyway"' (Logie, 2015, p 115; and see MSD, 2015).

This apparent indifference to the disproportionate impact of CIM may seem surprising given New Zealand has a political party – the Māori Party – specifically representing Indigenous peoples, a fact exemplifying some significant differences in the historical and political contexts of Australia and New Zealand. Indigenous peoples represent 16.5 per cent of New Zealanders, compared to 3.3 per cent of Australians (ABS, 2018; Statistics NZ, 2019). Following a Declaration of Independence by a confederation of tribal chiefs in New Zealand in 1835, the British Crown signed the Treaty of Waitangi in 1840. Although ignored for decades and subject to continuing debate, this treaty provides greater institutional and public recognition of Indigenous sovereignty and rights in New Zealand than Indigenous Australians enjoy, since they have no recourse to an historical treaty with the Crown and their calls for greater Indigenous political representation have frequently been ignored or undermined. New Zealand policy responses increasingly involve Indigenous representatives, consultation and/or Indigenous cultural concepts, and the Māori Party promotes a strengths-based, rather than a deficits-based, discourse when discussing Māori issues (see Humpage et al, 2020b). Indeed, the call for Youth Service providers actively encouraged Indigenous organisations to apply, with 11 out of the 42 providers eventually being tribally based and Māori-owned, while many others employ Māori staff (MSD, 2019b).

Māori traditionally have strong ties with the Labour Party, making the Māori Party's support of the National-led government from 2008 to 2017 controversial. The Māori Party made some policy gains through its supply and confidence agreements, but its relationship with the National Party likely limited its ability to critique CIM (Humpage et al, 2020b). However, like their Indigenous Australian counterparts, some Māori blame the welfare system for Indigenous disadvantage and thus support efforts to reduce so-called 'welfare dependency' (WWG, 2010a). The Māori Party, in particular, is generally rather conservative on social security issues, and this may have contributed to its voice being notably absent in debates about the policy and to the party voting to support the legislation introducing the Youth Service. This context helps to explain why, despite CIM's obvious racialised impacts, this policy was framed largely through a broader welfare dependency lens, one which Humpage's (2015) analysis of public attitudes towards the welfare state suggests was not particularly controversial in New Zealand.

Extending and consolidating Compulsory Income Management in New Zealand, 2015 to 2021

The youth development rhetoric used to justify the Youth Service, and the lack of racialisation of the policy, contributed to CIM being remarkably uncontroversial in New Zealand. This allowed the government to apply it to a wider cohort of young people through the *Social Security (Extension of Young Persons Services and Remedial Matters) Amendment Bill 2015* (MSD, 2015). This extended Youth Services and CIM to 18- to 19-year-old benefit recipients deemed to be 'at risk' of not moving into employment, while also tidying up other minor matters emerging from the 2012 legislation. Although the evaluation evidence available at this time was limited (see Chapter 3 for further discussion), it was used to justify CIM. First, new Minister of Social Development, Anne Tolley (2015, p 5285), emphasised that: '[a]n initial estimate shows that for every dollar spent on the existing Youth Service, the taxpayer's liability reduces by $2.53, and I expect that there will be a similar return on investment for this older cohort'. Thus, CIM was said to be saving the government money, as it had hoped. Second, it was also claimed to be saving children from their parents: '38 per cent of [Youth Service participants] had been victims of domestic violence, 76 per cent of them had been victims of emotional neglect, five per cent had been either homeless or victims of sexual abuse, and most of them had disengaged from mainstream education' (Doocey, 2016, p 11579). National MP, Parmjeet Parmar (2015, p 5285) went on to argue that:

> These findings are consistent with neuro-scientific research that shows that the portion of the brain that is responsible for impulse control, analytical thinking, judgment, and future-orientation gradually develops throughout early adulthood. So young people in their teens do need this structure, care, support, and guidance during those years, so they can learn the skills that are required for them to get into education or get into jobs.

This comment stresses the way in which those engaged in the Youth Service, some of whom were or are close to being legal adults, continued to be infantilised as a way of justifying the intensive case management intrinsic to CIM.

Notably, the Māori Party opposed the extension of the Youth Service in 2015, with co-leader Marama Fox (2016, np) stating that:

> The intent of the investment model, we absolutely support. If this [legislation] is to reduce the number of young people who are going to be long-term beneficiaries, we have no issue with that whatsoever, because we do want to have an aspiration where our people are not co-dependent on the Government.

However, Fox (2016, np) noted a number of operational concerns, as well as the fact that the extension 'is going to be targeted to young Maori parents more than any other group, and that these young Maori babies are going to be subjected to the stress of being hauled around from pillar to post. … It goes against the very human rights of our country'. It seems likely that, as the policy gains from its supply and confidence agreements waned, the Māori Party became more concerned with distinguishing itself from the National Party.

In contrast, although the Labour Party continued to vote against CIM, its arguments were far weaker in 2015 than they had been in 2012. It even acknowledged that some young people reported positive experiences (Ardern, 2016, np), and that the Youth Service 'takes our young people out of that toxic culture of Work and Income and provides them with the wraparound services and support that Work and Income, actually, should be offering' (Sepuloni, 2015a, p 5285). This may be one reason the Labour–New Zealand First government elected in 2017 did not abandon CIM. This is despite suggesting in 2012 that CIM was ideology-based not evidence-based and was a form of 'social engineering' (Prasad, 2012, np), and despite the Labour–Green (2017, p 4) confidence and supply agreement promising to '[o]verhaul the welfare system, ensure access to entitlements, [and] remove excessive sanctions'. The new government *did* establish a Welfare Expert Advisory Group (2019), whose report, *Whakamana Tāngata – Restoring*

Dignity to Social Security in New Zealand, could have justified a reversal of many of the Nationals' reforms, including CIM. The Labour government has also diluted the emphasis placed on actuarial risk modelling by acknowledging other forms of evidence, reduced the focus on sanctions, increased abatement thresholds, and expressed a desire to address the 'toxic culture' at Work and Income. Yet Neuwelt-Kearns and Asher's (2020, p 5) assessment of progress found that '[n]one of the 42 key [WEAG] recommendations, and only four of 126 detailed recommendations, have been fully implemented'.

It is possible that Labour's formal coalition with New Zealand First, a party that is conservative on social security issues, hindered its ability to implement the WEAG (2019) recommendations. This indicates how political 'interests' can act as an obstacle to as well as a facilitator of policy. However, several months after gaining an historic electoral majority in the 2020 election, which meant that Labour would govern in its own right, it has still not abandoned or even significantly modified CIM. When Labour opposed the extension in 2015, it requested only three amendments: that the additional employment and educational support available through the Youth Service be available to any young person who is NEET and is either on or applying for a benefit; that all 18- to 19-year-olds be notified when referred to Youth Service; and that YPP recipients should not have work or educational obligations placed upon them until their child turns three (in line with policy for the Sole Parent Support benefit) (Sepuloni, 2015b). Only the second change was implemented, with the support of the National Party. The first formal review of the Youth Service, conducted in 2018–19, prior to re-tendering in 2020, also did not bring radical change; although mentor/client ratios for both the NEET and YP/YPP cohorts were improved, CIM was considered out of scope (MSD, 2019a).

On the other hand, Labour in New Zealand did *not* extend CIM to other groups as the National Party had planned (and as the Labor government did in Australia). This is perhaps surprising since MSD has placed a greater emphasis on financial literacy among all social security recipients since 2016, including enhanced financial mentoring, peer-led support groups, and connecting social security recipients to Building Financial Capability services which focus on strengths-based financial planning (Torrie and Baillie, 2017). To some degree, then, the greater focus on supporting CIM participants in New Zealand compared to Australia has been extended to other groups *without* extending CIM. In contrast with Jenny Macklin's strong advocacy for CIM within the Australian Labor Party, there is also no policy entrepreneur promoting CIM within the New Zealand Labour government. Nonetheless, a high level of path dependency means that the policy has become sufficiently embedded to make radical change difficult – if, indeed, this is deemed desirable by a Labour Party that may feel it must follow centrist politics and policies to retain power.

Conclusion

This chapter has highlighted the often messy nature of policy making, where ideas emerge from multiple sources and coalesce to form policies that may share some characteristics with those elsewhere (overseas or locally) but are hybrids rather than exact replicas of any existing policy (Peck and Theordore, 2015; Stone, 2017). Although IM itself was new to both countries, it is arguable that it did not represent a *significant* departure from either countries' historical preferences for welfare conditionality. However, while CIM in both countries was driven by similar contextual factors (a desire to reduce social security costs and high levels of Indigenous/sole parent/disability/youth benefit receipt), a similar policy logic (restricting spending freedom to change individual spending behaviour) and operational similarities (the types of goods restricted, the use of Payment Cards), they emerged as quite different policies overall.

These differences result from the very specific local political contexts in which policy is made, including the way key interests aligned to provide the right environment for IM to be implemented, maintained and extended. In taking seriously Bacchi's (2009) discursive focus on problem definition, this chapter has noted how conservative governments in both countries actively commissioned inquiries and used their framing of the 'problem' to justify the implementation of CIM, drawing on discourses and self-evident myths that were naturalised to the point that it made backtracking by their Labor/Labour counterparts difficult. Despite IM's obvious racialised impacts, however, the policy was largely framed by a broader welfare dependency lens in New Zealand, one which Humpage's (2015) analysis of public attitudes towards the welfare state suggests was not particularly controversial in either country. This lens was clearly central to Australia's IM policy and is similarly accepted by many Australians. However, it was blurred by CIM's introduction as part of the NTER and only became more explicit when Labor reinstated the *Racial Discrimination Act* in 2010 and when actuarial cost predictions began in Australia from 2016 (Humpage et al, 2020b).

Overall, what this chapter has demonstrated is that there is remarkably little difference between centre-left and centre-right parties in Australia and New Zealand. Both have perpetuated the racialised, feminised and ableist implications of 'welfare dependency', despite the policy differences highlighted here. The next chapter indicates how successive governments have also selectively used (or ignored) evidence to garner public support (or at least avoid public criticism) and have failed to adequately consult those disproportionately affected by CIM, particularly Indigenous peoples. Later chapters in this book explore the intended and unintended effects of this negative framing on social security recipients.

3

Barriers to implementing Compulsory Income Management

Introduction

This chapter examines multiple barriers to the effective implementation of CIM programmes in Australia and New Zealand. Drawing on the views of Australian CIM participants and community stakeholders, this chapter argues that these implementation problems resulted from design and process flaws that could have been avoided if governments had given themselves genuine opportunities to listen to the needs of those individuals and communities impacted by CIM and had learned from research evidence. The first part of this chapter examines the impact of the top-down imposition of CIM on local communities in Australia. A major source of contention in trial sites has been the poor application of the chosen technology (whether the BasicsCard or Cashless Debit Card) without adequate regard to the needs or concerns of participants. Another source of conflict has been that so-called 'consultation' in specific geographical areas has been done with at best limited input from and consent of local communities, including IM participants. The limitations of government community consultation processes have had an adverse effect on community cohesion.

The second part of the chapter turns to New Zealand, where there was never any question that CIM was a top-down policy but where Youth Service mentors are meant to empower young people while at the same time tracking and surveilling their behaviour. This policy design causes considerable role confusion and frustration. Systems failures also mean the process of decision-making is lengthy and inconsistent, while technological failures created problems for both Youth Service providers and YP/YPP recipients.

The third part discusses how things would have looked had co-design processes been employed to further community and youth development goals. The chapter concludes that the evidence around implementation furthers the argument that the introduction of CIM was ideologically driven.

Implementation problems in Australia

Application of technology without consumer input

As noted in Chapter 2, the Australian Government introduced CIM via two forms of debit card: the BasicsCard, introduced in the Northern

Territory and then in multiple sites across Australia, including Playford and Greater Shepparton, where data were collected; and the Cashless Debit Card (CDC), later introduced in four sites for use at all stores. The CDC sites included Ceduna, another data collection location. Both forms of card were introduced with limited consultation with local IM participants. This lack of consumer input has caused significant practical difficulties for card users. Study participants in the BasicsCard sites of Playford and Greater Shepparton reported a number of concerns, including limitations on their financial autonomy and consumer choice due to many major stores (often including the supermarkets with the cheapest prices) not accepting the BasicsCard for payment, particularly in the early period of the CIM scheme. As Grant (Playford) noted:

> 'I moved to my house in [suburb] and IGA's my closest shop and they don't take the BasicsCard. That's when I started to get annoyed. I couldn't even do shopping down the road, so I'd have to catch the bus for shopping or meals.'

Other CIM participant concerns included the BasicsCard not being accepted outside the designated site, which limited users' mobility, and the stress caused by reliance on Centrelink to complete basic payments for regular services such as phone and other utilities. Overall, the card seemed to create major inconvenience for users, and if anything to undermine their financial management skills (Mendes et al, 2020). The emotional impact these problems had on CIM participants is explored further in Chapter 4.

In response to these issues, the CDC was designed to be more user-friendly than the BasicsCard, but also caused practical problems for users. Study participants in Ceduna reported concerns about technological limitations and inadequate coordination procedures on the part of the card provider:

> 'I went to the shop and went to pay for something and there is no money. … They don't know what happened. We got in touch with them [Indue] and they just said, oh someone else has had the same problem, and I said, "well, it's not good enough. It's my money. I need it". They just said, "Oh well, we'll try to locate it, and if we do, it won't be in until the next pay".' (Ellen, Ceduna)

In this case, technological problems led to significant hardship, despite this participant being legally entitled to their social security benefit. Broader concerns included the complex administrative processes involved in checking basic details concerning payments or balance, or in forwarding complaints or requests to Indue. Additionally, some users with limited IT literacy or a preference for using cash were seriously challenged by the sudden shift to electronic banking without substantive preparation or infrastructure support (Roche et al, 2021). Consulting with potential users of the cards and trialling the new technology prior to implementation could potentially have avoided these failures.

Poor communication about Compulsory Income Management

Interviewed CIM participants cited an array of issues related to the problematic implementation of CIM in their communities that resulted from poor communication about CIM from government officials. Many welfare recipients described being unaware of the introduction of CIM to their community, limited understanding of the reasons for their inclusion in the scheme, and confusion as to how and where to use the BasicsCard or CDC. Eric, from the community of Yalata near Ceduna, bluntly stated that: "They didn't ask us if we wanted it. … It was changed, all of a sudden."

Ellen (Ceduna) explained how they first found out about being placed on CIM:

> 'There was a little slip of a paper or a bit of cardboard or some type of notice thing that came through the post saying something about a basic card or something. Basically, a lot of us didn't know what the hell it was.'

Many participants were surprised to find out that they had been placed on a form of CIM by letter or a notification to their online Centrelink account. However, others were notified to attend an appointment at Centrelink:

Marnie (Shepparton):	I got an email on the Centrelink thing. Then I went in there and I was like, 'What the hell's this?' Then they said you have to be on the BasicsCard. I was like, 'Do I have to be?' They said yes. … Why? It doesn't make any sense.
Facilitator:	Yeah. Why do you think they put you on a BasicsCard?
Marnie:	I have no idea. … Everyone that I asked said, 'What the hell's that? … What the fuck's that?'

In these cases, placement on a CIM arrangement was immediate and seemingly irreversible. Tyson in Shepparton described how he was notified:

> 'I got an e-mail and a message on my myGov account, just saying that to be expected to be put on Income Management, because now I've been selected for Income Management. Then when I went in there, I spoke to the lady and she said to me that it's to help control your

money and help you manage it and stuff like that. … There was no option of not going on. I had to go onto it or I was getting cut off.'

This highlights that Centrelink staff were not routinely providing information about how CIM participants might seek exemptions.

Steph (Playford) had no prior warning of being placed onto CIM, responding with confusion and surprise to the new arrangements when checking her bank account:

Steph:	… like I got paid like half of my pay, and I was like what the fuck?
Facilitator:	So, you didn't know?
Steph:	No, they didn't let me know, and I was like what the heck? So, I went into Centrelink and I abused them – I was like 'Why did you only give me half of my pay? I'm meant to get this much money and I've only got this'. And they were like 'Oh, we'll have a look for you'. Made me wait nearly half an hour to an hour, like that's Centrelink for you, and they were like 'Oh, you're on the BasicsCard'. I was like "Well, thank you, dickhead – like you could have told me or something, rang me."

The abrupt implementation of CIM was also challenging for service providers supporting social security recipients to manage these new arrangements and to respond more broadly to the needs of communities. Stakeholders held views on how the implementation of CIM could have been improved to better consult welfare recipients, and also to involve them in the design and implementation:

> 'Well, I definitely think it would be improved if people were not just receiving things in the mail telling you that they're on it. That's not the way to go. I think people should be involved as much as possible; they should be fully informed along as they go. Things shouldn't be done *to* people; they should be done *with* people. So yeah … they should be fully informed about what's happening for them and know exactly why and not just be told well you have to be on this. … Talked to about it, informed and educated and then being a part of the decision.' (Dennis, Shepparton stakeholder)

Participants in this study remarked on the deep community divisions that were exposed by the implementation of CIM in Australia. In Ceduna, for example, opponents of CIM felt that those in positions of power, without direct experience or understanding of the impact of CIM – including its stigmatising elements and financial inconvenience – were making decisions about their day-to-day lives without their involvement or input. In contrast, proponents of CIM asserted that the policy was having a strong impact on reducing harms relating to alcohol use and gambling, that the wellbeing of families was improving, that consultations had been effective, and that CIM is a minor inconvenience for most social security recipients.

These circumstances have led to ongoing conflict in the Ceduna community. Community stakeholders claim that front-line social work professionals have left Ceduna due to overwhelming, and at times personal, criticism of their role in the implementation of CIM, while social security recipients have reportedly left the region altogether to avoid being placed on CIM. Conflict between community leaders and CIM participants has been ongoing, with extensive pressure being placed on Aboriginal community leaders in particular. A stakeholder gave an account of the impact of some of the conflict that has occurred in Ceduna:

Nancy (Ceduna stakeholder):	Certainly, at the beginning, the Ceduna Aboriginal Leadership Group were championing the card. So yeah, I was very much aware of that. I'm also aware that their lives became very difficult because they were copping a lot of flak from the community.
Facilitator:	What was that about?
Nancy:	People that didn't agree, didn't like them speaking on behalf of them without even consultation. Yeah, just the anti-card people that weren't happy that this group of Aboriginal people had stood up and said, yeah, we want this. … So, it's pulled people apart that used to be together. That's not a good outcome. They're professional people. People had to leave their jobs because they couldn't handle it anymore. … There was a lot of pressure going on. We have a very active Facebook and all of the social stuff, so that becomes intolerable for some. Others can stand up to it, but I think it really has been— some of those leaders have really suffered, without realising that consequence was coming their way. … I think the Commonwealth should have stood up and represented their own policy.

These comments from community stakeholders and CIM participants illustrate the degree to which top-down policy making without adequately informing participants and communities not only harmed those directly affected by CIM but also divided the communities. The next section examines the major and ongoing contention around the limited or poor processes used when consultation did actually occur in affected CIM sites.

Inadequate community consultation

This section draws on the interview data to explore the limitations of the government consultation undertaken around CIM. However, it is first worth noting that the argument presented here – that the IM measures introduced by the Coalition and Labor governments from 2007 to 2013 involved little, if any, *genuine* consultation with targeted communities or actual IM participants – is not unique to our study (Parliamentary Joint Committee on Human Rights, 2016). The measures can reasonably be described as top-down programmes that were 'simply imposed on the communities' (Bray, 2015, p 7). This contrasts with the model of CIM developed by the Cape York Institute for Policy and Leadership, headed by Noel Pearson, which was by comparison *more* community-based and -led through a partnership with the Commonwealth and Queensland governments. One month before the Northern Territory Emergency Intervention announcement, the Cape York Institute for Policy and Leadership (2007) proposed (and has subsequently implemented) a programme which similarly aimed to establish positive social norms and reduce 'passive welfare' in some of the remote Indigenous communities of Cape York. However, it differed from the federal CIM policy in several ways: communities 'opted in' to the IM scheme (through their local Aboriginal councils, or equivalent leadership groups), IM was only applied to a small number of community members as a last resort, and – of most relevance here – the policy was developed through community consultations that were, notwithstanding some critiques and limitations (for example see Scott et al, 2018), nevertheless more extensive than those experienced in other IM settings across Australia (Billings, 2010; Cape York Institute for Policy and Leadership, 2007). It was thus implemented with the knowledge and consent of at least some (though not all) community members (Scott et al, 2018). Chapter 2 also indicated that other Indigenous and non-Indigenous communities were experimenting with forms of voluntary IM, but no formal consultations were undertaken with such communities prior to the implementation of CIM in 2007.

As a result of significant criticism, and in response to early evaluation findings, the federal Labor government reported holding more than 500 consultation meetings with Northern Territory Indigenous participants, plus representatives of regional and major Indigenous stakeholder organisations, in June and August 2009 as part of the Future Directions process. Many participants in these meetings, particularly women, asserted that IM had resulted in more money being spent on necessities such as food, clothing, school-related expenses and white goods, and had reduced outlays on alcohol, drugs and gambling (Australian Government, 2009a; Macklin, 2009b). However, these were arguably little more than information sharing sessions. The participants were only offered two options: either to continue the existing IM model, or to allow individuals to request exemptions on the basis of demonstrated responsible behaviour. They were not given the choice of dismantling IM entirely, or of amending it into a voluntary scheme (Australian Government, 2009b; Bielefeld, 2014b).

Following criticism that the entire consultation procedure was flawed because it did not offer communities genuine participation in the decision-making process (Siewert, 2010), the government completed an extensive consultation process with Indigenous communities in the Northern Territory as part of the Stronger Futures programme, but IM was not discussed (Australian Government, 2011; CALC, 2012; Bielefeld, 2014b). However, it was apparent from the Stronger Futures parliamentary inquiry that Indigenous communities were divided on the merits of IM, with some community members labelling the measure as 'controlling' and 'dehumanising' (CALC, 2012, p 40).

Yet place-based IM (PBIM) programmes were still introduced in 2011–12 without any government consultation with targeted communities. Rather, the then Minister for Families, Community Services and Indigenous Affairs, Jenny Macklin, informed Parliament that the five sites had been chosen on the basis of high unemployment rates, and high levels of young people reliant on income support. Nevertheless, the Labor government did not consult with community groups in these locations to clarify whether the introduction of IM programmes was warranted, or how they might complement existing social service programs. The CEO of a major local welfare agency in one of these PBIM sites, Goulburn Valley Family Care, concluded, disappointedly, that 'Shepparton was not part of a place-based trial, but just a place required to host a trial for the Commonwealth' (Tennant, 2012, p 35).

In 2015, the Liberal-National Coalition government decided that, to be successful, the introduction of the more restrictive CDC would require evidence of support from local community leaders, including Indigenous leaders. Consequently, Alan Tudge (2015), the Parliamentary Secretary to the Prime Minister at the time, stated that the CDC would be trialled 'where there's at least an openness from the community leaders in a particular area who are wanting to participate in a trial'. In practice, this meant the government sought support from community members and organisations who ideally would have direct input into the programme design (Cantwell, 2015). According to Marcia Langton (2015), a prominent Indigenous supporter of IM at the time, the CDC was distinguished from the earlier forms of IM by substantial public support from local community leaders, including Indigenous community leaders.

The Federal government later claimed to have 'co-designed' the CDC trials in partnership with community leaders in each region (Department of Social Services, 2016; Orima Research, 2017; Porter and Tudge, 2017;

Turnbull, 2017a; Mavromaras et al, 2019a). For example, government representatives visited the town of Ceduna in far west regional South Australia (the site of the first CDC trial in March 2016) on multiple occasions to hold consultative meetings with leaders from local government, NGOs and Indigenous community organisations, including service providers in family violence, family support, education and health, plus police and local representatives of state and commonwealth government agencies. According to the government, the views expressed in these consultations were 'generally supportive of the concept of the trial in their community' (Johnston, 2015).

However, this was a limited form of community participation given that the consultations in Ceduna were restricted to selected community leaders, were not advertised in the local newspaper, and did not discuss whether or not to hold a trial or consider the merits of alternative or dissenting views. Rather, they addressed the practical and technical details of a trial, such as the geographical boundaries, the proportion of payments to be placed on the debit card, operational procedures for the card, and the type of additional drug and alcohol support services that would be required. As a result of these consultations, a group of community leaders in Ceduna, representing the local Council and five Indigenous organisations, signed a memorandum of understanding with the government for the trial to commence in Ceduna in March 2016 (Johnston, 2015). However, this process actively excluded from participation those local residents targeted for inclusion in the IM programme.

Critics of the CDC – such as the Australian Greens (and, particularly from late 2017 onwards, the Labor Party), non-government organisations (such as the peak welfare body, the Australian Council of Social Service [ACOSS]), Indigenous groups and various researchers – have persistently questioned both the extent of community support, and the content and process of community engagement in the selected sites. The conversations initiated by government bureaucrats with established community groups were limited and tokenistic, and, most importantly, rarely engaged likely or existing IM participants. Thus, community development terminology and strategies were expediently used to legitimise a pre-existing neoliberal agenda aimed at shifting responsibility for addressing social disadvantage from the state to individuals and voluntary organisations (Mendes, 2018).

A number of parliamentary inquiries (CALC, 2015; 2017; 2019a; 2019b; 2020) and official evaluation reports have acknowledged conflicting views concerning the extent of community consultations and support in CDC sites, and the existence of significant community divisions. For example, the official evaluation of the CDC in Hinkler reported significant community divisions over the trial. The report noted that some statements by supporters of the CDC had accentuated existing prejudices against groups such as the unemployed (labelled as 'dole bludgers', for example) and drug users. There was also criticism of the government's failure to engage with the many young people who would be participating in the trial (Mavromaras et al, 2019a).

Similar concerns around community divisions were reported in the official evaluation of the CDC in the Goldfields. That report indicated that a minority of participants continued to oppose the CDC after its introduction, and opposition was more prevalent amongst non-Indigenous participants. Influencing factors included the restrictions placed by the CDC on access to cash, the lack of targeting, which resulted in people with no addiction or finance problems being placed on the CDC, experiences of stigmatisation, and the perceived unfair racist targeting of Indigenous residents. Others opposed the CDC on the grounds that it was not the best means of tackling social harm, and they believed that at the very least there needed to be a broader set of support services and programmes in place. There were also mixed views about the effectiveness of consultations and information provision in the Goldfields. Most recently, the official evaluation of the CDC in Ceduna, East Kimberley and the Goldfields Region presented varied views on the extent and effectiveness of community consultations across the three sites. A number of CDC participants in all sites reported dissatisfaction with the nature of consultations, making particular reference to the dearth of information about trial processes, the limited cultural awareness involved in engagement, and a failure to maintain active engagement with community members once the trial had begun (Mavromaras et al, 2021).

This research confirms these findings that inadequate community consultation was common, and even when consultations were conducted, they rarely influenced policy outcomes. Across the three sites, the interviewees described a lack of clarity and reasoning around the selection of their community as a trial site and limited opportunity to participate in policy development. Leading government justifications for the location of CIM trial sites were predominantly based on the socio-economic disadvantage present in these locations over any consideration of the distinct needs, circumstances, or unique conditions or characteristics of the communities. Thus, trial site selection was viewed as poorly conceptualised and disconnected from the realities of welfare recipients and welfare services on the ground. A welfare programme manager in Shepparton, Marj, explained her perception of the site selection process:

> 'We kind of have visions of them standing back with a map throwing darts. I think, again, the rhetoric from government was very much around, like I said, the statistics, the geographic disadvantage. Certainly, we have a high Aboriginal population, but I never felt a very strong— they never received strong clarity about why Shepparton was, indeed, one of the selected sites.'

The Playford community similarly experienced its involvement in CIM trials as somewhat arbitrary, with no public debate or awareness as to which groups advocated for the initiative, and an acknowledgement that the socio-economic circumstances of the community were likely a part of the decision-making. A key stakeholder noted:

> 'I don't know who was championing it or who was pushing it. … Locally, Playford is seen as high single parent, high drug use, high unemployment, generational unemployment, high SEIFA [Socio-economic Index for Areas], so it was deemed to be the ideal place for a trial. … That's what would have made it the perfect candidate for this kind of a programme and for the compulsory component.' (Tracy, Playford stakeholder)

A federal Liberal Party MP explained how Ceduna was chosen as a trial site because elected local and federal officials advocated for it, and gained the support of local Indigenous leaders:

> 'I think when [Andrew] Twiggy Forrest came into our party room and actually told us about this idea he had for, I guess, the next phase of that, being the cashless welfare card, it certainly had my ears up. Alan Tudge [the then Minister] and I discussed this and we built up a degree of trust and cooperation with the Indigenous leaders. There's basically five main groups, being the Ceduna, the Koonibba, the Yalata, Oak Valley and Scotdesco, even though there's a number of little homelands dotted around, but that sort of covers off the bulk of the population that are living in, around and in the outreaches of that Ceduna influence. We'd reached some degree of trust and cooperation, and people could see some value in what we were doing. We just started discussing the idea of actually bringing the cashless welfare card in. We talked about what percentage is split on the income. We talked about the kind of extra support services that the Commonwealth would be prepared to put in if the community was willing to give this a go, because it was a trial.' (Patrick, Ceduna stakeholder)

While the local government self-selection of Ceduna as a trial site differed as to the manner in which Playford and Shepparton were chosen to participate in CIM, the majority of stakeholders and CIM participants across the three trial sites were adamant that there was little effective community consultation prior to, and during the implementation of, CIM in their community, and that when consultations did take place, government officials were largely uninterested in genuine engagement with community-level participants and welfare recipients. Kevin and Sue from the Ceduna trial site described their views of the consultation, or lack thereof, that occurred in their community:

Kevin:	We never really got officially notified [of the introduction of CIM] until 2016. But I got wind of it beforehand, obviously.
Sue:	Yes, we heard it was coming.
Kevin:	Yes, but it was never ever— there were never any public meetings or any consultation about it. It was just, this is coming, and that's it.
Sue:	All of a sudden, it's here.
Kevin:	I wrote to [Mayor] Allan Suter about it a couple of times. What's going on here, there's been no public meetings about it, or anything like that. He was adamant that we'd be consulted, but there'd been no public meetings. … There was very little consultation. They will say that there was consultation, and my argument is it was probably two to three years before they brought this in, they had Stronger Futures meetings here. Now, in that, apparently, there was discussions about Income Management, but at the time, the only Income Management that was available was the BasicsCard under a voluntary programme. So, they will say, 'Oh, we consulted about Income Management', but they never consulted about anything mandatory.

Reflecting on the consultation process in Ceduna, Kevin and Sue viewed the process with scepticism and mistrust. From their perspective, the consultations were not objectively interested in, or valuing equally, the views of all who participated, particularly welfare recipients who would be most impacted by the policy:

Kevin:	The main meeting what they held for the public was down at the Ceduna Footy Club grounds on a Saturday morning and we had all the rednecks and all the boofheads there.
Facilitator:	So who was leading that meeting?
Sue:	[Minister] Alan Tudge, yeah.
Kevin:	The Lord Mayor of the town, I was standing near the Lord Mayor. He didn't give anybody a chance to say or state their opinion – he just over-talked everybody.
Sue:	He was even trying to talk over the two Elders. He was hanging onto that microphone to give them the least amount possible of time to talk.
Facilitator:	Yeah, okay.

Kevin: We walked out of the meeting eventually. Said, 'We've had enough of you, I can't fucking bear to listen anymore, see you later'. … It was totally choreographed. The only questions that got asked were the ones that they wanted to have asked. Tudge was purposely avoiding the people with the hard questions.

In Ceduna, most consultation occurred at a governance and leadership level, involving the federal government, the local council and key community governance bodies. The decision to introduce the CDC to Ceduna was made in consultation between government and the major Aboriginal communities in the region, with the knowledge that, at a community level, it would be an unpopular policy. Discussing the Shepparton community's opportunity to be heard during CIM community consultations, Glenys (Shepparton stakeholder) similarly explained that the community was given too little warning to respond adequately, and that this was part of an ongoing pattern with social policy initiatives:

> 'they didn't get any warning … they gave warning when they were about to introduce it and they learnt from that. What they learnt was don't give warning, people will complain. Just introduce these things in a sneaky underhanded manner, and you won't have the community outcry.' (Glenys, a Shepparton stakeholder)

Stakeholders and CIM participants also described consultation efforts in Playford as poor, with minimal effort to engage community members or provide information prior to introduction:

> 'Certainly the impression that we got is that the consultation had been pretty thin on the ground and awareness was— I think even among service providers who were spoken to, there wasn't a sense that there had been a lot of public discussion beforehand. It was more that the decision was made and it was rolled out and there was very little awareness raising beforehand by the government.' (Theo, Playford stakeholder)

Overall, government consultation processes in Australia have rarely directly engaged with IM participants, or given priority within policy development processes to considering their lived experience of the programme. While the government continues to insist that the CDC involves a 'bottom-up approach' in partnership with local communities (Canavan, 2019, p 94), what the government terms 'co-design' seems to be, in reality, little more than an information-sharing exercise with selected groups of community leaders. This has not only resulted in problems with implementation, as discussed earlier, but also appears to have exacerbated existing community divisions and conflict around the causes of and potential solutions for social disadvantage. While the next section highlights that New Zealand's implementation problems differed, it will later be argued that genuine co-design and community development processes could similarly have avoided key barriers to implementation of the community and youth development goals articulated by governments in both countries.

Implementation problems in New Zealand

As in Australia, significant problems emerged when implementing CIM in New Zealand due to it being driven by ideology rather than evidence from consumer or community experiences. Given CIM is a national policy in New Zealand and was not trialled in some areas before others, there was no attempt to formally consult with specific communities about where Youth Service providers were to be placed. Existing research evidence about the Youth Transition Services (YTS) initiative established by the previous Labour-led government in 2004 also appears to have been ignored. This initiative aimed to have all 15- to 19-year-olds in work, education, training or other activities that contribute to their long-term economic independence and wellbeing. By 2008, when the National-led coalition government came to power, 14 YTS operated across the country, of which a positive evaluation was published just a few months before the government was elected (MSD, 2008).

This evaluation concluded that YTS might be decreasing the number of 18- to 19-year-olds receiving working age benefits compared to those not engaged in the services which was, of course, the key rationale for developing the new YTS and adopting CIM. Most importantly, however, the evaluation reported that: 'Overall, YTS was well received by youth participants, as shown by the overwhelmingly positive findings of the youth focus groups and interviews' (MSD, 2008, p 26). This contrasts with the much more mixed findings from interviews for this study with YP/YPP recipients (see the discussion later in this chapter, and Chapters 4 to 6) and MSD's research with YP/YPP recipients (MSD, 2019a; Momsen, 2021). This is perhaps not surprising since YTS 'employed staff who were trained for youth work, were youth-friendly, had experience working with youth, were well-known locally and had good existing networks or ties within the local communities' (MSD, 2008, p 26). Fundamentally, the fact that they were not also monitoring young people's compliance with obligations or recommending decisions about social security entitlement likely contributed to their success. As discussion in the next section highlights, the dual roles of Youth Service employees have contributed to many implementation problems.

There was no clear alternative model to CIM that the government could have adopted, as was the case with the Australian Cape York model. Nor did the National-led coalition government undertake any research or seek consumer input to understand whether there was widespread mismanagement of money amongst young social security recipients before implementing CIM (Fletcher et al, 2013). In this context, a public servant working closely with the Youth Service noted that when it later trialled the delivery of commercial food boxes to YPP recipients, the food box company and MSD staff: "were absolutely blown away by the knowledge that these young mothers had about budgeting, menu planning and about just general shopping as far as their young family went … these young mothers were really adequately prepared to look after their money and feed their families."

The National-led government might have been more aware of the skills and aptitudes of young people if it had paid more attention to submissions made about the legislation that introduced CIM. Fifty out of the 85 written submissions received by the Social Services Select Committee on the *Social Security (Youth Support and Work Focus) Amendment Bill 2012* opposed the reforms overall, while of the 37 submissions that commented specifically on Money Management, 29 were in opposition (MSD, 2012a). Common concerns were the universal application of CIM to all young people, the risk of encouraging dependence rather than independence, and the extraordinary powers conferred on the Chief Executive of MSD to determine whether young people were financially competent, particularly given the absence of comprehensive financial literacy education in schools (and thus among the general population).

No formal public consultation was undertaken, and only ten written submissions and three oral hearings were reported for *the Social Security (Extension of Young Persons Services and Remedial Matters) Amendment Bill 2015* (MSD, 2015). This extended Youth Services and CIM to 18- to 19-year-old benefit recipients deemed to be 'at risk' of not moving into employment, while also tidying up other minor matters arising from the 2012 legislation. The then new Minister of Social Development, Anne Tolley (2015, p 528), claimed that: 'An initial estimate shows that for every dollar spent on the existing Youth Service, the taxpayer's liability reduces by $2.53, and I expect that there will be a similar return on investment for this older cohort.'

However, ongoing evaluation of the YTS was patchy and findings mixed. The first evaluation in 2015 found that the YTS was effective for YPP recipients, in particular at improving educational attainment, reducing time on benefits and increasing employment outcomes. Results were mixed for YP recipients, however, with short term improvements in educational participation and attainment, and modest impacts on employment outcomes not translating into less time on benefit. Further research focused specifically on the voluntary part of the service for NEETs was more critical (MSD, 2019a). In an interview, Tolley indicated that she was "very frustrated" by such evaluation results, because they did not provide the evidence needed to extend CIM to working-age adult social security recipients (and other groups, such as newly released prisoners) as the National government had hoped, "because you're dealing with that age group, actually the effects of it you don't see for five or six years. So you've got to hold your breath and hope that you're on track making small changes".

Similarly, the first formal review of the Youth Service, conducted in 2018–19, prior to re-tendering in 2020, highlighted a number of operational issues but did not bring radical change. Following comprehensive consultation with providers, Youth Service participants and other stakeholders, the government targeted the NEET service to those most at risk (particularly those leaving state care) and lowered mentor/client ratios for both the NEET and YP/YPP cohorts. Notably, issues relating to CIM (including 'legislative changes relating to age, client social obligations, Youth Service Support Unit (YSSU) structure, MSD In-house resourcing/structure' were considered out of scope (MSD, 2019a, pp 3–4).

Finally, in 2021, MSD published internal research on Money Management. It made no attempt to 'evaluate the effectiveness of money management as a way to improve the financial stability and financial capacity of young New Zealanders receiving the YP/YPP' (Momsen, 2021, p 6), but did acknowledge many of the operational issues this study documents in this and later chapters. The research paradoxically indicated that a majority of providers and young CIM participants agreed with the concept of IM but did not like the way it was implemented – particularly restrictions on agency associated with the Payment Card and the $50 In-Hand Allowance. Its finding that providers were more favourable than young people towards CIM failed to acknowledge the interest providers have in maintaining a system that financially profits them, so the research, not surprisingly, recommended that IM should not be abandoned completely. The modifications to CIM proposed do look more like the youth development models discussed in later sections of this chapter, but the design problems associated with front-line workers both surveilling and attempting to empower young people would be maintained (Momsen, 2021).

It is in this context that the remainder of this section focuses on operational problems that front-line workers in NGOs faced as they tried to implement the CIM policy. In addition to finding that many aspects of CIM sat in tension with the youth development focus of these organisations, the interaction between IT processual systems and front-line workers was also problematic, resulting in delays and inconsistent decision-making for young people and further frustration for workers. Lack of contractual requirements for qualified social or youth workers and inadequate training also contributed to implementation problems.

Empowering or coercing youth? Organisational design flaws

As noted in Chapter 2, the Youth Service is a strange hybrid, attempting both to support and empower young people through a youth development model and to track and monitor their activities for compliance with CIM. This involves Youth Service employees reporting to the Youth Service Support Unit (YSSU) when YP/YPP recipients have completed educational, budgeting and parenting obligations, as well as recommending financial incentives and/or sanctions. Those interviewed described how this CIM compliance framework sat in tension with the youth empowerment aspects of their job. For instance, most Youth Service employees believed young people should be required to meet obligations of some kind but thought that these should focus on more meaningful outcomes. Interviewed Youth Service employees also noted that important activities such as volunteering, family responsibilities or cultural obligations do not 'count' according to the reporting system, even if they do matter to the young person and help to demonstrate relevant maturity, skills and knowledge (Humpage, 2018). Two Youth Service mentors thought the educational obligation was completely inappropriate for young people with learning disabilities, because they are often unable learn in the same way or at the same speed as other young people.

Interview participants also described how the compliance framework failed to account for individual goals, including a desire to work rather than study – in contrast to Australia, New Zealand CIM participants do not have work obligations because, given their age, Minister Paula Bennett wanted them to focus on education and training only. However, Youth Service employee, Phil, noted that some young people have "got the qualifications, they're still with us, so unless they do another course – as I said, they don't want to because they're over it, they're over the education. [This leads to] the churning of doing a course for the sake of doing a course". Yet the CIM compliance framework requires them to meet education obligations to achieve incentive payments and avoid sanctions.

One Youth Service employee described getting very angry when MSD newsletters reported a significant increase in the number of young people in education or exiting a benefit. This is because she felt that these outcome measures reveal little about youth wellbeing or empowerment: some young people may have met the education obligation but not completed the course, or they might have come off a payment not because they moved into work but simply because they felt the stigma or red tape was not worth the effort. Welfare advocate interviewees reported knowing of many young people in the latter group who are living rough on the street or in similarly precarious situations. However, current reporting does not allow the exact number of such people to be calculated or for them to be followed up in any way (Humpage, 2018).

The fact that Youth Service providers – or indeed young people themselves – were not consulted prior to the development of the compliance framework suggests that CIM was never really about empowering young people, as government documents purported. An earlier MSD document had lauded the YTS for using a 'strengths-based practice model' that:

> is holistic and focuses on developing a youth's opportunities and supports them to realise their potential through building networks and connections across communities. This model is in contrast to a deficit approach with a focus on problems and what is lacking – such as what qualifications the young person had failed to achieve, a history of truancy, and/or involvement with the criminal justice system. (MSD, 2005, p ii)

We believe the high level of targeting of NEET and the application of CIM to YP/YPP recipients, key components of the Youth Service, reflect such a deficit approach. This may well be why the Green Party noted in its minority report to the Social Services Committee (2012, pp 17–18) that: 'We have spoken to several respected providers who have not tendered as they believe it [CIM] would compromise their ethics.'

There is also no evidence that the specific needs of Māori youth were addressed when designing the CIM policy, despite the fact that Māori are disproportionately more likely to receive YP/YPP. Although Chapter 2 highlighted how the introduction of the CIM policy was far less racialised in New Zealand compared to Australia, the call for Youth Service contracts did prioritise providers with experience working with Māori. Yet some Youth Service providers based in *iwi* (tribal) organisations noted how the rigid frameworks governing the Youth Service made it difficult for them to meet the needs of young Māori. Compliance frameworks were described as:

> 'red tape in terms of what they [young people] have to achieve while receiving this benefit, because it is still structured by Work and Income. So we have to sit here as case managers but also as *iwi* providers, which is where we can target those really cultural aspects of a service.' (Shaniah, New Zealand Youth Service employee)

Yet the cultural knowledge and value such providers bring is not useable in ways that benefit young Māori. To address their concerns, far greater devolution of power to *iwi* providers would be required so that they can decide how to best meet the needs of young Māori.

The policy decision to establish Youth Service providers as the public face of social security entitlement for young people and yet to maintain the real decision-making power within the YSSU, which is part of MSD, indicates that avoiding costs to the state in the future was more important to the government than empowering youth or enabling Māori providers to support their young people. Yet this two-tiered system for decision-making proved extremely challenging for many Youth Service employees trying to implement CIM. For some, this was because they developed relationships with the young people they worked with:

> 'I do struggle with the whole sanction thing, being— I don't know whether [this is because of] the more emotional side of having read the family breakdowns, [but] it's like now we're just lumping another thing onto this kid who is trying to deal with all of this mental health stuff and now we're telling him they are going to get less money to try and survive on. That plays on my mind quite a bit.' (Tony, New Zealand Youth Service employee)

Indeed, the YSSU was established to avoid Youth Service employees making *final* decisions regarding entitlement, incentives and sanctions, exactly because government officials were concerned that their relationships with young people might influence their decision-making.

Some Youth Service employees appreciated the 'distance' between themselves and the final decision-making because it meant they could act as advocates for their clients and 'blame' any negative decisions on YSSU: "it means my relationship is a lot safer with that young person and they can separate the two roles" (Jackie, New Zealand Youth Service employee). However, some reported that young people and their supporters (often family members more familiar with the Work and Income approval system) did not always understand or believe that the mentors could only recommend decisions, and did blame the mentors themselves (Humpage, 2018). On the other hand, some Youth Service mentors were frustrated that the YSSU did not appear to 'trust' their recommendations and appeared to want to second-guess decisions that they had made according to the set criteria and with greater knowledge of the particular case histories of young people: "If we are saying that this young person needs this and we've done all our checklists, I don't want to fight for an hour and a half to get this approved" (Jackie, New Zealand Youth Service mentor). Jackie went on to describe YSSU as "really quite dismissive. I don't know if you've been to YSSU offices, it's just a whole lot of people in front of screens so they don't have that empathetic relationship with the young person".

Many of the interviewed Youth Service employees felt that, if CIM was truly about empowering young people towards positive behaviours, then mentors who have intimate knowledge of the young person's background would be better placed to make such decisions (Humpage, 2018; see also Momsen, 2021). For instance, Shaniah said:

> 'It would work so much better if we were given more other responsibilities … in terms of the decision making around sanctioning or suspending a benefit because we're there almost weekly, daily sometimes, so we can see the effects first-hand and we still have to go and ask for permission to say, look, we want a sanction; the paperwork and admin side of it that takes so [long] by the time that happens it's about two to three weeks later. So that's a very long time for them to be— for income to be just so inconsistent. Week to week is hard enough for those— the best of us.' (Shaniah, New Zealand Youth Service employee)

Shaniah also felt that Money Management dominated the whole Youth Service structure and that that was where "a lot of the concerns or issues stem from, is the structure of it".

A further design flaw exacerbates this problem: there is no requirement in provider contracts that all or a significant proportion of mentors be trained in social or youth work, which again counters the purported youth development focus. The authors acknowledge, however, that some Youth Service staff *are* trained in youth work or related disciplines and have the relevant cultural and professional knowledge and skills to successfully work with young people. Moreover, interviewees revealed an internal youth worker qualification programme specific to Youth Services has been developed by MSD. Most of the Youth Service mentors interviewed also saw themselves as advocates for their clients and attempted to develop a trusting relationship with young people to support them in establishing life goals and skills. Although not all YP and YPP recipients viewed their mentors as succeeding in this goal, many did, and were grateful for the assistance they had received. However, there were also some reports of assistance not being forthcoming or only being reluctantly provided, while one YPP recipient with experience of two different services said she felt as if she was treated as a 'number', rather than a human being, by both services. Welfare advocates interviewed confirmed that young people they have assisted complained that some providers 'talk down to' young people and are often reluctant (or unable due to ignorance) to provide information about entitlements (Humpage, 2018).

This is troubling given Chapter 2 noted that the minister who introduced the Youth Service and CIM to New Zealand, Paula Bennett, made clear that she did not want young people engaging with Work and Income, presumably due to its 'toxic culture'. At least three Youth Service mentor interviewees had previously worked for Work and Income, and while they were relishing the opportunity to engage more deeply with clients through Youth Service, welfare advocates felt that those previously trained in Work and Income environments were not always suitable for the youth mentor job, because they focused more on compliance than youth engagement (Humpage, 2018). Indeed, Youth Service manager, Elaine, said that since she had chosen to employ only youth worker-trained staff, "engagement levels with our young people have just skyrocketed". On the other hand, Youth Service employees who have not previously worked at Work and Income usually have little knowledge of social security entitlements. Welfare advocates reported numerous cases of young people not being told of their full entitlements because Youth Service mentors were unaware of or reluctant to reveal such information (Humpage, 2018). This problem has been exacerbated by the fact that, while Youth Service staff were given "pretty intensive training" (Adina, New Zealand Youth Service employee) about entitlements by Work and Income when the service was first established, training for new staff is largely in-house and is not regularly provided by Work and Income/MSD officials – although there is evidence that this may have changed following the 2019 review of the Youth Service (MSD, 2019a).

Inconsistency in the qualifications and ongoing training of Youth Service employees is one factor contributing to a further design problem: the considerable variability in how providers deliver Youth Service contracts. Although some providers go to great lengths to make their service appropriate for their particular clientele, the diversity of providers may mean that a young person in one part of the country receives different information, access to rights, or restrictions on consumption from another living elsewhere. For instance, some providers take their clients off CIM as soon as they have met the obligations that allow them to do so, regarding it as the young person's right to decide whether they wish to continue voluntarily, while others require young people to stay on CIM (or prevent their coming off it by failing to disclose that possibility) if they believe the person will spend their money inappropriately (Humpage, 2018). One provider does now allow recommendations for sanctions to be submitted by mentors without a report from and engagement with a social worker because "if someone is going to miss out on money" (Elaine, New Zealand Youth Service manager), they want to ensure the reasoning is absolutely clear.

Systems and technological failures

The implementation challenges emerging from organisational design problems are enhanced by the poor processes and integration of the Youth Service with MSD information technology systems, contributing to extremely slow and inefficient decision-making by YSSU. In particular, Youth Service employees said that YSSU decisions about obligations, incentives and sanctions are lengthy and unpredictable depending on which or how many YSSU staff are involved. As one of the participants quoted in an earlier section highlighted, sanctions take so long – at least days, sometimes weeks – to be actioned by YSSU, that the relationship between 'inappropriate' behaviour and the sanction is often not obvious to the young person involved that the mentors think it unlikely sanctions would have any effect on the spending behaviour of YP/YPP recipients. Decisions for incentives generally appeared to be made more quickly yet one Youth Service employee still said there was a running joke about who would have the biggest back-pay in incentives because delays in payment were common. Again, there was some uncertainty as to whether incentives really modified behaviour. While young people appreciated the $10 per week they gained, many did not see the incentives as either large enough or as appropriate levers for changing their behaviour in the long term (Humpage, 2018).

Although not specific to CIM, interviewees said that approval to receive a YP/YPP payment can also frequently take weeks, requiring young people to rely on family members, friends, landlords or – in at least one case reported by a welfare advocate – prostitution to cover costs during this period; another young woman was reported to be living in a boarding house where an advocate believed she was being groomed for sex work. In a further case reported by a different advocate, a young pregnant woman with a history of self-harm and no other source of income was 'couch-surfing' and going hungry while she waited for her payment to be approved (Humpage, 2018).

Sometimes such delays result from young people having not supplied the documentation needed, but providers indicate that this is difficult for some young people to obtain. For instance, an advocate said that young people who have been in the care of Oranga Tamariki (New Zealand's child protection agency) will have a birth certificate on file, but they might not have a copy themselves. YSSU, however, requires that the young person provide this rather than checking to see if the document can be passed on from Oranga Tamariki, even though the agency is within MSD's remit (Humpage, 2018).

Similarly, YP applications are often hindered by independent assessments to prove family breakdown, with some young people waiting weeks and with welfare advocates reporting that, if a parent was willing to have the child live with them, YSSU often assumed that it was safe or appropriate for the young person to do so. Alternatively, they indicated that breakdown reports typically focus on the young person's relationship with their natural parents, even if the recent breakdown was with another family member or a foster parent. These difficulties in merely applying for financial assistance are clearly not in line with a youth development focus and are worsened by reports that when a young person mistakenly presents at Work and Income to apply for YP/YPP, they are often simply told that Work and

Income cannot help, rather than being referred to a specific Youth Service for assistance (Humpage, 2018).

Welfare advocates indicated in interviews that, because they have contacts within YSSU/MSD and because they are well-versed in social security law, they are often able to go directly to YSSU to escalate a system or decision issues, while Youth Service mentors are expected to follow a hierarchy, first within their organisation, then with regional contract managers who would take the matter to YSSU. Although interviews with Youth Service mentors suggested some were escalating more directly, they still complained that escalations were no longer addressed immediately and could take days to be dealt with. As one Youth Service employee, Tony, said:

> 'YSSU don't see the faces of these people and they don't see people who are [bringing young people in], yelling at us over the desk to hurry up and do our jobs. Yeah, we're going to go up in the next wee [short] while and have a chat with them. But it's no fault on either side, it's just that when you don't have that person in front of you, you're not seeing how distressed they are.' (Tony, a Youth Service employee)

The fault, of course, lies with decision-making systems that were not built on input from those who would be directly affected by them, leading to many young people being placed in trying circumstances that harm their wellbeing (Humpage, 2018). For instance, even decisions for approving hardship grant applications were slow and variable. Karina (New Zealand Youth Service employee) explained:

> 'There is no normal at the moment. Originally it could take a whole day, it could take two days … we're talking about emergency hardship. They've done really well to bring that timeframe down. Some of them, last week, was half an hour. So that was brilliant. Some of them are still a day. Yeah, there's really no consistency in that.' (Karina, a New Zealand Youth Service employee)

Another Youth Service employee summed up the tensions created by the CIM design: "I think we're constantly fighting against YSSU … because [w]e're advocates for our clients and we're trying to get what's best for them and make sure that they're entitled to everything. Full and correct entitlement. But when we go to YSSU, it's kind of a constant argument" (Tony, New Zealand Youth Service employee).

In trying to explain these delays, the Youth Service employees suggested these were in part linked to what appears to be insufficient staff numbers at YSSU for the workload involved in monitoring YP and YPP recipients on CIM, as well as NEET clients. This problem was worsened by high staff turnover, which means many staff are always 'getting up to speed' with their new job. More generally, there is also a perception that YSSU does not fully understand providers and their clients, meaning that misunderstandings are common (Humpage, 2018). As a result: "We'll have the same kind of situation. A youth coach will go to YSSU, get it granted for this client. The same situation will happen two days later and that client doesn't get the same" (Tony, New Zealand Youth Service employee). However, the next section highlights that technological issues also contributed to these processual issues.

The final area where implementation was significantly flawed was the technology used both by Youth Service providers and by young people subject to CIM. First, the Activity Reporting Tool (ART) database used by Youth Service providers was not well-integrated with MSD's IT systems, contributing to confusion, double-handling and inconsistent decisions. In particular, Tony (New Zealand Youth Service employee) noted that Youth Service and YSSU templates don't align with one another:

> '[what] we tick boxes [for] doesn't match their paperwork. I think that one was really quite a huge revelation for us, is that they'll [YSSU] come back and ask another question and we're like, "But it's not on our list." It's on their list, but it's not on ours. So don't muck around, just give us the one.' (Tony, a New Zealand Youth Service employee)

According to a policymaker interviewee, this was not possible due to security protocols protecting benefit recipients' private data. However, requiring Youth Service providers to use a different IT system significantly impinged upon their ability to help YP/YPP recipients. For instance, neither Youth Service mentors nor YP/YPP recipients can access updated account balances for their young clients. A mentor said:

> 'We get a one-page summary, and we get that— so today will be yesterday's payment summary. So we don't know what's happened overnight or first thing in the morning … sometimes those payment summaries lag, so they are really off. Payment summaries don't show childcare subsidies, so we can't even give that information.' (Karina, New Zealand Youth Service manager)

Although Karina said things had improved since MyMSD was introduced, in the past, "That was the majority – 80 per cent of the work that we would do would be checking payment cards". Nonetheless, YP/YPP recipients cannot always access MyMSD for various reasons, so continuing to have out-of-date payment summaries meant extra work for mentors who had to call YSSU on behalf of young people. It could also lead to considerable stress for CIM participants who were "ringing us from the supermarket about to use their payment card and it's been declined, and they're ringing us and we haven't got any accurate [information] – and so they're still standing at that checkout waiting for us" (Jackie, New Zealand Youth Service mentor).

As with the Australian CIM participants, YP/YPP recipients also faced many struggles with the electronic Payment Cards not working correctly or being able to be used at the types of retailer they frequent. These matters and the emotional impact they have on CIM participants are explored in the next chapter. Overall, design flaws, systems failures and technological problems combined to make implementation very challenging for Youth Service providers.

Towards co-design and genuine developmental processes

While social security is not usually known as a site for community or consumer engagement in policy design, both Australia and New Zealand adopted the language of either community or youth development when promoting IM. This was more obviously the case in Australia, where 'consultation' with communities was attempted. In New Zealand, however, the government contracted non-government providers, including Māori providers, already working with young people in their communities and used youth empowerment rhetoric to promote CIM, suggesting youth development was a key goal. This chapter has highlighted that in practice, community or youth development processes were not applied, resulting in significant implementation problems.

This was a major policy failure, given increasing use of co-design processes, particularly for understanding complex problems that have proved difficult to overcome through standard policy making. Co-design, which is sometimes called co-production, refers to a bottom-up policy development and decision-making process whereby policymakers partner as equals with marginalised groups such as service users and carers (Dillon, 2021). Their experiential knowledge and capabilities are utilised through a process of mutual education to define a social problem, identify needs to be met and an associated range of potential service options, plan and implement a programme, and evaluate the outcome. Co-design processes emphasise the importance of facilitating participation by diverse groups and of ensuring access for all who want to participate, which often means paying service users for their time and/or funding skills training for them. Additionally, the result of a co-design process must be subject to negotiation with participating groups, and cannot be predetermined (New Economics Foundation, 2008; Beresford, 2013; Social Care Institute for Excellence, 2015; Future Social Service Institute, 2018; Yeates and Amaya, 2018).

Co-design processes are generally informed by community development (CD) principles (Mendes, 2019). Here, community development refers to the employment of local community structures and networks to address social needs and empower groups of people (Boyle et al, 2010; Coote, 2015). A policy process based on CD principles would involve the devolution of policy development to local groups with local expertise to define problems and identify effective solutions (Clague, 1997). Not surprisingly, both the Australian and New Zealand governments have increasingly used the language of co-design in their engagement with Indigenous peoples (Closing the Gap Refresh, 2018; Ministry of Health, 2018; Commonwealth of Australia, 2020; National Indigenous Australians Agency, nd; Te Arawhiti, nd). Co-design offers an opportunity to bring together western and Indigenous knowledges in community engagement and to incorporate key Indigenous values into policy design, which may in turn improve policy outcomes (Mules et al, 2017; Te Morenga et al, 2018). It should be acknowledged that co-design is *not* the same as self-determination, and that government interest in this issue may simply be a way of shifting responsibility for Indigenous outcomes and avoiding tougher conversations about the devolution of social security spending to Indigenous groups, as well as broader sovereignty issues (Pearson, 2000; Ngāi Tūhoe Service Management Plan, 2012; Uluru Statement from the Heart, 2017). Given the experiences in CDC sites in Australia, there is a clear need to ensure that co-design processes recognise that 'community interests' are heterogeneous and to avoid reinforcing existing inequalities through inadequate recognition of different levels of power and engagement across various interest groups (Dillon, 2021).

Nonetheless, it is likely that some of the considerable implementation problems described in this chapter could have been avoided if co-design had been a feature of the policy process. In the case of the CDC in Australia, a genuine CD process would have involved extensive consultations through open democratic meetings or smaller panels scheduled at times and venues easily accessible to most residents to discuss how the CDC might benefit the community. These meetings would have offered residents multiple options, such as the CDC combined with new services and supports to address identified social problems, such as substance abuse and gambling, or alternatively would have offered just the new support programmes. This engagement would have particularly targeted members of three groups: income support recipients who would be subject to the trial plus representative service user organisations, including groups that oppose the CDC; the key government and non-government community services that currently work with these disadvantaged groups; and representatives of Indigenous community groups, given the disproportionate representation of Indigenous Australians in IM programmes. The CD principles outlined earlier would be applied to ensure respect for competing views, and to protect the privacy and/or safety of participants as required. Alternative consultation processes would be developed with Indigenous communities, given their emphasis on consensual rather than majority vote decisions (Ife, 2016).

Additionally, formal consultations with the three groups mentioned would have been a major component of the planned evaluation framework in order to examine whether IM had led to better outcomes for IM participants and the local community in general, and to determine future service and policy strategies (Mendes, 2018). A further important point made by the Australian interviewees is that community support for CIM is not static and has evolved across the lifespan of the CIM trials; some individuals and organisations have changed their position after a number of years of observing its impact. Changes in support for the policy should be captured throughout the CIM trials and the subsequent evaluations.

Although New Zealand's CIM was a national policy and thus not rolled out one community at a time, there was still plenty of room for improved community and Indigenous engagement to ensure that the purported goal of youth development was achieved. For instance, a first step in co-design would have been to formally consult with existing Youth Transition Services, who were well-connected within local communities and aimed to provide a forum for ongoing strategic planning and co-ordination of services for young people (MSD, 2008). In the Otorohonga district, for example, a small region in the middle of the North Island, the YTS was a significant part of a broader youth development model led by Dale Williams, then Mayor of Otorohonga, which reduced youth unemployment to zero for several years running (Wilson, 2015). The key components of the Otorohonga model later became the basis for the national Mayors Taskforce for Jobs (2021) Youth to Work Strategy, which aimed to improve local pathway development, access, retention and achievement of youth outcomes within education, training and employment. This model was frequently referenced by those opposed to the introduction of the Youth Service and CIM in parliamentary debate, but it was disregarded by the National-led government. Further, because Minister of Social Development Paula Bennett was keen to establish obligations for young people focused only on education, not work, the Otorohonga YTS 'did not place a bid in the initial tender process' (Social Services Committee, 2012, pp 12–13). This was a great loss, given the model's huge success in reducing youth unemployment in its place of origin.

MSD could also have learned from other strengths-based programmes run through YTS, including ones that partnered with, rather than took over the role of, Work and Income to require young people on the Independent Youth Benefit (the predecessor of the Youth Payment) to engage with mentoring services (MSD, 2005, p 3). This would have avoided implementation problems resulting from a newly contracted range of Youth Service providers having to quickly upskill to provide advice on social security entitlements. Other YTS were one-stop-shops where youth could access social, health, employment and legal services under one roof, including from services founded on Māori values. For instance, at The Pulse in Whangarei, a worker built relationships with young people by engaging with extended family members, encouraging them to take an active role in their young person's advancement and helping other unemployed family/*whānau* members move into employment and/or training. The Whānau worker also had links with the social housing agency to enable young people to access safe housing (MSD, 2005). This reflects the Māori view – which was being implemented in policies such as the Whānau Ora (Family Wellbeing) strategy around the same time as the Youth Service was introduced – that we need to move beyond individualised notions of 'empowerment', and "endorse a group capacity for self-determination". It is also key to define wellbeing holistically, incorporating the spiritual and inter-relationships between mental and physical health (Taskforce on Whānau-centred Initiatives, 2010, p 30; see also Humpage, 2018).

While YP recipients, in particular, are often estranged from their families (with family breakdown being one of the main criteria for receipt of the payment), Youth Service workers interviewed provided numerous instances when greater engagement with the wider family and community would be beneficial for improving a young person's outcomes. For instance, changing spending behaviours – one of the key goals of CIM – was difficult when family members contradicted, verbally or demonstratively, the advice given or, in some cases, deliberately exploited young people by using their Payment Card with or without the young person's knowledge. A co-design process could have begun by engaging with and building upon these existing initiatives within communities and upon Māori cultural values. The New Zealand government has already engaged in co-design processes relating to Māori young people, so this idea is by no means far-fetched (Wehipeihana et al, 2018; Ngā Puhi Iwi Social Services, 2019).

Green Party MP Jan Logie noted in her interview that scaling up the Otorohonga model to the national level may not have been possible, but that each Youth Service *could* have been based more squarely within its own community. She also placed a stronger focus on building relationships with schools, employers and other relevant organisations. While it is likely that this would not resolve some of the problems with inconsistency in implementation raised earlier in this chapter, empowering local communities (including Māori communities) through the types of consultative body described earlier would be more effective in supporting young people to transition from school into higher or vocational education and work than the coercive and compliance-based approach associated with CIM.

Conclusion

This chapter has argued that paternalistic policy processes in both Australia and New Zealand have meant that alternative models and evaluation evidence were ignored, and that the expertise of local communities and the people being placed on CIM were side-lined. Even the planned partnership with local community leaders to introduce the CDC in Australia did not alter the fundamentally top-down nature of CIM as a measure imposed on specific geographical areas and communities. Community consultation was led by bureaucrats from the Department of Social Services, which mostly occurred only after key policy development decisions were made, was usually limited to providing information about the logistics of introducing the CDC rather than seeking feedback on whether or not the CDC was an effective policy initiative, and which targeted only a limited group of leaders who were not necessarily representative of their communities. In New Zealand, such consultation with local communities or Māori was not even attempted. It is highly likely that this contributed to significant implementation problems as CIM was rolled out.

This chapter has indicated that inadequate consultation in Australia divided communities rather than bringing them together, while in New Zealand, Youth Service providers faced design and system failures that made it hard to focus on the development needs of the young people they are tasked with empowering. CIM participants themselves have also faced difficulties accessing their social security entitlements due to implementation problems, notably with technology. The next chapter explores how CIM has harmed the wellbeing of many individuals and communities, contributing to social stigma.

4

Identity and emotion

'Usually people think that you've done something wrong to warrant it. I don't think people look at you positively for being on welfare. There's so much propaganda and stereotypes around. … I don't think people would see my card and think, "She's done a university degree, she worked, she's tried hard". I don't think so. They would look at the Indue card and … just assume I don't want to work or I'm on drugs, or they would just assume bad things that aren't really true.' (Tahlia, Hinkler)

Introduction

CIM has been touted as a measure to bring financial stability to welfare recipients' lives, improving the health and wellbeing of individuals and communities in the process. In reality, however, CIM can have contradictory and even counterproductive effects. As the previous chapter showed, CIM introduces new financial pressure into many participants' lives. This is particularly true in Australia, where welfare recipients in (CDC) trial sites have struggled to make basic purchases and pay essential bills. Building on this picture of financial difficulty and deprivation, this chapter explores the impact of CIM on participants' wellbeing and sense of self. It shows that while financial stress and reduced financial control are key concerns for many participants, the infantilisation and stigmatisation that CIM involves are also powerful stressors. Together, these factors can contribute to significant reductions in participant wellbeing, harming cardholders, their families and their communities.

This chapter has five parts. First, key insights regarding the influence of financial deprivation on physical and psychological wellbeing are reviewed, underlining the importance of available funds, personal autonomy and social connectedness for good health. Second, it is shown how CIM infantilises and disempowers participants. Third, participant experiences of social stigma are explored, underlining the role of public discourses in shaping these experiences. Fourth, it is revealed that (as the extant scholarship would predict) this combination of financial deprivation, infantilisation and stigmatisation has profound negative impacts, corroding participants' social and emotional wellbeing and inflicting radiating harms. The chapter concludes that – while a minority of individuals experience improved financial and material stability under CIM – the social and emotional impacts of the policy have been largely negative.

Socio-economic disadvantage and wellbeing

The relationship between unemployment and reduced wellbeing is well documented (Kokko et al, 2000; Paul et al, 2009; Wanberg, 2012; Hiswals et al, 2017), as is that between financial deprivation and poor health (Vetter et al, 2006; Weinstein and Stone, 2018). People living in poverty typically experience higher rates of physical and mental illness (St Vincent de Paul Society, 2013; National Rural Health Alliance, 2017), while unemployment has been associated with low self-esteem, depression and anxiety, as well as higher rates of self-harm and suicide (Smith, 1985; Kokko et al, 2000; Wanberg, 2012). Given the significant overlap between these groups, unemployment-related health deterioration has often been attributed to financial stress. Financial deprivation has been shown to compromise access to healthy food, safe accommodation, quality education and adequate healthcare, including psychological support. As Abeyta et al (2017, p 693) summarise, 'money can help people meet basic needs for survival, since it can be exchanged for shelter, food, and clean drinking water'. In addition to ensuring physical needs are satisfied, however, finances can play a critical role in making sure that basic *psychological* needs – including the need to feel autonomous, competent and socially connected (Abeyta et al, 2017; Weinstein and Stone, 2018) – are met.

Autonomy – often operationalised by feelings of independence (Weinstein and Stone, 2018) – is vital for psychological health, but difficult to achieve in conditions of financial scarcity. As noted above, reduced access to funds places significant constraints on individuals' life choices and behaviours. People living on the economic margins are often limited in their ability to make choices regarding everything from what to eat for dinner (Huang et al, 2016) to whether to relocate in search of employment (Marston et al, 2019). Conditional welfare policies, which place additional restrictions on income support recipients (Immervoll and Scarpetta, 2012), can add to this experience of disempowerment as individuals lose control over large and small aspects of their daily lives. As Malenfant et al (2007, p 816) observe, '[t]he sense of having lost control over one's life situation is thought to play a significant role in … health deterioration during periods of unemployment'.

There is also growing evidence that stigma is an important part of this picture (Rantakeisu et al, 1999; Walker, 2014; Dougherty et al, 2017; Peterie et al, 2019b). Unemployment and poverty attract significant social stigma in many countries. Income support recipients in particular are often perceived as a burden on society (Sutton et al, 2014), causing many to experience their joblessness as a source of shame. As a largely *social* emotion which hinges on the appraisals of others (Walker et al, 2013), shame can contribute to reduced feelings of autonomy and competence as individuals see themselves through others' eyes (Cooley, 1902; Goffman, 1963).

There is also mounting evidence that both poverty and unemployment can contribute to reduced wellbeing via reductions in social connectedness. Scholars have long recognised that most forms of social participation require funds, and that financial deprivation thus forces people to reduce their social activities (Jahoda et al, 1972; Jahoda, 1981; 1982; Morris and Wilson, 2014; Stam et al, 2016). It is known that '[s]pending money on experiences (eg, dining at restaurants, going to concerts) can bolster a sense of relatedness' (Abeyta et al, 2017, p 693), yet the majority of people living in poverty or on income support payments have little if any disposable income for 'luxuries' of this kind.

Stigma and stigma-induced shame are again implicated here. Stigmatised groups are more likely to experience social exclusion and ostracisation, but they may also utilise social withdrawal as a stigma management strategy. As Peterie et al (2019b) note, stigmatised welfare recipients often avoid social encounters in which they might face public humiliation, yet such isolation can add to their long-term disadvantage – adversely affecting job search, political solidarities and wellbeing, even if it provides short-term emotional relief (see also; Howe, 1998; Vinokur and Schul, 2002; Malenfant et al, 2007; Contini and Richiardi, 2010).

In light of these findings and the consistent assertion that conditional welfare policies *intensify* experiences of social suffering, the social and emotional impacts of CIM policies – which have introduced a new suite of restrictions and stigmas – warrant focused attention. As the remainder of this chapter will show, many participants in this study experienced CIM as a form of infantilisation and stigmatisation. As such, they experienced reductions in social and emotional health which undermined the policy's stated objectives vis-à-vis individual and collective wellbeing.

Infantilisation

(In)dependence

A key theme in both the Australian and New Zealand interviews was the sense of infantilisation that CIM produced. Part of the concern for the people interviewed was that the restrictions and practical challenges associated with the scheme made participants more reliant on other people. This theme was particularly strong in Australia, where the technical and system issues described earlier saw participants who had previously been financially independent turning to friends and family members – including parents – for financial help. This unintended consequence contradicts the official aim of the policy, which is to increase financial independence.

Numerous Australian interviewees recalled instances when – unable to finalise a transaction or make an online payment transfer – they had had little choice but to ask a loved one for assistance:

> 'I filled up my car and then I went in to pay for it and my card declined. Then they said that I couldn't leave and I had all these other cars parked behind me so I had to move my car which made me feel worse. I had to ring my parents to ask them to come and pay for it.' (Dave, Hinkler)

For some adults, accepting financial help – particularly from parents – felt like a regression to childhood: "[I] had to ask my father to just cover my rent, which felt a bit, like, embarrassing and humiliating. It really makes me look bad, if you know what I mean? Not being able to pay my rent … I'm not someone who pays things late" (Tahlia, Hinkler).

While reliance on family and friends was more common amongst New Zealand participants in the often long wait for social security entitlements to start, there were also cases where they had to ask family members to purchase certain goods because the Payment Card could not be used. For these interviewees and others, CIM had made them *more*, not less, financially dependent. Where they had previously been able to rely on payments that were theirs as an entitlement, they were now forced to appeal to the sympathy and generosity of others – in some instances literally turning to charity because they had nowhere else to go.

This distinction between entitlement and charity – between 'rights' and 'compassion' – is an important one. Conservative leaders have at times insisted that 'liberating' welfare recipients from 'dependency' on government and encouraging them to instead access community and familial support will help disadvantaged individuals reclaim their dignity (Bush, 2002; Berlant, 2004; Woodward, 2004). Yet the power dynamics implicit in 'compassion' can be far from enabling (see Berlant, 2004; Peterie, 2017; 2019). The emotional experience of accessing an entitlement is extremely different from that of receiving charity, and not all families are safe environments in which material and emotional resources are forthcoming.

Numerous interviewees described how they felt infantilised and demeaned appealing to the generosity of others in a way that they didn't when accessing state entitlements. Interviewees who turned to formal charities for assistance expressed gratitude for this help, but also described the experience as evidence of their growing hopelessness:

> 'You want low of low, I was having to get meals at charities. I was getting St Vincent de Paul – which were wonderful, wonderful people – to come and bring a box of food and pet food because I couldn't feed my pets. I had St Vincent de Paul and I had the RSPCA come and

> drop off a 10-kilo bag of cat food, that kind of thing. I love them to bits but they shouldn't have been doing that because I shouldn't have been in the situation.' (Callum, Playford)

These experiences of accessing charity were distressing – lowlights of participants' lives to date – and did little to build psychologically-necessary feelings of autonomy and control.

Similarly, several interviewees reflected that in rendering them dependent on informal social networks, CIM had made them more vulnerable to exploitation:

> 'One of our friends, … he's like, "if you need fuel or you need anything just let me know and I'll use your card and give you the cash". … [H]e would be like, "oh, because you gave me fuel and I had to go up there and all this, I'll charge $20 or more extra on top for my time". That's unfair on that person.' (Anthony, Hinkler)

Many interviewees mentioned having made arrangements with parents or landlords to buy, for example, all household groceries using their cards as an alternative to paying board. Yet it was clear that these supports were not safely available to all people, as they were premised on the existence of trusting relationships. Several participants told us that some businesses and landlords were, for example, "taking advantage of poor people with this system" (Anthony, Hinkler). This was seen in New Zealand, where some landlords – who were paid to provide meals and board to their tenants – had stopped providing food, confident that they would nevertheless continue to receive their full tenancy income through Money Management's automatic payment system. The system thus enabled micro-economies of exploitation.

In making participants more reliant on others, CIM corroded autonomy. It frequently caused shame and humiliation, left some with insufficient support, and exposed others to exploitation. As discussed later, this had the self-defeating consequence of pushing some disadvantaged individuals further to the margins of their communities.

Bureaucratic encounters

In both Australia and New Zealand, the process by which CIM participants can apply to receive a larger portion of their benefits in cash also added to feelings of infantilisation and impotence. Australian interviewees described their anger at being required to justify purchases that it was within their means to pay for, simply because the required funds were on their payment cards. Ashleigh (Hinkler), for example, explained that she had organised a temporary change to her rental payment plan to allow her to cover the cost of her son's paediatrician appointment:

> 'I had no spare money to pay for the appointment. So I organised with my [real estate agent] that I didn't pay rent that Friday. I paid $30, so all that I [had] left owing was $300. So for the next three weeks I would pay $430. That was all good between us.' (Ashleigh, Hinkler)

Centrelink (the statutory social security agency in Australia), however, disputed this arrangement, arguing that she should pay the extra $100 for the subsequent three weeks from her unquarantined funds, which would have introduced new financial stress:

> 'I just felt very violated, as though I was doing the wrong thing. … I am an Australian citizen and entitled to this money, raising my two Australian citizen children. If I want to pay whatever amount I want to pay to my rent for a roof over my head, I'm entitled to do that; you can't control how I spend my money.' (Ashleigh, Hinkler)

For Ashleigh and others, the constraints imposed by CIM made it harder to make responsible financial choices.

New Zealand participants faced similar bureaucratic frustrations. Under Money Management, participants can only use their payment cards at approved businesses. As numerous interviewees mentioned, most approved outlets sold food and children's items; purchasing other essentials like adult clothing was difficult, particularly for those in regional areas where there were few local stores. In order to receive additional unquarantined funds, participants had to explain to their mentors and YSSU why they needed these items, and why they had not saved for them. This was required even when participants wished to buy basic items, such as new underwear to accommodate body changes after a pregnancy: "I remember I went and I had to tell them I have to save up for an $8 bra, this is a bit sad. I need new undies, I had a baby, blah blah blah, got no money, you know?" (Manaaki, New Zealand).

This level of justification contributed to feelings of shame and embarrassment in some participants who were at times already self-conscious about their personal needs and expenses. These New Zealand interviewees stressed that, as new mothers, they were in dire need of additional support, yet instead faced the humiliation of increased questioning and bureaucratic scrutiny. Stakeholders, including Youth Service mentors and advocates, typically agreed that these requirements were unnecessary and counterproductive.

While interactions with welfare services could thus contribute to participants' feelings of infantilisation, it is important to note that New

Zealand participants – who dealt primarily with Youth Service providers – typically felt more supported in these interactions than their Australian counterparts. Indeed, many New Zealand interviewees were complementary of their service providers and had developed close relationships with their Youth Service mentors:

> '[M]y youth coach and even others here are really good in regards to helping you meet your goals. Just as long as I suppose that you're honest, completely honest with them, and just straight up and upfront about what's going on in your life, and what it is that you need. I feel that this isn't a place of judgement, so yeah, I feel like it's quite good.' (Tangaroa, New Zealand)

Knowing that someone genuinely cared, she explained, could be a powerful enabling force in a young person's life.

> 'I think what it is really is for someone to just find somebody who cares enough to put them first, really. I think I can say that on behalf of a lot of people. If you don't have somebody who cares enough to just take that time out to help you, you're pretty stuffed.' (Tangaroa, New Zealand)

As previous chapters have explored, Youth Service providers are non-government organisations contracted to coordinate budgeting and parenting programmes, vocational training and educational referrals for young welfare recipients. While they also make recommendations regarding financial benefits or sanctions, the provision of mentoring and support is central to the Youth Service model and stands in stark contrast to the punitive and compliance-based cultures of both the government agencies of Work and Income in New Zealand and Centrelink in Australia.

For Australian participants, dealing with street-level bureaucrats embedded in these punitive cultures *added* to the stress of CIM. Several interviewees describing harrowing interactions with Centrelink staff in which they were denied the basics of human dignity:

> 'I've got degeneration in my spine and I could hardly walk … I remember several times I came in [to Centrelink] and I had to lean on the front desk and they just said, "Take your hand off the desk." I said, "I can't". "Take it off now or we'll get the guard." I said, "I can't, I've got spinal problems". Then I took it off and then I grabbed a chair, and she said, "No, you're not going to sit," … so I went on my knees. I was at the front desk on my knees talking to her.' (Alistair, Playford)

Participants at CDC trial sites similarly shared stories of Indue staff engaging in something akin to gaslighting (a form of psychological abuse where victims are made to doubt their own sanity) when they called their helpline asking for assistance:

> 'Even when you ring them up after the card has declined, they just deny it. They say "oh, nothing has declined on our end. We can't see it where it's declined". And it's like, "I've got a receipt here, it declined". They are like "no, no, we can't see it on our end, it didn't decline." "No, it did, I've got it right here." They're like "no, no, no". It just makes you feel like you are a child, essentially. It's quite eye-opening, especially the way that they treat you. They are nice and friendly on the phone, but then as soon as there is an issue, it's like not their fault, it's not happening, it's not true, they are trying to make you out like a liar and it's not on. You don't feel like a person anymore.' (Aileen, Hinkler)

As Aileen stressed, the emotional impacts of this treatment were severe: "It just makes you feel useless, as if you're not a part of society anymore, like you're segregated, like you're one of those [who] goes into that corner." Again, participants' autonomy and associated psychological health were thus harmed.

Discursive positioning

Beyond these experiences of dependence and patronisation, interviewees explained that their inclusion on the CIM programme had, in itself, altered their perceptions of themselves as adult members of Australian or New Zealand society. Being placed on the cards, interviewees explained, was akin to being told that they were not trusted to behave responsibly or to manage their lives independently: "[S]uddenly they're put into this category where they're not able to have autonomy. ... The society doesn't trust them enough to have autonomy through perhaps no fault of their own. So I guess that sort of feeling of that society doesn't trust me to spend my money ... pervades" (Andrew, Ceduna).

To be included in the programme was to receive a social judgement – to be told that they were *undeserving* of adult privileges.

This idea that CIM participants were viewed as 'naughty children' who needed supervision and management was a recurring theme in the interviews. People who had successfully managed tight budgets for years felt angry and humiliated by the intimation that they were financially irresponsible: "It kind of feels like you're a six-year-old who can't manage your own money and you've been given just some little bit of card that your mum's like, 'oh, here, just have this'. It's leftover money. You know? It feels like you're really irresponsible" (Tamsyn, Playford).

Young people placed on the card in New Zealand experienced similar emotions. As YPP recipient, Manaaki, emphasised: "I think what they need to understand is that as soon as you have a kid you're forced to grow up and you're not actually a normal 16-, 17-, 18-year-old— well, for most cases you're not. You have to grow up, you just have to."

Many of the New Zealand participants were mothers themselves – working to juggle household expenses and care for dependents – yet they were treated as children. Younger participants in both countries resented the assumption that they could be controlled simply because they were young. As Kane from Playford said, welfare recipients in their late teens and twenties were not viewed as "proper adults". "[U]s being adults now, we want control of our own stuff to be independent", Sharmaine (New Zealand) said.

This experience of CIM as a social judgement was largely related to the restrictions the cards imposed. At the most basic level, being placed on CIM meant participants lost autonomy over their own money, despite their status as adults. Yet, as the next section will explore, this subjective experience of judgement and infantilisation was also associated with the dominant narratives that surround the policy.

Stigmatisation

Public discourse

Significant stigma surrounds benefit receipt in most OECD countries, including Australia and New Zealand (McDonald and Marston, 2005; Baumberg et al, 2012; Taylor-Gooby, 2013; Humpage, 2015; Patrick, 2016;). As Chapter 2 outlined, CIM policy narratives in Australia have built on pre-existing stereotypes – maligning welfare recipients as lazy and unmotivated (Marston et al, 2019; Peterie et al, 2019a), but also as 'problem citizens' engaged in anti-social behaviours such as drug and alcohol abuse (Staines et al, 2020b). Single mothers receiving income support payments have been subject to particular stigmatisation (Grahame and Marston, 2010; Peterie et al, 2021). In New Zealand, discourses have been less overtly vilifying, but have nonetheless furthered inaccurate stereotypes by assuming all young welfare recipients lack financial management skills and thus require state supervision (Humpage, 2018).

Questions regarding media effect and the power of political speech are complex, and the available evidence shows that the relationships between political and media discourse and public opinion are highly nuanced. It is often assumed that popular representations are the *cause* of community hostilities and prejudices towards outgroups. One orthodox view of political and media affect, for example, is that 'negative government and media representations … foster negative public perceptions and fears, which in turn provide justification, legitimation and electoral support' for hardline social policies (Klocker, 2004, p 14). Many communications scholars, however, have challenged 'propaganda model' (Herman and Chomsky, 1988) understandings of audience effect, arguing that they risk understating audience autonomy and 'prod-user' activities (Sullivan, 2013). Confirmation bias models have also gained traction in these debates, as researchers have shown that people are more likely to accept and adopt narratives that support their views. As Heshmat (2015, np) explains, '[c]onfirmation bias suggests that we don't perceive circumstances objectively. We pick out those bits of data that make us feel good because they confirm our prejudices'. Put differently, 'moral intuition comes first, strategic reasoning second' (Haidt, 2013, p 286; see also Haidt, 2012).

Whatever the lines of influence, political and media discourse can – at a minimum – provide citizens with valorised arguments that support and sustain prejudices. While it is unclear if discourse can straightforwardly *cause* stigma, there is evidence that 'elite' talk and text (van Dijk, 1993) can contribute to false beliefs and fan into flame the sparks of prejudice (Pedersen et al, 2006). As Bissell and Parrott (2013, p 224) explain with respect to media reporting, for example, 'content may activate stereotypes, making them more readily available for subsequent information processing and perception tasks (priming)'.

In describing their own social and emotional experiences surrounding CIM, interviewees in this study frequently referenced popular portrayals of welfare recipients in political and media discourse. In Hinkler, for instance, interviewees noted that the card had originally been touted as a measure to combat addiction and associated unemployment, but that proponents had later pivoted to suggest a need for action to reduce child abuse and neglect. It seemed to Dawn (Hinkler) that local MP Keith Pitt's policy justifications were secondary to his ideological commitment to the card: "[H]e keeps changing his mind of why he pushed for the card. Originally it was for the drug problem in town. … Now it's all about the children. It's all for the children." While MP Pitt's commitment to the policy was unwavering, the rationales he used to justify it oscillated, such that they seemed to be driven by political considerations.

Interviewees explained that these official discourses came to define the meaning of CIM within their communities. Longstanding stereotypes of welfare recipients as 'bludgers' who preferred not to work are prominent in Australia (Marston et al, 2019). With the introduction of CIM, these stereotypes were overlaid with additional aspersions. Being on the BasicsCard came to mean being "someone who just blows away money on absolute crap" (Grant, Playford). It was "that card for people who can't manage their own money" (Drew, Shepparton). Similar tropes surround the policy at

CDC trial sites, where government and media discourses have given new shape to older prejudices against welfare recipients:

> 'I'm scared that they're going to think "oh, she's one of the ones that's buying drugs and alcohol instead of spending money on her kids," even though I'm there to buy groceries. ... Because the government has said "it's for the kids. It's for the kids so the parents aren't doing drugs and alcohol".' (Fiona, Hinkler)

In New Zealand, interviewees spoke less about political and media discourses, perhaps because New Zealand's Money Management policy has received considerably less media attention than Australia's schemes. Nonetheless, many New Zealand interviewees, like their Australian counterparts, believed that the policy narratives surrounding CIM were based on false and stigmatising assumptions which damaged their status in society (see discussion later in this chapter and in Chapter 6).

Public markers

In both Australia and New Zealand, the distinctive nature of the CIM payment cards was a recurring theme in the interviews. Interviewees stressed that their cards made them easily identifiable as CIM participants, which – in the context of the pejorative policy narratives described earlier – contributed to more direct experiences of stigmatisation and humiliation.

For participants in both countries, the problem with the cards was twofold. First, they looked different from regular bank cards, and second, the payment process for people using a CIM card was slightly different from that for bankcard users. In Australia, BasicsCard users complained that their cards were "bright green" and that they had "to swipe it and then do the pin number" (Marnie, Shepparton), where other customers could tap and go. Participants on the CDC made similar points. Their cards had "a big Indue logo" (Aileen, Hinkler) on them, were a distinctive shade of grey, and could not be used for contactless payments (although plans to introduce this functionality were announced in May 2020, in light of the COVID-19 pandemic [Ruston, 2020]). In New Zealand, interviewees noted that their payment cards were green, visibly branded, and required a unique signing procedure:

> 'Because it's a big green card that says "payment card", everyone knows what that card is, like it's so obvious you're on a benefit. It's just embarrassing, and I find when you're in the line you'll swipe it, ... wait for someone to come, sign it, and everyone's just like "Come on". I do care, but it's just, well, I've got to get my food so this is how it

has to happen. … You know everyone's like, "oh, they're on the dole, I go to work and do this and that and just to pay for their benefit".' (Manaaki, New Zealand)

Across all sites and schemes, the underlying concern was the same: the cards made CIM participants publicly identifiable in a context where cardholders were viewed with stigma and disdain.

In Australia, numerous interviewees had received disparaging comments from members of their communities who – in light of the aforementioned portrayals – deduced they had problems with drugs or alcohol. Young Hinkler mother, Aileen, described her humiliation when fellow shoppers at a local supermarket assumed she was a "junkie":

> 'I was at the shops and one of the [self-checkout] machines – it was a bit of an older machine and I was trying to get the chip to read and it wouldn't read. I'm putting [the CDC] in and out and in and out and it just would not read. Usually, after the third attempt, it asks you to swipe. With this card, it doesn't. So after the third attempt, the self-serve light on the top started flashing and I had to wait for the lady to come over and then I had two tradies [tradespeople] just behind me and they were like, "oh, that's one of them junkie cards". I was already a bit panicky because the card wasn't working and I just burst into tears … I've never touched drugs in my life.' (Aileen, Hinkler)

As Mick (Ceduna) explained, the cards meant there were "no secrets", as an individuals' social security status was visible to all: "[S]traight away you get branded. 'Ah, bludger, dole bludger'."

Disparaging comments did not only come from fellow customers. Interviewees also described instances when retail staff had made snide comments or treated them differently because of the cards. Anthony (Hinkler) recalled a service station attendant remarking, "oh, you're one of them," when he purchased petrol using the CDC. Another observed that retail staff would ask to check his bags for stolen goods before he left a store, something that was rarely required of shoppers who did not pay with a CIM card. The constant assumption, this interviewee explained, was "you guys steal and you're a drug addict. … It's humiliating, that's for sure" (Cindy, Hinkler).

Similar stories peppered the New Zealand interviews, where participants observed that their payment cards inspired withering looks and judgemental comments:

> '[T]he supermarkets' customer service – I think they make people feel really bad for having a payment card. I've got a lot of friends that

> I talk to that have payment cards and they all say the same thing, that payment with the payment card, when the people look at you they look at you like "oh". … If I'm being really honest, it actually makes me feel like absolute rubbish. Makes me feel really self-conscious and scared to do it again.' (Clare, New Zealand)

The stigma of being on welfare, several interviewees stressed, was particularly pronounced for YPP participants, who faced the added stigma of being teen parents: "as a young mum, you already feel like you're frowned upon" (Aroha, New Zealand). Another participant, Pania (New Zealand), posited that Māori participants using these cards faced even greater prejudice: "[If we had] blonde hair and white skin, and we went in there and we had a payment card … [w]e wouldn't have people looking at us like, 'oh my God, look at her'." Social stigmas, Pania implied, built upon each other, creating and reinforcing increasingly denigrating stereotypes, which attached to (racialised and gendered) bodies.

Interventions of this kind underline the potential toxicity of the paternalistic narratives used to justify CIM (see Chapter 2). In asserting that the state should monitor and control how social security recipients spend 'taxpayer funds', political discourses provide implicit moral authorisation to members of the public who might wish to do the same. As Tahlia (Hinkler) reflected, the whole policy approach felt "vindictive, like we're paying you out of our tax money, so you've got to tell us exactly what you're spending with it".

In sharing these stories, participants observed that transaction problems – such as the system failures described in the previous chapter – at times contributed to these scenes of humiliation. Australian interviewees explained that when payment problems occurred, they drew the attention of store staff and attracted interest from other shoppers. As such, they could prompt disparaging comments and negative encounters. Even when overt comments or confrontations did not occur, however, being unable to finalise a purchase caused considerable stress and was frequently experienced as "embarrassing", "humiliating" and "shameful".

One mother of four in Bundaberg, Queensland described her anguish and mortification when – after years of going without to provide for her family – she tried to purchase some much-needed clothing for herself:

> 'I never buy anything for myself so for me to go to Just Jeans to buy myself some clothes, I felt bad enough about that as it was. Then for the payment to not accept, I just – I felt like scum of the earth [cries]. I felt like it didn't matter that I was doing the right thing but, you know. I don't go out, I don't drink, I don't gamble. I don't even buy fucking scratchies [lottery cards] [laughs]. … [The shop assistant] had

a look at the card, and it declined. I don't know if it was a look of pity or of disgust.' (Deidre, Hinkler)

For CDC users, the unreliability of the cards made shopping stressful. Many interviewees were apprehensive shopping at untested businesses, which (as will be discussed) had implications for their local economies. As Tahlia (Hinkler) explained, "you do get that fear of being humiliated in front of everybody".

BasicsCard users and some New Zealand interviewees shared these fears. Given only authorised businesses could accept these cards, many of their difficulties surrounded ascertaining which retailers were participating in the scheme. Tyson (Shepparton) described his embarrassment when he was unable to complete a grocery purchase because the store did not accept the BasicsCard:

> 'I went and did a whole shop and I went to the registers to pay and it declined three or four times. The manager came out and had to speak to me. … I was very embarrassed, to be honest. I didn't know what to do, I just sort of put my head down and was like, "I can't really do much, I'm sorry". … That was in a shop full of people also wanting to be served, so it was very embarrassing. I sort of just walked out of the shop and walked home.' (Tyson, Shepparton)

Alistair (Playford) described a similar incident trying to buy underwear:

> 'The lowest point was when I wanted to buy some underwear that was on a really good special … I put the card out and they looked at me and said, "We don't take that". I just felt like a piece of shit – excuse the French. I said, "Why?" They said, "Because at the moment there's no agreement".' (Alistair, Playford)

For these interviewees and others, the public embarrassment of payment failures had serious repercussions. It built on the stress and hardship caused by being unable to access basic goods and services, with significant social and emotional consequences.

These experiences of public shaming saw participants adopting a range of strategies to mitigate against stigmatisation. These included actively trying to hide or camouflage cards, and monitoring fellow shoppers: "I'm embarrassed every time I have to use it at the supermarket, which is about the only place I do use it. I sort of look around and see who's behind me in the queue. I don't want anybody to see me using it" (Daphne, Ceduna).

Several interviewees described angling their cards away from onlookers so that their distinctive features were hidden:

> 'I don't want the grief of other people saying these nasty comments so I always try to be careful when I do use it as to who's looking. … You never used to have to worry about it, like you'd just whip out your bank card and pay and not have to worry about what anyone is going to say or do around you and now that's something you have to think of. … I have it facing with the back of it up the front so no-one can see the word 'Indue' on it. It's facing the floor sort of thing, so I just kind of hide it.' (Tash, Hinkler)

Others had painted their cards, covered them in coloured contact paper, or used strategically placed stickers to hide provider logos. As Aileen from Hinkler explained, "[t]here is still anxiety there, but it kind of makes me feel like maybe some people won't notice".

In addition to these strategies, however, many interviewees altered their shopping behaviours and reduced engagement in community activities to avoid situations in which they might experience stigma. Some participants limited their shopping to quieter hours or chose self-checkout machines where staff would not see their cards: "It made me feel like everyone was looking down, like I was a junkie but I'm not. It just felt really embarrassing, so I wouldn't do my shopping until 10 o'clock at night, because no one's hardly out at that time" (Marnie, Shepparton).

Others described postponing grocery shopping for as long as their supplies could last, or making all of their purchases in a single shop to avoid the need for multiple embarrassing checkout experiences:

> 'I felt like the money that went onto my Payment Card— I felt that I needed to spend it all in one go, kind of thing, each week on groceries so that— the whole stigma thing; so I didn't actually use it over and over again. … Whereas now that I'm off it, I find that I can spend half of what I spent on groceries when I was on the Money Management and now I can actually save.' (Aroha, New Zealand)

As the following section will show, however, as these behaviours escalated, they contributed to social isolation, with some participants becoming increasingly disconnected from their communities and social circles. This had implications for their psychological health.

Social and emotional wellbeing

Community involvement

In both Australia and New Zealand, interviewees' limited access to cash created practical barriers to their participation in community life. Interviewees explained that neighbourhood events and activities rarely accepted EFTPOS payments. Many Ceduna participants, for instance, described their sadness at being unable to participate in the local Oyster Festival or attend the Royal Adelaide Show, where the cards were not accepted: "People go from here to Adelaide, you know, and want to take the kids over there and they can't buy anything with [the] Indue card, they've got to get cash" (Paddy, Ceduna).

Hinkler participants and their families felt similarly excluded from the thriving local markets, where many had bought fresh, locally grown produce prior to their placement on the CDC:

> 'I want [my son] to grow up like that, too – where he's around the community and he's around farmers and he's around all of those kinds of people as well, because you do really have a lovely time and it's a nice day. So you kind of feel a bit excluded.' (Aileen, Hinkler)

As Drew from Shepparton explained, CIM prevented cardholders from participating in many of the very activities that "would benefit someone trying to get out and be more social and engaging in [the community]". Even participating in local sporting clubs was difficult because "you can't afford the registration fees, you can't afford the … shoes" (Drew, Shepparton).

Interviewees on parenting payments felt their exclusion from local community activities particularly acutely. Many stressed that it was their children who suffered when family-friendly activities became inaccessible. Younger children in particular didn't understand why they could no longer participate in hobbies they had previously enjoyed:

> 'Tell me how that's not making my children suffer, by not being able to give them a sporting thing. He loves to run, he loves to jump, he likes doing all that, he loves being outside. But to me, I don't know how I'm going to afford to put him into football or whatever he wants to do, because they all want cash up front.' (Pearl, Hinkler)

As Tarleen (New Zealand) explained, CIM meant previously affordable activities were no longer accessible, and children had to do without:

> '[The Payment Card] is restricting in every way. … If you want to take your children out and you need five more dollars but that five more dollars is on your Payment Card, then you can't do that. So you've got to find something that's either free or extremely cheap.' (Tarleen, New Zeland)

Children were thus adversely affected by constraints on their parents' spending.

Parents also noted that, in limiting their access to cash, CIM made it harder for them to parent effectively. As several interviewees recounted, CIM made it harder to teach financial responsibility:

> 'Anywhere in life, you're given tools to teach people or to learn how to do things. One of the things the kids need to learn is how to manage money. If you haven't got access to a bit of money to give to them to teach them how, they're never going to learn.' (Kevin, Ceduna)

It also made it difficult to instil community values, such as the importance of supporting small businesses and buying fresh local produce:

> 'The way I want to encourage [my children] to grow up is to buy things locally. We like going to markets and supporting local businesses, like farmers and stuff like that. It's pretty much like the cashless card people are saying you can use your card at Woolworths, but that's not how we want to raise— well, that's not how *I* want to raise my kids. I want to raise them to support local things.' (Fiona, Hinkler)

Where CIM policies purport to help children by constraining parents' allegedly problematic behaviours, many participants instead reported that the cards thwarted them in their efforts to raise healthy, happy, community-minded citizens. This, in turn, contributed to psychologically damaging feelings of ineffectuality and incompetence.

Limited access to discretionary cash not only stopped interviewees from participating in community activities; it also made it difficult for participants to adhere to norms of reciprocity, which in turn compounded feelings of social exclusion and ostracism. In Australia, for instance, Tamara (Hinkler) explained that buying a round of drinks was part of her family culture – the way she and her immediate family expressed love and thanks. With no means of purchasing alcohol, she therefore struggled to communicate gratitude:

> '[I]f I wanted to buy a round of drinks for my parents and my uncle, I can't unless I use my other card, but I can't do that because all the money that goes into my actual bank account goes towards the bills that I have to pay from that. I've got no money left over whatsoever to actually indulge on giving something to my family. My parents have done so much for me – they helped out so much when I first had [my child] … it's time that I could start giving back to them, but I can't.' (Tamara, Hinkler)

Indigenous participants in both Ceduna and Shepparton raised similar concerns, observing that sharing resources was an important cultural value and that CIM was insensitive to these norms: "I think, as far as finance goes, you've got the whole collective identity going on … we were collective. The food was shared and clothes were shared. We'd be asking anyone 'are you right, sis? We've got everything'. So, I think this Income Management is a complete clash" (Mikaela, Shepparton stakeholder).

Western concepts of financial stability and independence thus had limited relevance for some participants, whose preferred economic practices were markedly different from those CIM sought to impose (as we also discuss in Chapter 7).

Participants in New Zealand shared similar concerns, explaining that Money Management made it harder for Pasifika and, to a lesser degree, Māori participants to meet cultural obligations. For instance, a lack of available cash made it difficult to attend *tangi* (funeral services) or to meet familial or church expectations to contribute *koha* (a gift or contribution). As Pasifika participant, Sharmaine, said: "[J]ust helping out with family gatherings and funerals sometimes … giving a *koha* and if you can't give it, you feel shame, like sad."

While some participants experienced these obligations as burdensome and were pleased to be free of them, others were ashamed of their inability to contribute.

Where inadequate access to cash prevented interviewees across Australia and New Zealand from engaging in community life and participating in cultural activities, participants at CDC trial sites in Australia reported an additional dimension to this social exclusion. The unreliability of their cards – as well as restrictions against using them anywhere alcohol was sold – deterred participants from restaurants and cafés, damaging relationships between friends and partners.

In Hinkler, for example, Mary explained that she and her partner – who could afford few other luxuries – used to save and go out for dinner once a fortnight. These shared meals (often affordable pub specials) were a chance to enjoy each other's company and nurture their relationship; they were a way to "give ourselves a little treat, because it was something nice that we could do as a date" (Mary, Hinkler). With the introduction of the CDC, Mary explained that this was no longer possible:

> '[A] lot of the pubs, even the RSL and places like that, they don't [accept the CDC], and it sort of gets to a point where you feel like everything is just too hard. It's like, why do we even bother, if we go there and get knocked back, what are we going to do? It's not like we can go and grab cash and pay for it. It's not like we've got a whole lot of money to spare to be able to do anything. … And my partner's social anxiety, having to worry about how he may handle that [public embarrassment]. It just becomes all too much.' (Mary, Hinkler)

Other interviewees shared similar reflections, noting that most restaurants and bistros sold alcohol and were therefore inaccessible to people on the card. Date nights, friends' birthday dinners and girls' coffee dates were often automatic declines, contributing to social isolation and reduced wellbeing.

Emotional wellbeing

In light of participants' experiences of financial stress, infantilisation and stigmatisation – as well as their perceived social exclusion under the policy – it is unsurprising that many interviewees indicated that CIM had harmed their physical and emotional wellbeing and sense of self.

As the previous chapter explored, the introduction of CIM to Australia has been marred by numerous technical and system issues, which have brought new financial instability into some participants' lives. These impacts have been particularly acute for participants at CDC trial sites, where reports of both card failures and online transfer problems have been common. Interviewees at these sites explained that these issues – and the possibility of rental defaults and overdue amenity bills they introduced – caused significant stress. Interviewees lived in a constant state of vigilance, unsure when their cards might decline and whether essential online payments would be successful:

> 'It's just made life so much more difficult than what it was. I mean, I used to think it was hard living fortnight to fortnight not knowing how much money we'd have left over, but this is so much harder. I don't even know if my bills are going to get paid on time. That has never been a problem for me.' (Dawn, Hinkler)

Concerns about housing security were particularly common:

> 'It's been making my anxiety go through the roof, because every time I transfer rent over I'm wondering, is this going to be the day where it bounces back? Is this going to be the day that I'm not going to be able to pay my rent? … That sort of anxiety is always there in the back of your mind.' (Catriona, Hinkler)

In this context, many interviewees invested large amounts of time and emotional energy trying to avoid the most serious consequences of system failures. Interviewees described compulsively checking online banking records and making regular phone calls to check the status of their bills. As Riley (Hinkler) put it, being on the card was "exhausting": "I'm tired all the time because I just constantly worry."

For some participants, including those with pre-existing mental health conditions, this stress and nervousness could contribute to crippling anxiety.

In a number of cases, debilitating physical symptoms – including vomiting and panic attacks – made it hard for participants to function. Aileen (Hinkler) told us that she lost three-and-a-half kilograms of body weight during her first week on the card:

> 'I could not stop throwing up; just the anxiety of using the card and trying to switch payments over, worrying about which payments were going to get paid, is my landlord going to kick me out, what's going to happen? Am I going to get a blacklist on my name? This will affect my credit rating and everything in the future.' (Aileen, Hinkler)

Sue (Ceduna) described crying and having "a full-on breakdown" at Centrelink as she tried to set up her card. A third interviewee, Marlee (Hinkler), explained that both she and her partner now suffered regular panic attacks because the stress of managing their finances had become too much:

> 'It's become at least a fortnightly thing – one of us at least are having a physical panic attack. And his get bad enough where he will spend the whole day in a panic attack, and then, come night-time, he's throwing up because he's been in such a state of stress.' (Marlee, Hinkler)

The physical and psychological impacts of CIM were therefore significant, but – as the next chapter will explore – even vulnerable participants struggled to access exemptions and were routinely forced to continue under the scheme.

As described above, card restrictions and limited access to cash saw many participants across all interview sites excluded from community activities, which in turn weakened their social networks. Experiences of financial stress could further damage participants' relationships – introducing new tension and conflict into the family home:

> 'I'm stressed. My partner is stressed, and it's probably not the healthiest of relationships when it comes to stress. Everything else is fine, but once one of us gets stressed, the other one feeds off that and it's just like the whole house hears about it then. Then we overreact. … There's some weeks where [my partner's] clients aren't paying so there's no steady, predictable, reliable income. … Then when one of the kids mucks up, because we're already stressed, we overreact to the situation even though we're trying not to. But it's just like, how much pressure can we take before we explode?' (Dawn, Hinkler)

Multiple interviewees noted that, while proponents of CIM regularly suggested it could help women in family violence situations, the programme also had the potential to enflame already dangerous dynamics. One New Zealand interviewee, Tangaroa, had seen this play out in her own neighbourhood:

> 'They're coming at this other partner like, "well, why the fuck can't you talk to your case manager, trying to get off it?" "Why can't you get the money, what the fuck's wrong with you?" Then they'll smash them. Then it's just, like, "no, I'll fucking take that card," but they can't do anything because it's a signature. But then you've got the really clever ones who know how to do the signature. So regardless of what it is, it's not going to end the actual proper issues.' (Tangaroa, New Zealand)

Several interviewees who had experienced family violence in the past concurred: the limitations CIM imposed could enrage an abusive partner, and fleeing would be more difficult with little available cash.

When financial pressures created or aggravated mental health problems, this also impacted participants' families:

> 'It sends the anxiety higher. The depression kicks in ... and the obsessive-compulsive behaviour, it's terrible. Then that puts more pressure on the family, too. They say that the CDC doesn't affect anybody who's not on it. Well, it affects my partner, it affects my kids, it affects my [home] owner, it affects my community. ... My partner at the moment is struggling because he can't help me. This card's not supposed to affect him but it does affect him because it affects me, which means it affects our whole entire household.' (Riley, Hinkler)

These experiences, building on incidents of public humiliation and stigmatisation, had a profound impact on participants' self-worth, which could in turn cause or exacerbate mental health problems. As Riley reflected, "with my anxiety and depression and everything at the moment, I keep thinking that I'm failing [my children], and my partner, too". New Zealand participants did not describe such extreme cases of stress and anxiety, for reasons discussed below.

Stability and capability

While stories of stress and anxiety recurred in the interviews, a minority of participants – mainly young welfare recipients who had not previously managed their finances independently – indicated that CIM had *reduced* their stress levels. These were interviewees whose bills were paid automatically from their benefit before they saw the funds, and who were relieved they no longer had to worry about overseeing these payments. As a New Zealand

Youth Service employee explained, knowing that rent and utilities would always be paid could "take away some stress" from less experienced money managers (Tony, New Zealand Youth Service employee).

A young New Zealand mother, Clare, shared this view. Receiving social security benefits already made her feel guilty, she explained. Only having to manage a small portion of her payment eased her fear of making irresponsible purchases:

> '[W]hen I first went onto it, I felt quite guilty for being paid for, like, getting an education, you should just want to get an education because it's free, so it's pretty good. But I don't know, I feel like I'd freak out if I had a lot of money in there because I wouldn't know what to do with it and stuff. I guess it's pretty tense.' (Clare, New Zealand)

Several Australian interviewees expressed similar sentiments. Sylvie (Hinkler), for example, had a condition that prevented her from budgeting independently. Automatic bill payments made her life simpler:

> 'I have my rent and everything that I've got to pay, I have it coming out automatically through Centrepay. Because that's how I prefer to have it, otherwise I just won't pay it. I'll rather spend the money or put the money towards something else than paying rent or something else. … Before I was on the card, I was reminded every week or every fortnight to go pay it by my mum. I've got a short-term memory – I don't remember some things – so if rent [didn't automatically] come out, I probably wouldn't remember it.' (Sylvie, Hinkler)

Such gains, however, were contingent on these systems functioning correctly, which – as earlier shown – did not always occur. Indeed, one interviewee recalled that when the Centrepay system failed several weeks earlier, she hadn't noticed the additional money in her account and had accidently spent it on other items. Despite the Centrepay system, she was now behind on her rent.

This incident reflects another concern – which was heard from both stakeholders and CIM participants in Australia and New Zealand – regarding whether CIM builds genuine financial *capacity* or in fact contributes to increased participant dependence on welfare services. As Drew (Shepparton) reflected:

> '[T]he most basic way of using of the BasicsCard is to have a Centrepay set up. So, if you have bills, fortnightly bills or monthly bills that will come straight out of your BasicsCard. That in turn doesn't teach you to pay rent. … When people do finally get off Centrelink, what have

> they learnt? You know what I mean? You go through a hard time and you end up on Centrelink and then you get out of that, and if you're used to this system of your money gets managed for you then you don't really learn how to dig your way out of that hole and work it out.' (Drew, Shepparton)

In addition to relying on automatic payments, many New Zealand participants also came to depend on their Youth Service mentors for assistance monitoring their quarantined funds. While such mentors provide support in many cases (such as avoiding applying financial sanctions where possible), card balances could not be checked via ATM, and internet access was often not available or affordable for disadvantaged welfare recipients. This lack of access to up-to-date account details saw some participants regularly calling their mentors for basic account balance information. Others simply did not monitor their funds.

As noted earlier, numerous interviewees stressed that CIM had made them more dependent on family support. These stories indicate that CIM can also entrench one of the very issues it seeks to address – making welfare recipients more, not less, dependent on the social security system.

Identity and self-worth

There is long-standing agreement in the sociological literature that other peoples' perceptions deeply influence individuals' perceptions of themselves. In 1902, Cooley posited that people view and judge themselves from the (imagined) perspective of others. If they believe that others view them positively, they experience pride. If they judge that they are seen negatively, shame is the response. In a similar vein, symbolic interactionists such as Goffman (1963) have posited that individuals constantly curate and perform socially favoured identities to garner acceptance and approval. When these performances fail, or when approval is not forthcoming, embarrassment, shame and humiliation result.

As this chapter has shown, CIM participants in both Australia and New Zealand are typically viewed unfavourably, and participants are acutely aware of this stigma and stereotyping. The majority of the Australian interviewees pushed back against public narratives that maligned them as problem citizens, asserting their enduring contributions and conformity to social norms. Nonetheless, many recognised that experiences of infantilisation and stigmatisation had damaged their sense of self:

> '[W]e've heard all over the TV and news it was only going to be for those who did the wrong thing and exploited the system and things like that, and then next thing you get the letter. … What did I do wrong

to exploit the system? I didn't think I did anything wrong. It makes you question what you've done or it makes you question things you have done and everything.' (Tash, Hinkler)

Feelings of guilt and shame – even while investing significant energy into doing 'the right thing' – were common, and took a toll on participants' wellbeing:

'Mental health wise, I was going pretty good until I got the card, and then it instantly just makes you feel like you are guilty of doing something when I'm out there. My son is in kinder programme at the moment, so whenever he is in school … I'm going out and I'm handing out resumes, but the second that you pull [the card] out, you just instantly feel guilty.' (Aileen, Hinkler)

These negative self-perceptions could have dire consequences, contributing to serious mental health problems including suicidal ideation:

'I don't understand this. Is it because I'm a bit backward? I don't understand this. I go in, come out, and I'm all in tears. I just don't want to go home. I just want to stand in the middle of the road and get run over, mate. That's how I feel.' (Doreen, Shepparton)

As Alistair (Playford) summarised, "it made me feel useless".

While CIM participants in New Zealand were less likely to report these negative outcomes personally, welfare advocates indicated that Money Management had been psychologically costly for some clients. Others indicated that the waiting period until entitlement for Youth or Young Parent Payment came through was particularly difficult, with one advocate highlighting that young women, in particular, had to find alternative ways to earn money, including methods they might not have otherwise chosen:

'Like I knew the girls that I was working with last year, if I didn't get them their entitlements met, then they were going on those sort of [web]sites and they really didn't want to. One of them was dancing, one of them was— well actually three or four of them were actually going [on] the sugar daddies sites, because actually that was the only other way they had to make money as a 17-year-old that had no means to income, [and] was studying full-time.' (Michael, New Zealand advocate)

Another advocate, Sharon (New Zealand), agreed that young people are forced into potentially risky situations to survive while waiting for payment to come through:

> 'Sex work: if it's not for paid money, it's for a roof over their head. Yes. Stealing, the young men. They're very resourceful, as far as survivig. … But that's teaching them a way of life that you're not meant to be teaching them … "I've been offered a job, but I've got nowhere to live, so I can't take the job". … A roof, a roof, food. Yes, those kind of essentials need to be there, before they can move forward on any level.' (Sharon, New Zealand advocate)

Sharon also felt that Youth Service providers did not do basic check-ins with young people:

> 'We [the welfare advocacy service] do a basic check, okay. Then the young person would say "well, I am meant to go to the doctor, because … I'm high risk of suicide. But I can't afford it, so I'm not going to go. I am meant to have these meds, but I can't afford it, so I'm not picking them up". The Youth Transition Service [which was abolished when the Youth Service was established], I would have imagined, before that, would have gone there and said "hey, what are your needs? You obviously need housing, food, clothing, whatever else. How's your health? What do you need – do you have any costs?" Which is kind of the questions we ask. Really basic wrap-around stuff. But they [current Youth Service providers] don't do that.' (Sharon, New Zealand advocate)

Some young people end up homeless as a result. Amelia (New Zealand advocate), described how Work and Income (New Zealand's social security agency) turned down a young mother's request for a food parcel and said:

> '"Go back to your youth provider," and she ended up homeless, with her and her baby … she had actually given up – with one of them, she had given up the custody to her mother for the first child. This was the second one she was trying to hold onto. … When I got involved: "Oh well, you know, she's got to tick these boxes to get her benefit back on". By then she's homeless with this baby. … Luckily her mother has taken her in, in the meantime. [But] we found out that both of her children could have been attending a day care, which would have took the pressure off the mother, with a disabled child as well. So they're really complicated lives.' (Amelia, New Zealand advocate)

These lives are further complicated by rule-bound systems that fail to address individual needs, sometimes contributing to young people taking their own lives: "[T]he wee [little] girl that suicided here last year, she was Youth Parent Payment and … she was constantly denied entitlements when she really needed them for the baby. And life just got too hard for her" (Michael, New Zealand advocate).

These examples suggest that CIM policies alone do not create the stigma and shame that makes some CIM participants feel worthless. They are, however, part of a broader restrictive and punitive social security system that denies welfare recipients the dignity and respect that everyone deserves.

Conclusion

These qualitative interviews in both Australia and New Zealand shed light on the socio-emotional impacts of CIM, highlighting, in particular, the shame and stigma associated with the scheme. Interviewees stressed that government-issued debit cards signalled to others in public and commercial encounters that they were a 'problem to be fixed'. While it is possible that the experience of being on CIM led participants to rate themselves as stronger money managers that they would have otherwise been, the interviews overwhelmingly indicate that CIM has hindered rather than helped participants to manage their financial affairs. Furthermore, they demonstrate that CIM has reduced many participants' sense of autonomy, wellbeing and overall locus of control.

There are many factors that make up financial wellbeing, such as possessing an ability to save and having low levels of personal debt. Psychological and emotional factors also have an impact, with research indicating that those who have responsibility for the day-to-day management of their money have higher levels of mental health and wellbeing (Kempson et al, 2017). It is therefore disappointing that these established connections between mental health and social identity, self-determination and financial wellbeing have been missing from public and political debates regarding the merits (or otherwise) of CIM.

The experiences documented in this chapter contradict political discourses that portray CIM as a means of *increasing* individual responsibility and wellbeing. In practice, CIM appears to *undermine* rather than support the stated policy objectives of creating more autonomous, independent individuals who will be more likely to transition into employment. As has been argued elsewhere, and is again highlighted in this study, the primary challenge for those placed on conditional welfare schemes is not *managing* money, but a fundamental *lack of money* to meet everyday needs. The policy implication that follows from this conclusion is that social security debates in both Australia and New Zealand should be more focused on the adequacy of income support payments, rather than on controlling discretionary expenditure.

From an institutional perspective, what is lacking in CIM schemes is a basic recognition of people's capabilities, their sense of determination and their various strengths. Misrecognition adds a level of cultural insult to people's economic injury (Fraser, 1997), reinforcing the importance of Sennett's (2003) work on the corrosive effects of social inequality on the capacity to sustain mutual respect between citizens. Mutual respect needs to be built into policy design and implementation if it is to be sustained.

The next chapter extends the discussion of rights and respect to consider the sociolegal aspects of the policy and the attempts research participants made to exercise their procedural and redress rights in both Australia and New Zealand.

5

Procedural, consumer and contractual rights, and access to justice

Introduction

This chapter presents a sociolegal analysis of cashless welfare cards, considering the content of CIM laws and policies in Australia and New Zealand and how these are experienced in everyday life by cardholders. This study reveals a gap between official (idealised) narratives about how compulsory IM schemes function and about government income support recipient's everyday experiences. This reflects a long-held tradition in law and society scholarship of focusing on the distance 'between the law-on-the-books … and the-law-in-action' (Calavita, 2016, p 109). To make these gaps apparent, the legal framework governing IM programmes must be set out. Scholars working within critical social policy are also concerned with gaps between what is represented by policy frameworks and how this translates into people's lived experiences (Bacchi, 2009, pp xviii–xix).

The research for this book found that the autonomy of IM cardholders was adversely affected with respect to purchases of a range of everyday items that extended beyond those officially prohibited (Marston et al, 2020; Humpage et al, 2020a). Payment problems created by IM cards often caused people to be unable to acquire goods and services when these were needed, and rendered IM cardholders in Australia unable to pay a range of bills. As will be discussed in this chapter, this undermined long-valued consumer rights and contractual freedoms. This chapter also examines procedural rights for cardholders to exit or make complaints about IM schemes, and how these processes are experienced by those who have to use them.

This study shows that IM exit and exemption processes raise significant access to justice issues. For example, not only were there protracted timeframes for determining exit and exemption requests under the Australian CDC scheme, but cardholders also needed to acquire documentation from third parties at their own expense to submit their applications. The number of people who have been able to regain their autonomy through the legal frameworks governing IM exits and exemptions in Australia has been small (Australian Government, 2021c; 2021e). In New Zealand, exit from the Money Management programme typically occurs through participants aging out of the scheme, though IM has reportedly led some young people to withdraw from the social security system altogether or, tragically, take their own lives rather than be subject to the programme (Humpage et al, 2020a, p 13). In this sense, the risks associated with compulsory IM are high indeed.

Consumer and contractual rights of welfare recipients under Income Management

Prior to the introduction of IM cards, recipients of social security payments were free to purchase goods and services from merchants and service providers of their choice as and when they wished. The consumer and contractual rights of government income support recipients have been substantially altered through IM programmes. Contractual freedom has long been a valued right in common law countries, where freedom of contract is understood to mean that: '(1) contracting parties should be free to agree to whatever agreement they wish; and (2) people should be free to decide to enter into contracts with whoever they please and should not be compelled to enter contractual relationships' (Carter, 2012, pp 6–7). Although there have often been 'exceptions and qualifications' to contractual freedom (Carter, 2012, p 7), IM represents a new type of legislative exception with respect to the quarantined income of social security recipients, because they are no longer free to enter into contracts for whatever goods and services they want with whomever they wish to purchase such goods and services from using their cashless welfare cards (Bielefeld, 2013; 2014b; 2018b). In the present research, cardholders using the BasicsCard or CDC in Australia or the Payment Card in New Zealand experienced expenditure prohibitions on a range of everyday goods and services and delays in their purchasing capacity. The IM cards created consumer problems and contractual freedom of cardholders was undermined.

Australia's BasicsCard

As mentioned in Chapters 1 and 2, IM via the BasicsCard was initiated as part of the Northern Territory Emergency Response and was then later introduced into Place Based IM trial sites in other jurisdictions. Part 3B of the *Social Security (Administration) Act 1999* (Cth) governs CIM, under which 50 per cent of fortnightly social security payments are typically quarantined to the government-issued BasicsCard. This percentage can be higher, up to 70 or 90 per cent, depending on the IM category a person is subject to (see Sections 123UC to 123UFA). In addition, 100 per cent of lump sum payments are quarantined. Expenditure of these funds is limited to legislatively defined priority needs (Section 123TH), and quarantined funds cannot be spent on prohibited items, namely alcohol, tobacco, pornography and gambling (Section 123TI). The legislative objectives of BasicsCard IM, set out in Section 123TB, are to:

- ensure payments first go to 'priority needs';
- create 'support in budgeting to meet priority needs';
- ensure limited funds are available for purchase of alcohol, tobacco, gambling and pornography;
- reduce the chance that 'recipients of welfare payments will be subject to harassment and abuse in relation to their welfare payments';
- 'encourage socially responsible behaviour, including in relation to the care and education of children'; and
- 'improve the level of protection afforded to welfare recipients and their families.'

The vast majority of people on the BasicsCard are subject to it as a compulsory measure (Australian Government, 2021e), with autonomy-eroding effects. There is no sunset clause under social security legislation limiting the length of time that IM via the BasicsCard is to operate. Because of this, cardholders who cannot earn sufficient income to pay for necessities could be kept on the card for many years to come.

Although the Australian government has previously proclaimed the merits of the BasicsCard (Commonwealth of Australia, 2007, p 6), consumer purchasing problems were apparent from the earliest days of the programme (Gibson, 2009, p 4), with government-commissioned research indicating that these problems persisted over time (Bray et al, 2014, pp 137–8). Recipients with a BasicsCard who have wanted to make more expensive one-off purchases, such as whitegoods, have needed to go through time-consuming and demeaning bureaucratic permission-seeking processes (Lattas and Morris, 2010, p 82).

In addition, EFTPOS failures have occurred with some regularity (including, for example, as a result of power outages or other technology failures) where the BasicsCard operates, leaving people to go without essentials (Allam, 2020; Hynes, 2020). The BasicsCard can only be used at government-approved shops, restricting the market from which cardholders can make necessary purchases. Shrinking the market for people on low incomes limits their ability to stretch their money as far as possible, and can also hamper job seeking, health care, and other basic functionality.

Exemplifying these problems, Grant (Playford) explained that getting groceries was now more expensive because they needed to factor in the cost of travel to an outlet that accepted the card: "I moved to my house in Clearview and IGA's my closest shop and they don't take the BasicsCard. That's when I started to get annoyed. I couldn't even do shopping down the road so I'd have to catch the bus … for shopping or meals." Tamsyn

(Playford) said that shopping with the BasicsCard required "more effort" because of the difficulty finding places that accepted it.

Another BasicsCard holder, Alistair (Playford), opined that IM meant they "couldn't get things … on specials in certain shops". He described his frustration at trying to purchase discounted underwear and having the shop refuse to accept the BasicsCard (Alistair, Playford). Alistair also explained how the BasicsCard hampered his attempts to save money by buying in bulk: "It's still very demeaning, it limits our life. It's … like apartheid, where people are forced to live in a particular place, to live a particular way." He would have preferred to keep bulk buying food at Costco for his family of six, which the BasicsCard precluded. As Tyson (Shepparton) also spoke about, having a BasicsCard transaction repeatedly declined deprived cardholders of access to basic goods.

Feelings of frustration at having their consumer choice and budgetary autonomy eroded were common for BasicsCard holders, as Grant (Playford) explained: "I have to keep calling up just to pay a certain bill. It would take forever to get a hold of them and even longer to get the bill to be paid." Similarly, Drew (Shepparton) stated that the BasicsCard "makes it harder for people" by setting up too many "hoops for people to jump through" and that "just seems to jack up the height of the hurdles" in life. Obtaining essential medication was also made more challenging by the BasicsCard: "I had to go in and get my medication … but the pharmacist … kept saying you can't use the BasicsCard to pay [for] the prescriptions. You couldn't find anyone who would … take this BasicsCard for anything" (Callum, Playford). Callum was also unable to pay for vet services or petrol. Difficulty buying petrol was a common complaint among the interviewees.

None of the items the interviewees mentioned trying to buy had anything to do with substance abuse, pornography or gambling addiction, and the restrictions put in place to prevent such purchases ended up meaning that cardholders were unable to purchase what they needed, when they needed it. This chapter now turns to the similar problems faced by CDC holders.

Australia's Cashless Debit Card

As discussed in Chapter 2, the Forrest Review recommended a 'Health Welfare Card' that would quarantine 100 per cent of social security payments (Forrest, 2014, pp 100–8). The government modified this and introduced it as the CDC. Initially trialled in Ceduna and the East Kimberley region, the CDC has since been extended to additional trial sites. Part 3D of the *Social Security (Administration) Act 1999* (Cth) governs IM via the CDC. The legislation provides that CDC-restricted funds cannot be spent on alcohol, gambling, and some gift cards described as 'a cash-like product that could be used to obtain alcoholic beverages or gambling' (Section 124PM). In

Ceduna, the East Kimberley region and the Goldfields, the CDC applies to a broad range of social security payments defined as 'trigger' payments (Sections 124PD, 124PG, 124PGA, 124PGB). In the Hinkler region, the card applies to people who are 35 years old and under who receive a 'jobseeker payment, youth allowance ... or parenting payment' (Section 124PGC).

Generally, 80 per cent of fortnightly social security payments are quarantined to the CDC (Section 124PJ), which is issued by the for-profit financial services provider Indue Ltd. Cardholders in Ceduna and the East Kimberley region can apply for a reduction in their restricted portion. A further CDC trial site, the Northern Territory, was added in 2021, and those in this jurisdiction have 50 per cent of their fortnightly income quarantined to the CDC, a change introduced by the *Social Security (Administration) Amendment (Continuation of Cashless Welfare) Act 2020* (Cth) (hereafter the *CDC Continuation Act*). After the government failed to garner sufficient support in the Parliament to install the CDC as a permanent mandatory measure in the Northern Territory in December 2020, special voluntary arrangements were put in place for the CDC trial in that jurisdiction. However, as of March 2021, the vast majority of people on the CDC are subject to it as a compulsory measure (Australian Government, 2021c).

Before the *CDC Continuation Act* entered into force, the objectives of the CDC under the *Social Security (Administration) Act 1999* (Cth) were to:

- reduce the amount of cash 'available to be spent on alcoholic beverages, gambling and illegal drugs' (Section 124PC[a]);
- 'determine whether such a reduction decreases violence or harm in trial areas' (Section 124PC[b]);
- 'determine whether such arrangements are more effective when community bodies are involved' (Section 124PC[c]); and
- 'encourage socially responsible behaviour' (Section 124PC[d]).

The 2020 Act also introduced a new Section 124PC objective: to 'support program participants and voluntary participants with their budgeting strategies'. The same legislation repealed the former objectives in Sections 124PC(b) and (c). This changing of two legislative objectives after five years of trials signals that policymakers are still searching for a compelling rationale for the CDC.

These CDC legislative objectives represent the policy problem as inherent deficiency in welfare recipients, with these people portrayed as irresponsible and undisciplined. At the time of writing, there is still no evidence to demonstrate that the broadly applied compulsory CDC achieves the government's stated policy objectives, nor that the cohort of cardholders generally exhibit the behavioural deficiencies the government claims to address with the CDC. However, the passage of the *CDC Continuation Act* ensures that the trials will run until at least December 2022.

Although the government maintains that the CDC can be used at any merchant the government has not blocked, this research indicates that many goods and service providers refused the CDC (Marston et al, 2020). Interviewees experienced these restrictions as undesirable and unnecessary burdens. Interviews revealed a gap between official information about how the card would work and how the CDC affected cardholders in practice. The legislated CDC objectives stress the need to encourage 'socially responsible' conduct, yet this research found that the card frequently prevented interviewees from paying bills, including bills for groceries, utilities, car repayments, car insurance, petrol, optometrists, kindergarten, tutoring, school photos, and school uniforms. Interviewees often reported that payment of rent within the CDC/Indue system was particularly difficult. This could result in serious legal ramifications for cardholders' housing security:

> 'I've … tried to pay my rent because I pay it to a private landlord, and so you're waiting for it to go through and waiting for it to go through. Then I think it was two days later, next minute, that amount had been bounced back in my account and I'm looking at it and I'm like, "why has that bounced back?" Then you ring them up and they say, "oh, it's just a minor teething issue, just keep trying" … but that's two more days my rent's due, you're telling me it's a minor teething issue to breach a contract. That's breaching your contract, especially when you're paying late.' (Aileen, Hinkler)

Aileen (Hinkler) described the CDC as an unreliable system for bill payments: "It takes longer for BPAY [a bill payment service] to get paid. It takes longer for normal bills to be paid if they get paid and don't bounce back". For Aileen, having her consumer rights restricted through the CDC was infantilising and dehumanising: "It just makes you feel like you are a child essentially. … You don't feel like a person anymore."

This study indicates that CDC holders experienced the card as imposing restrictions on a wide range of purchases they would otherwise have been able to make. For example, Andrew (Ceduna) explained that "straight off … I was much more limited to how much fruit and veg I could buy' because 'the fruit and veg truck that came through didn't have EFTPOS". Fiona (Hinkler) stated that the CDC prevented her from buying food at her preferred shop: I "can't shop at Costco any more", which she described as "a big thing", since previously she could "just buy bulk". This had helped her stretch her social security payments further to cover necessities.

Many cardholders experienced transaction declines in mainstream supermarkets: "You go there, do all the shopping. Then get to the checkout, run it all through the checkout and then go, no, it won't let me pay for it" (Tim, Hinkler). Similarly, Riley (Hinkler) explained how she put her "groceries through and the Indue card declined … twice", then she was "sent to the front desk and … told … the Indue card was the one they were having the most dramas with and asked … [to] pay some other way".

CDC holders indicated that purchasing affordable second-hand goods was difficult, and indeed, sometimes impossible. As Dawn (Hinkler), who is a mother of four, explained: "We have a three-legged kitchen table at the moment because I don't have enough cash left over to buy a second hand one. It's just ridiculous … it's like we can't hunt for a bargain because all of the best ways to do that have been blocked from us."

Interviews revealed that obtaining medicine was also more challenging with the CDC: "I had to go to the chemist and get medicine. I went to use my cashless card and it didn't work. … It wouldn't accept it at the EFTPOS machine" (Tash, Hinkler). Cindy (Hinkler) indicated that the CDC could create problems for women who were menstruating, pointing out that when "you need to go to the shops to get your monthly things", if the CDC was not working, "you can't … and it's a problem".

CDC restrictions on consumer choices for people with disabilities and visual impairments presented particularly onerous burdens. For example, Ellen (Ceduna) who is on a Disability Support Pension explained that 'my backyard is just atrocious with weeds … because the bloke I pay, he only does cash. … It makes it really hard'. Tahlia (Hinkler) relayed the problems she had purchasing reading glasses once she was on the CDC: "I had to buy … reading glasses, because I'm working … on the weekend. I have difficulty with my eyesight, so I had to buy glasses … and I couldn't use my Indue card." Tahlia found the permission seeking process for trying to get the necessary reading glasses "humiliating", questioning why she needed to tell a stranger that she needed glasses. "It feels like you're … suddenly reporting to a parent again … it takes away from your independence and your autonomy … it feels vindictive. It doesn't feel like they're doing that to help you" (Tahlia, Hinkler).

The government has represented the CDC as a new and improved form of IM, however, the CDC shares some problems with the BasicsCard in terms of consumer restrictions. CDC-induced bill payment problems were common across both trial sites where interviews were conducted. The problems caused by the CDC/Indue system were outside the control of cardholders, yet they were the ones left carrying the heavy burdens caused by card malfunctions, delayed payments, system errors, EFPTOS failures, and power outages. Anthony (Hinkler) concluded: "It's punishing the poor people by the card not working." Many interviewees felt like their rights had been violated by being put on the CDC.

New Zealand's Payment Card

In New Zealand, IM cards are restricted to Youth Payment (YP) and Young Parent Payment (YPP) recipients. These people are placed on the Money Management programme where the bulk of their income covers bills; rent, board, utilities, and other debts (Work and Income, 2020a). The government's intention is to ensure that the core needs of the young person are met through these arrangements. Young people on Money Management in New Zealand have access to a maximum of $50 cash per week (Work and Income, 2020a), and have any additional money quarantined to a Payment Card. The Youth Service provider monitors the social security recipient's expenditure via the Payment Card, which can only be used to purchase 'approved items' (Work and Income, 2020b), and cannot be used to purchase 'alcohol, cigarettes, tobacco, gift cards, vouchers, lotto tickets, appliances, or electronics' (Work and Income, 2020c). However, in practice, young interviewees indicated that the card often could not be used to purchase petrol either, limiting their mobility.

The Money Management programme is legislatively authorised by the *Social Security Act 2018* (NZ). Certain types of social security payments made to young people, including 'any youth support payment', are required to use 'a money management manner of payment' (Section 341), which Schedule 2 defines as 'a manner of payment, prescribed in regulations made under Section 418(1)(k), that is designed to assist certain young people to manage their money effectively'. Youth support payments are made subject to obligations, including that the young person supply details about their living costs to the MSD or their Youth Services provider so they can be placed under Money Management (Section 162). Young people who fail to comply with their obligations can be sanctioned (Section 275). The Money Management programme is targeted towards young people deemed to be 'at significant risk of long-term welfare dependency' (Section 165), defined in Section 165(9) as the risk 'that the person will, for an indefinite period, not be able to obtain full-time employment and will be likely to remain wholly or largely dependent for the person's financial support on all or part of a main benefit under this Act'. Young people are exempted from Money Management if the MSD considers that the person has satisfied the criteria for managing their own social security payments (Section 342). However, the interviews for this study indicated that young social security recipients were frequently unaware of their legal rights.

Interviews with people on the Payment Card indicated that they experienced problems purchasing consumer goods due to restrictions on where the card was accepted. For instance, Tui (New Zealand) explained that the Payment Card would "be better if we could use it at The Warehouse [a low-cost retail chain] to buy clothes for us and our babies". Another similarly indicated that they were having difficulty purchasing a washing machine on the Payment Card (Charlotte, New Zealand). Several interviewees saw the restriction on purchasing petrol as problematic: "They need to make it so you can get petrol as well" because under the Money Management scheme "you only get $50 in your bank and if you use it all on petrol then it's like nothing after that" (New Zealand 15). This was a pressing issue for those living in regional areas where transportation by car was essential.

The Payment Card presented difficulties in paying for family outings, too, often resulting in parents needing to find low- or no-cost substitutes. Parental freedom to contract with preferred goods or service providers was thus undermined. As was the case with Australian forms of IM, some of those on the Payment Card regretted not being able to bulk buy to stretch their money further. As Tangaroa (New Zealand) explained, she wanted to be able to shop at "certain places where it's cheaper to buy bulk", but this was not possible "because they don't accept payment cards". Some interviewees also said that the Money Management programme and the Payment Card restricted them from contributing to funeral costs or other family obligations (Sharmaine, New Zealand). This research found that programme participants often needed to spend their small amount of discretionary cash on essentials, given that the card is not universally accepted.

The degree of Money Management scrutiny over necessary purchases could also be awkward and intrusive. One female interviewee, Manaaki (New Zealand), reported that she had to seek permission from her programme mentor to buy underwear after having a baby. That underwear purchases needed to be explained and approved in this way was demeaning, and undermined consumer and contractual freedom.

The interviews revealed that leaving young people with very limited access to cash could make them vulnerable to exploitation (Humpage et al, 2020a, p 10). An advocate indicated that some people having their board paid through Money Management were not receiving the income due to them because the landlord was not providing what was needed: "It is handy to ensure that their board is paid, because that roof over their head is very important, but then sometimes that roof has been paid for and that child's not even staying there because they're not happy being there" (Hannah, New Zealand advocate). This is telling in terms of the lack of consumer protections that the IM system provides for cardholders and how detrimental this can be for them. Hannah thought that better quality control was needed with respect to boarding arrangements for young people on the Money Management programme:

> 'The provider doesn't go to them and say, do you think that your $150 in board you're paying is worthwhile? Do you actually get food, or

do they provide this, is it nice and warm? ... it's just ... you've got a place to stay, it's this amount ... we'll direct that out of your benefit.' (Hannah, New Zealand advocate)

Another issue Hannah identified was that the weekly cash allowance permitted under the Money Management scheme was inadequate for the needs of young parents:

'young parents ... found it very hard to try and get nappies, and the end result is other people having to help them all the time, to clothe, [provide] napp[ies], milk powder, all that sort of thing for the young one, because that doesn't come under their board, and only being allowed $50 on your card means that doesn't go far.' (Hannah, New Zealand advocate)

Although paying for rent, board and utilities is important, there were times when prioritising these bills led to young people being unable to afford other necessities. All needs must be adequately provided for if people are to have the best chance at securing better futures.

Exit, exemption, complaints and review

As made clear in Chapter 4, many of the people under IM who participated in this study experienced harm to their health, wellbeing and autonomy, as well as social exclusion. These experiences and other consumer and contractual difficulties described so far in this chapter led some cardholders to seek exemptions and exits from these programmes where this is provided for in the legislation. This research shows that where such exemption, exit or review options are available, cardholders are confronted with substantial barriers when it comes to accessing justice; they commonly described the processes involved as unfair.

Procedural fairness is an important aspect of modern governance. The Australian Law Reform Commission (ALRC) (2015, p 393) explains that procedural fairness 'means acting fairly in administrative decision-making. It relates to the fairness of the procedure by which a decision is made'. Unless legislative intention clearly indicates otherwise, citizens are entitled to expect that public power will be exercised in accordance with principles of procedural fairness rather than arbitrarily or capriciously (ALRC, 2015, pp 393–4). At common law, the content of procedural fairness includes the right to a 'fair hearing' and freedom from bias in the decision-making process (ALRC, 2015, p 392). Although some legislative incursion into traditional common law rights has occurred, courts commonly interpret legislation so as to protect a right to procedural fairness (ALRC, 2015, p 394). Scholars have suggested that the degree to which a process is fair may be measured against several criteria, including 'consistency' in decision-making, 'suppression of bias', and 'accuracy' (Tyler, 2006, p 118).

Processes put in place by the Australian government regarding IM exemptions and exits are complicated and time-consuming for cardholders, leading to low rates of successful exemptions and exits (Australian Government, 2021c; 2021e). The legal framework of compulsory cashless welfare cards in Australia and New Zealand has also presented cardholders with few options in terms of exiting the scheme. This is unsurprising given the dominant political narrative about the virtues of IM. However, in Australia, persistent NGO advocacy in relation to BasicsCard and CDC problems have led to exit and exemption processes being put in place, though still very narrow ones. Where cardholders have sought to engage in these processes, they have often experienced problems in terms of procedural fairness. The following sections address the processes for each IM scheme in turn.

BasicsCard

The *Social Security (Administration) Act 1999* (Cth) sets out categories of IM in Sections 123UC to 123UFA. Two compulsory IM categories from which people may seek an exemption are 'disengaged youth' and 'long-term welfare recipients' (Sections 123UCB and 123UCC, respectively). Social security recipients in these categories can seek an exemption if they are eligible under Sections 123UGC (where a person does not have dependent children) or 123UGD (where a person does have dependent children). In explaining these legislative criteria, the government stipulates that 'youth and long term payment recipients' without dependent children may receive an exemption if they 'are a full-time student or apprentice', 'had less than 25% of [their] basic rate of payment for at least 4 of the last 6 fortnights', or 'get Special Benefit and are 16 or older' (Australian Government, 2020). People with dependent children who are 'youth and long term payment recipients' may receive an exemption if: they can demonstrate that they are 'financially secure', their 'children's immunisations are up to date', and their 'children are participating in age appropriate activities' (Australian Government, 2020). The legislative language used to reflect the concept of financial security is that there must have been 'no indications of financial vulnerability in relation to the person' in the 12 months before they lodged their exemption application (Section 123UGD). This criterion can be difficult for social security recipients to satisfy, given low payment rates.

Exemptions remain in place for a maximum of 12 months, and the exemption can be withdrawn if the person's circumstances change (Australian

Government, 2020). Social security recipients therefore need to expend a great deal of effort if they want to regain their budgetary autonomy for a limited period before reverting to IM. Collecting the documentation required to submit an exemption application can be time-consuming and challenging, and it is therefore unsurprising that the number of exemptions granted is small. As of 1 January 2021, government data indicate that there are 27,982 social security recipients on IM, where payments are generally made using a BasicsCard (Australian Government, 2021e, pp 1–3). More than 23,000 of these people are subject to the compulsory IM 'disengaged youth' or 'long term welfare payment recipient' measures, categories in which people can apply for an exemption. Yet, at 1 January 2021, only 2,059 exemptions are clearly recorded in government IM summary data (Australian Government, 2021e, p 3).

Non-Indigenous social security recipients are far more likely to be granted an exemption than Indigenous recipients (Australian Government, 2021e, p 3), and Indigenous peoples are grossly overrepresented in the programme (Department of Social Services, 2018). This reflects a longstanding pattern of racially disparate outcomes in access to IM exemptions (Bray et al, 2014, p 98). Although the government has now stopped recording the percentage of people on IM who identify as Indigenous in its IM data summary documentation, as of March 2018, Indigenous social security recipients comprised 78 per cent of the IM cohort who were on the BasicsCard (Department of Social Services, 2018). As of 1 January 2021, Indigenous social security recipients are recorded as receiving 520 of the 2,059 exemptions granted (Australian Government, 2021e, p 3). This disparity in access to exemptions indicates that there are issues with accessibility for First Peoples, which may include 'language, literacy and knowledge barriers' (Commonwealth Ombudsman, 2012, p 1), but may also reflect 'paternalism and discrimination' in 'discretionary decision-making' (Bielefeld, 2012, p 548).

In this research, interviewees relayed that their pathway off the BasicsCard was usually brought aging out of the IM scheme, rather than formal exemption or review. Steph (Playford) explained how they had no interest in continuing under IM once their time in the compulsory category was over, despite being offered $250 extra every six months if they volunteered for IM (an incentive that has since been discontinued). She stated that the additional $250 was "not worth the risk … not worth the money … not worth the time … not worth the headache" (Steph, Playford). Her rent had not been paid on time by the government once they had been forced onto IM, which caused her considerable distress. Callum (Playford), who had been contemplating pursuing an internal review, which is permitted under Part 4 of the *Social Security (Administration) Act 1999* (Cth), was informed by Centrelink that there would be an approximately 18-month wait if he went ahead with it. Such a significant delay is undoubtedly a disincentive to pursue an exemption. The difficulty of pursuing an IM review or appeal was confirmed by stakeholder feedback, where it was said that, if you pursue these processes, "you've got to fill out paperwork, you've got to prove yourself over and over again. The benefit of the doubt is not in your favour" (Tracy, Playford stakeholder). Some participants had tried to get off the BasicsCard and IM, but the government refused to grant them an exemption. Others were not aware that they had procedural rights in applying for an exemption or review. As Tyson (Shepparton) explained: "They didn't even let me know that you could get exemptions from it … they just pretty much said, 'you have no other option, you're on the BasicsCard'". Some people were afraid of government retaliation if they pursued complaint or review processes, so even though they did not want to be on the BasicsCard, they endured IM.

In Australia, numerous complaints have been made to the Commonwealth Ombudsman's office regarding wrongful payments from IM accounts (Commonwealth Ombudsman, 2013, pp 43–5; 2015, p 40). These wrongful payments have left people on low incomes with even less money to meet their needs, with restoration of that wrongfully denied income taking a long time (Bielefeld, 2015, p 107). Complaints have been made to the Ombudsman about ways that IM harms rather than helps people with respect to securing their priority needs (Commonwealth Ombudsman, 2014, p 32). Numerous complaints have also been made about the quality of decision-making regarding exemptions from IM (Commonwealth Ombudsman, 2012). After investigation of these complaints, the Commonwealth Ombudsman concluded that: 'Some … decisions … reviewed did not address all of the required legislative criteria and lacked a sound evidence base', and 'letters designed to explain decisions were inadequate and unclear and failed to inform Centrelink customers of their review rights' (Commonwealth Ombudsman, 2012, p 1). The Commonwealth Ombudsman continues to monitor IM and CDC trial sites with interest (Commonwealth Ombudsman, 2017, p 56). IM via the BasicsCard persists despite many years of complaints to the Commonwealth Ombudsman. Although these complaint processes have been useful in rectifying some problems experienced by some individuals or organisations, thousands of people are harmed by IM who may not come forward. For them, access to justice and restoration of their financial autonomy remains elusive.

Cashless Debit Card

In the CDC programme as it was first conceived, there was no legal exit or exemption process. However, Sections 124PHA and 124PHB of the *Social Security (Administration) Act 1999* (Cth) now set out the CDC wellbeing exemption and responsibility-based exit criteria. These criteria provide the government with discretion as to whether someone can leave the programme. Legislation clarifying criteria for the Section 124PHB exit process was enacted under the *Social Security (Administration) Amendment (Cashless Welfare) Act 2019* (Cth), after the initial vague criteria proved to be administratively unworkable.

The government may exempt a person from the CDC where satisfied that there is 'a serious risk to the person's mental, physical or emotional wellbeing' (Section 124PHA). There is no definition of 'a serious risk' in the relevant law, or details of what type of medical or other documentation will suffice for the wellbeing exemption. This can make it difficult for people wanting to escape the CDC. For example, if a specialist's letter is required to substantiate a CDC holder's medical condition or disability, but the visit to such a specialist requires substantial funds that the cardholder does not have, this can present an insurmountable barrier. As an advocate interviewee explained: "a lot of people applying for Wellbeing exemptions that are on JobSeeker can't afford to get those reports done from specialists" (Ella, Australian advocate).

Interviews with Australian cardholders who had sought a wellbeing exemption revealed that the government had not informed people prior to lodging their wellbeing applications what standard of proof was required to substantiate their applications, and that medical letters from their GP would be deemed inadequate. They were only informed of this requirement for specialist documentation after their applications were rejected. In terms of procedural fairness, people should have been informed about what type of medical documentation would be required before their applications were lodged, and, ideally, given additional financial support necessary to meet these requirements. These departmental findings regarding GP evidence were also peculiar given that a GP can have detailed long-term knowledge of their patient's condition and would be well placed to make observations about their mental health before and during the CDC trial.

Interviewees who had sought a wellbeing exemption indicated that the requirement to see specialists to secure the evidence desired by the government was burdensome. For example, such specialists can be located far from the CDC trial sites. If travel is required to access a specialist, but the cardholder is provided no additional funds for this purpose, this can present difficulties, especially for people with disabilities that include mobility restrictions. In effect, these documentary requirements can render the exemption inaccessible, leading to budgetary autonomy being unjustly denied.

Under Section 124PHB, the government may facilitate exit from the CDC if satisfied that 'the person can demonstrate reasonable and responsible management of the person's affairs (including financial affairs)', considering the following:

- 'the interest of any children for whom the person is responsible';
- 'whether the person was convicted of an offence against a law … or was serving a sentence of imprisonment for such an offence' within the previous 12 months;
- 'risks of homelessness';
- 'the health and safety of the person and the community';
- 'the responsibilities and circumstances of the person'; and
- 'the person's engagement in the community, including the person's employment or efforts to obtain work'.

The person is also required to satisfy any criteria the Minister may stipulate in a 'legislative instrument', which gives the Minister discretion to add further criteria in future.

Some cardholder interviewees reported that having to use the CDC and Indue system heightened their risk of housing insecurity as a result of problems paying rent (Marston et al, 2020, pp 10, 36, 103). Some people experienced rent payments bouncing back into their accounts, resulting in delayed rent payments and breach of their contractual obligation to pay on time. Although the CDC/Indue system was itself creating the risk of homelessness through late rental payments, that same risk could then be used, unjustly, to deny exit from the CDC. What authorities deem necessary for community 'health and safety' is also susceptible to a very broad interpretation. Numbers of 'reasonable and responsible management' CDC exits remain relatively small. As of 1 January 2021, only 334 of 1,462 applications had been granted under Section 124PBH (Australian Government, 2021c, p 3). People on the CDC who were Indigenous were far more likely to have their exit application denied (Australian Government, 2021c, p 3). This is concerning, given that First Peoples are heavily overrepresented in the programme.

Importantly, Sections 124PHA and 124PHB offer no clear legal *right* to exit the CDC. There is merely an opportunity to apply to be exempted from or exit the CDC, provided that the application is submitted using the required forms with accompanying documents to substantiate the claims made.

Many IM participants on the CDC were unclear about the process for seeking an exemption, the criteria used to make these decisions, and who to contact for clarification. As Dawn (Hinkler) explained:

> 'I'm told that in July [2019] there's a chance to get off it, but you've got to jump through hoops to do it. There's no real solid information about that either. All they've said is that, "oh, you can apply through the Department of Social Services," but nobody knows what you have to do to get off the card.' (Dawn, Hinkler)

CDC holders were often uncertain whether a person needed to apply for an exit or exemption through Centrelink, Indue (which administers the CDC), or the Department of Social Services (which initially operated an email account that cardholders could use if they were encountering CDC problems, now discontinued). Applications are now determined through another Department, Services Australia (formerly the Department of Human Services). Some interviewees reported frustration at being sent from one entity to another without their problems being resolved. Dawn (Hinkler), who also has mental health difficulties, stated that she was given inaccurate information about the exemption process by Indue: "I called Indue. … They were all … 'oh, there's no way to get off the card, sorry we can't help you'. … Yet in the policies and procedures it says there is a mental health exemption."

When people sought to engage in the exemption process, they were frequently discouraged from doing so by officials, revealing significant access to justice issues. As Ashleigh (Hinkler) relayed: "I found they already have a wellness exemption and that lady on the phone said that I wouldn't qualify for it. I told her that I would go to a therapist and have a report written. She said, 'no, it's still not going to [succeed]'." A fair hearing requires that a person be permitted to gather evidence, lodge an application, and then receive a determination as to whether the evidence submitted meets the standard required. Similarly, Ali (Hinkler), who also has mental health challenges, explained she too had experienced bureaucratic blocking of her exemption application:

> 'I … tried to apply for a medical exemption because I got reports … documenting my anxiety and stuff, but I was told … that I'm ineligible. … They didn't ask for any proof … I said, I've got a psychiatrist, a psychologist and a social worker, who do you want evidence from?" They said, "well, it doesn't really matter because you're not eligible",' (Ali, Hinkler)

Tom (Hinkler) was informed by Centrelink that they "would need to be in absolute dire situation to be considered to be taken off the card". Moreover, Aileen (Hinkler) indicated that authorities were unwilling to process their exemption application:

> 'They flat out just tell you, no; there's no way off the card. I … asked if I could apply for an exemption, they said "why?" They said "you don't need an exemption; it pays for all your bills". I said "well, it hasn't been". They said "oh, no, it's just teething issues at the moment. Wait until later on when you have been on it for a while".' Aileen (Hinkler)

Bureaucratic strategies that discourage people from lodging CDC exemption and exit applications are a way to keep more people on the card, but such strategies violate the legislated procedural rights of cardholders to lodge applications with evidence of their circumstances and have them fairly considered.

Follow-up interviews conducted with some cardholders from the Hinkler region in 2020 who had applied for a CDC exemption or exit indicated that the process had been deeply problematic, with lengthy delays – sometimes up to 13 months – before the Department deigned to make a decision. Some people from Hinkler stated that they thought it would be quicker to age out of the CDC scheme at 36 (an age limit unique to this trial site) than have an exemption or exit application succeed through the government's processes. The protracted timeframes for determining exit and exemption outcomes had an adverse effect on people's mental health:

> 'I've applied for a wellbeing exemption and ... I've still had nothing done. The social worker's holding everything and keeps telling me I need more evidence. ... My wellbeing is deteriorating. I've been unmedicated ... for three years. I'm now back on meds. I'm in therapy and I'm seven weeks into having this card ... it's exhausting. I'm tired all the time because I just constantly worry. ... It makes you feel helpless and everywhere you turn you can't get help ... no matter how many people you speak to ... you're blocked at every door, basically, which makes it even harder. It sends the anxiety higher, the depression kicks in.' (Riley, Hinkler)

For some people, the state of their mental health meant they felt too unwell to be able to engage in the wellbeing exemption process: "Someone's got to sit there and look at you and go 'no, you're not unwell enough, you can stay on it' ... to ... go through all of that stress and then possibly be knocked back is daunting" (Mary, Hinkler). Similarly, Australian advocate, Ella, pointed out that a lot of people they spoke to on the CDC avoided the exit and exemption process because "they can't handle the mental strain of it. It's just too daunting, it's too hard. With what they're living with already". Cardholders commonly stated that the exit and exemption processes were onerous.

Some interviewees considered the exit and exemption processes to be unfair, stating that regardless of what their exemption or exit documentation demonstrated, the government's agenda is to keep people on the CDC, so they would be unlikely to succeed with an application:

> 'Yeah, everybody in the government departments like DSS [Department of Social Services], DHS [Department of Human Services], I think they all have a script to run by. I think that they're told not to veer off that script and hang on and keep everyone going as long as they can

hold them off, try and stop them basically from getting off this card. Yeah, so it makes people feel even worse.' (Riley, Hinkler)

Another cardholder similarly stated: "There is like no chance of anyone getting through, so I haven't even tried" (Alicia, Hinkler). There was a belief that the system was stacked against people trying to exit the CDC, that decision makers charged with assessing applications were biased in favour of keeping as many people as possible on the CDC programme, irrespective of individuals' needs or budgetary capacities.

Some cardholders said they did not apply for an exemption or exit because they felt that to do so would destroy the last remaining traces of their privacy. Others who had applied reported that the level of questioning they were subject to about their expenditure was intrusive and judgemental. For example, Ali (Hinkler) relayed how the department official managing her exit request inquired not simply whether groceries were regularly purchased but, much more specifically, that "they asked questions about the kinds of food I eat". Another person was questioned about why they had chosen a particular car insurance company over others (Cindy, Hinkler). Some cardholders expressed concerns about where such information was going to be distributed and how it might be used in future.

Some cardholders explained that CDC transaction declines were the reason given for their responsibility-based exit applications being denied, but that such declines did not always show up when the person checked their Indue account online. Transactions can be declined for a range of reasons, such as insufficient funds, PIN number error, technology outages or other system failures. There were numerous instances of technology outages reported by CDC holders throughout the fieldwork period which several interviewees reported were later used to refuse an exemption or exit application. As Mia (Hinkler) lamented: "They take no responsibility for any of their stuff ups." When Mia asked for a copy of her Indue statement with evidence of these transaction declines she was informed that she could not have it because it was an internal working document. Mia said it was unfair for them to be judged deficient at budgeting due to alleged transaction declines and not to be given evidence of them.

Interviewees with experience of the exit and exemption processes consistently said these should be fairer and that it should be easier to opt out of the CDC if being on the card was not working for them. As Riley (Hinkler) explained:

> 'you should be able to opt out and it should be easy. … Especially if you can produce your bank statement to show that you pay your bills and you do your groceries. … You should be able to opt out if you can show you do the right thing.' (Riley, Hinkler)

Another interviewee elaborated on how the exit and exemption process was neither fair nor respectful: "When you have to speak to them about it … they're quite often very rude. They tend to try to disregard any of your concerns, belittle you … they try to make you feel like you're stupid basically. It's a far too lengthy process, far too complicated process" (Mia, Hinkler).

Due to difficulties with the process, some people found the only way to exit the CDC was to get Members of Parliament and Senators involved. Applying political pressure in this way was more effective than persevering with legal processes that are not user friendly, especially for those with literacy and health challenges. Some people trying to exit the CDC indicated that they had complained to the Commonwealth Ombudsman.

In late 2020, Sharon (Hinkler) was seeking an appeal from an internal review of the Department's refusal of their exit and exemption applications, which needed to be made to the Administrative Appeals Tribunal (AAT). She was underemployed rather than unemployed, and she expressed a strong preference for budgeting with cash. She also suffered from anxiety, and her sense of shame at being on the CDC was so intense she could not bring herself to use it in public, afraid that a work colleague or other community member may think she have the kind of behavioural problems the government says the card was designed to address. If Sharon were thought to have substance abuse problems, this could jeopardise her employment. A small proportion of Sharon's total income had been quarantined to the CDC, yet this sum had grown, and she wanted to access the money as cash. Sharon described the CDC exit and exemption processes as "unfair", and explained how she had submitted evidence of bills being paid with her responsibility-based application, including bills for her children's needs, but her application was rejected. She stated that the grounds for rejection given by the Department were inconsistent with the documents submitted with her application. The process had consumed more than a year of Sharon's life and had still not resulted in restoration of her budgetary autonomy:

> 'I've done nothing wrong. My bills are paid. If I was … a horrid person, yeah, okay … but they need to do a proper assessment. … They're playing with people's lives … I'm trying to do the best I can to get through on what I've got and to be told that I'm not meeting the needs of my children and I'm financially incapable just destroyed me … I thought what, why and how? They don't know me. I showed proof of all my bills being paid. I'm in no debt. I owe no one money, and to make those accusations and presumptions on me without the proof, it's just beyond a joke. I don't get it … I'm getting so angry and frustrated with the system.' (Sharon, Hinkler)

Although the government describes the CDC as 'helping' and 'support' (Porter and Tudge, 2017; Ruston, 2019), Sharon said "I feel I'm not a person anymore because of this system". The autonomy-eroding impacts of IM were experienced as dehumanising, debilitating, time-consuming, and exhausting. Another cardholder similarly disagreed with the government narrative about the CDC being a support, stating: "This is not a support. This is a punishing, demeaning mechanism used to control people" (Ali, Hinkler).

A further cardholder whose exemption application was denied lamented: "It's screwed with my head … it's traumatised me deeply" (Tim, Hinkler). Tim went on to explain: "Every time you submit something, they'd change the goal line and ask for something else." According to Tim, the process was harder for those who were not very familiar with computers: "I'm not really tech savvy, and I had dramas trying to download my bank statements and stuff, and I had to go into the bloody thing – into the bank office and … get … on the net", with charges incurred for bank statement printouts. The reasons given as to why Tim's application was denied included that he had declined CDC transactions on their record. However, for those whose preference is managing their budget with cash, as was the case for Tim, the shift to digital banking created budgeting problems because they were less able to know the state of their finances at any given time. As Tim explained, with the CDC, "you've got to have phone credit to check your bloody balance and … there's no Indue machines around that you can go stick your card in and get the balance".

Common to all interviewees who had sought a CDC exit or exemption was the unreasonable slowness of departmental decisions on their applications. Cardholders viewed this as unjust, and it reflected the legal maxim 'justice delayed is justice denied' (Gladstone, in Sourdin and Burstyner, 2014, p 46). One cardholder had their exit application denied after more than 12 months of waiting. When asked if they would apply for a departmental review or utilise the AAT, they wryly concluded: "I could probably try these review processes and I'd age out before I got the result" (Mia, Hinkler). At the time of writing, aging out is an option reserved only for the Hinkler cohort of cardholders. Some cardholders reported calling the government every week or every fortnight to try to see what the hold-up was with their applications. Time burdens associated with the process were significant.

Some cardholders relayed that their exit requests appeared not to have been read closely by those attending to them, giving cause for concern about whether their submitted evidence had been properly considered by decision makers. For instance, a same-sex couple had an exit request denied and the statement of reasons mis-gendered one of them. These interviewees concluded: "They did not read that application" (Anthony and Declan, Hinkler). They had applied for a financial responsibility-based CDC exit and were told their application was unsuccessful partly because they had not submitted evidence of mental health problems, a criterion only relevant to the wellbeing exemption. Some cardholders also reported being given inconsistent or inaccurate information about discussing or appealing their exit rejection correspondence.

Money Management

In contrast to Australian IM programmes, there is no exemption process available for young people placed on New Zealand's Money Management programme. The only way to exit the Payment card is to age out of the scheme or for young people to have met all their behavioural obligations to the satisfaction of the MSD. A government employee, Robin, explained the reasoning for official reluctance to have an exemption process, stating that it would have undermined the intention of the policy and made programme delivery more difficult: "Particularly with something like this, and with the particular group that we're talking about, once you get into the exemption thing, it can easily just run away with you and you've lost what it is ... you're trying to achieve when you come down to the delivery side." The government also wanted to avoid the need to review an exemption process "as to whether it's actually working and what the impacts of the exemption regime might be" (Robin, New Zealand government employee).

While YP and YPP recipients can seek review of decisions relating to whether or not they are eligible for entitlement, there is no review process available regarding the decision to put someone on the Money Management programme. Essentially, this means that if they apply for YP or YPP they must accept that they will be on Money Management for at least six months. However, New Zealand interviewees revealed that even gaining access to a social security payment could be an arduous process.

The process in place for complaints/review of decisions about access to social security entitlements is as follows: first, the matter is subject to an internal review, which culminates in a decision by the Benefits Review Committee as to whether the matter has been resolved by that internal review. Complaints and applications for review are strictly time-limited.

With regard to complaints about matters other than entitlement, young people are supposed to raise these, in the first instance, with their Youth Service provider, who may, at times, be the cause of the problem. This can leave young people in a precarious situation.

An important issue highlighted by the interviewees is that people on the Money Management programme frequently had no idea that they could complain or seek a review of a decision. Although programme participants are given a brochure when they first enter the Youth Service that mentions what the process is, many young people on these benefits require literacy support, or misplace the brochure at some point during their time on the programme. One advocate, Michael, expressed concern about the information withheld from young people about their review rights and other basic social security rights, explaining that when people went to the "Youth Service … they … can't get help, and … weren't being told about review of decisions, they weren't being told about … their basic and essential … entitlements" (Michael, New Zealand advocate). He found it unacceptable that young people were being given inaccurate information and lodged a complaint with the Minister. Many young people had never received a social security benefit before and were unfamiliar with the local social security advocacy organisations that can assist with complaint and review processes. This lack of awareness may have been exacerbated by the Youth Service being set up as a separate structure from Work and Income. Some advocates interviewed believed this was one factor inhibiting YP/YPP recipients and their families from thinking that these organisations might be able to assist them with Youth Service difficulties.

Nevertheless, the New Zealand MSD (2021b) has confirmed that there have been numerous complaints about Money Management, and its 2021 *Experiences of Money Management in the Youth Service* report concluded that young people subject to it do not view the programme favourably (MSD, 2021a, p 36).

Citizenship, autonomy and access to social justice in the welfare state

Scholars suggest that autonomy has a deeply relational quality, and that people can only experience autonomy through relations that support this (Anderson and Honneth, 2005, p 127). This is borne out in the context of compulsory IM, where the autonomy of cardholders is deeply diminished. Anderson and Honneth (2005, p 129) explain that 'personal autonomy requires the resources and circumstances necessary to lead the life one determines to be worthwhile'. Compulsory IM programmes routinely deny this to the captured cohort of cardholders.

In Australia and New Zealand, IM programmes are costly, with significant opportunity costs in terms of evidence-based alternatives. Although vast sums are redistributed through the welfare state, the existence of 'welfare state societies' does 'not eliminate large-scale suffering and deprivation' (Young, 2011, p 54). Within such societies, full citizenship and rights to autonomy have been unevenly distributed (Young, 2011; Dwyer, 2019). Policymakers have long excluded dependent persons from equal citizenship (Young, 2011, p 54). However, 'dependency should not be a reason to be deprived of choice and respect' (Young, 2011, p 55). Every person, irrespective of their socio-economic status, deserves to experience 'dignifying care', which includes respect for their autonomy and restoration of their agency if this has been undermined (Miller, 2012, pp 5, 79). This includes the restoration of their contractual freedom and consumer choice.

This research has revealed that consumer choice restrictions through compulsory IM present problems unforeseen by policymakers, many of whom show scant regard for the perspectives of those with lived experience of the challenges of being subject to IM. Such a reduction in the rights of welfare recipients caused many to question their status as citizens, reflected in cardholder comments that, because of compulsory IM, they had been reduced to second-rate, third-rate or fourth-rate citizens. The voices of those who are placed on compulsory IM cards indicate that these payment mechanisms present daily difficulties, regardless of the jurisdiction in which they reside. Such cards were not universally accepted at EFTPOS machines, and purchase of basic items was prohibited in practice, even when they were not under legal restriction.

Although Australian and New Zealand IM systems permit 'cardholders to apply to have a greater portion of their income made available in cash', interviewees explained that these 'approval processes' are 'prohibitively complicated and slow' (Humpage et al, 2020a, p 8). Cardholders indicated that this posed serious problems when low-cost or second-hand goods were available in limited quantity, for a limited time, or at a time-limited discount. Restricting access to affordable consumer goods for people on the lowest incomes is socially unjust.

An essential prerequisite of exercising one's rights is being aware of them, but interviews with IM cardholders in both countries revealed that many lacked awareness of their procedural rights of complaint, review, exit or exemption. As Cunneen and colleagues (2014, p 235) explain: 'Without some knowledge of rights and the avenues of potential assistance, the prospects of realising legal entitlements are obviously very low'. Some Australian cardholders interviewed for this study did not seek an exemption because they did not think the process was feasible due to it being too time-consuming, too difficult, and too financially burdensome in terms of obtaining the required documentation. They indicated that they were already 'time poor' due to: difficulties paying bills now they were on IM cards; undertaking workfare requirements as a condition of access to their social security payments; parental responsibilities; carer responsibilities; and searching for employment. Putting in place procedural rights that are, in practice, largely inaccessible fails to afford justice.

Some CDC holders who declined a follow-up interview about exits/exemptions explained that they did not see the point in applying because they could not trust that government processes would lead to fair outcomes. Although they did not want to be on the CDC, they felt the government's agenda was to keep as many people on the CDC as possible, irrespective of their personal financial capacities and needs. This feedback was illuminating in terms of ascertaining how cardholders see these processes. Cardholders who agreed to follow-up interviews about their experiences with CDC exit and exemption processes reported that these were extremely difficult. This, too, raises procedural fairness concerns.

Conclusion

The problems raised in this chapter bring to the fore the challenge of ensuring that governance 'engages with human subjectivity and agency in life enhancing ways' (Hunter, 2015, p 5). Interviews revealed important insights into everyday experiences under compulsory IM. While such programmes are described by governments as mechanisms for instilling responsible behaviour, interviews indicate that this outcome is frequently thwarted by problems participants encounter in everything from bill payment to securing sufficient food and providing for their families. Overturning contractual freedom frequently came at a high cost to those on IM programmes, and placed people at risk of not securing essentials in a timely way.

Moreover, many people had no idea what their legal rights were with respect to exit, exemption and review of government decisions. Indeed, some people affected by compulsory IM saw the law as a means by which their rights have been removed rather than a vehicle through which their rights can be exercised. This made them less inclined to pursue their exit, exemption, and review rights. The research revealed that IM exit, exemption and review processes were routinely experienced as unjust by those who sought to utilise them, with many cardholders expressing no faith in the capacity of these systems to lead to the fair treatment they were entitled to. If governments aspire to legitimacy and effective governance this is deeply problematic, because public perceptions of the authorities' legitimacy are 'closely intertwined with the procedures they use when dealing with the public' (Tyler, 2006, p 165).

6

Resistance and reform: individual and collective agency

> 'I have an anxiety problem, that was hard for me to do. But it meant something, so we all just did it, even though it was all hard for us all. Yelled our lungs out. I was blowing a trumpet and everything.' (Sue, Ceduna)

Introduction

So far, this book has shed light on the experiences of people impacted by CIM. It has shown that CIM disempowers welfare recipients, denying them control over their finances, corroding their rights, and ultimately damaging both their wellbeing and their capacity to participate in community life. Against this backdrop, this chapter considers cardholder resistance – understood in this context to mean refusal to accept the material conditions of 'being on the card' and/or the devalued social status attached to being arbitrarily categorised as 'irresponsible'.

Understanding dissent in social policy research is necessary for at least two reasons. First, on a theoretical level, it is important because power and resistance have been influentially conceptualised – most notably by Foucault (1978) – as mutually constitutive. From this viewpoint, any study of power that does not also consider resistance risks oversimplification and, indeed, misrepresentation. Second, on an ethico-political level, accounting for dissent ensures that the agency of those in question is recognised. To represent welfare recipients as the two-dimensional victims of a malevolent state would be to ignore their complexity and capabilities, and thus inadvertently contribute to their denigration in public discourse.

This chapter has six parts. First, it provides a brief overview of resistance as a sociological concept and, in doing so, constructs a theoretical scaffolding for the chapter. Second, it explores how the sociopolitical context of CIM in Australia and New Zealand thwarts overt forms of resistance and pushes cardholders towards more covert means of dissent. In parts three and four, it describes these 'everyday' forms of resistance, focusing, respectively, on cardholder efforts to circumvent restrictions, and cardholder attempts to contest the policy's framing. Part five then turns to open public protest in Australia, exploring the interplay between everyday and public resistance, and why a similar movement has not emerged in New Zealand. The chapter concludes by situating these examples of resistance within our growing understanding of CIM as an instrument of power.

Theorising resistance

Historically, the study of resistance – like the study of power – has focused on 'highly visible, collective struggles against structures of power' (Hynes, 2013, pp 562–3); put differently, scholars have conceptualised resistance primarily in terms of open and overt acts of defiance. In his influential book *Weapons of the Weak* (1985), however, Scott drew attention to the more clandestine or 'everyday' forms of resistance used by those in positions of economic precarity and political marginalisation and, in doing so, fundamentally shaped our understanding of resistance efforts.

Scott's work was notable for its recognition that exploited and vulnerable people often face negative consequences if they engage in open resistance. Scott shows that marginalised individuals – unable to afford these consequential costs – find subtler and safer ways to express their opposition:

> Tenants may bitterly resent the rent they must pay for their small plot, but they must pay it or lose the land; the near-landless may deplore the loss of wage-work, but they must scramble for the few opportunities available; they may harbour deep animosities toward the clique which dominates village politics, but they must act with circumspection if they wish to benefit from any of the small advantages which that clique can confer. At least two aspects of this grudging, pragmatic adaptation to the realities merit emphasis. The first is that it does not rule out certain forms of resistance, although it surely sets limits that only the foolhardy would transgress. The second is that it is, above all, pragmatic; it does not at all imply normative consent to those realities. (Scott, 1986, p 15)

Through subtle 'everyday' acts, Scott argues, vulnerable groups resist oppressive forces while avoiding the backlash that open rebellion might prompt.

Significantly, Scott (1989, p 37) posits that these everyday forms of resistance mirror the power they oppose:

> The various practices that might plausibly be claimed to represent everyday forms of resistance are legion. To an outside observer it might appear quixotic to assemble them under the same heading. Their variety is nothing more than a mirror image of the variety of forms of appropriation; for every form of appropriation there is likely

to be one – or many – forms of everyday resistance devised to thwart that appropriation.

Scott's model suggests that material domination will inspire material and physical acts of resistance, while status domination will prompt the production of 'hidden transcripts' that seek to combat this affront (Johansson and Vinthagen, 2016). As Scott explains, the 'denial of status (humiliation, disprivilege, assaults on dignity)' is frequently met with 'hidden transcript or anger, aggression, and a discourse of dignity' (Scott, 1989, p 56).

In the decades since Scott's work was originally published, orthodox conceptualisations of resistance have expanded to incorporate both open and everyday forms, such that it is now widely accepted that even the subtle actions of marginalised groups can be politically meaningful (Scott, 1986; 1989; 1990; Hollander and Einwohner, 2004; Johansson and Vinthagen, 2016; Baaz et al, 2017). In ensuing debates regarding what, precisely, constitutes resistance, various definitions and typologies have been offered. Debate is ongoing regarding whether an action must be intended and recognised as resistance to qualify as such, yet scholars are largely united in understanding resistance as an *oppositional* act – no matter how small – which has the potential to undermine existing power relations (Hollander and Einwohner, 2004; Johansson and Vinthagen, 2016).

As the remainder of this chapter will demonstrate, this research is valuable for understanding the resistance efforts of CIM participants. The social, political and emotional conditions in which cardholders exist present significant barriers to open resistance and make subtler forms of dissent – from resisting material domination by circumventing card restrictions to resisting status domination by advancing discursive counter-narratives, or expressing deviant emotions – more likely. Nonetheless, these actions exist on a continuum with more and less open displays of resistance, and, in the right conditions, both can contribute to and exist alongside open protest and activism. Notably, while different forms of resistance were a common theme in the Australian data, only resistance via circumnavigating CIM rules was discussed by New Zealand interview participants.

Barriers to open resistance

Exclusion from community consultation

As Chapter 3 highlighted, community consultation was tokenistic or non-existent in both Australia and New Zealand. Indeed, as Australia's Parliamentary Joint Committee on Human Rights (2016, p 60) observed in their review of the *Stronger Futures* framework, '[i]ncome management in the Northern Territory has never been implemented with the agreement of, or following consultation with, the communities in which it applies', yet 'consultation is recognised as critical in the effectiveness of any income management regime'. The introduction of place-based CIM programmes was also marked by inadequate levels of government consultation with targeted communities.

Significantly, several interviewees observed that – in addition to being excluded from these official consultation processes – their attempts to contribute to public debate at the time had been subject to censorship. In Hinkler, for instance, Anthony recalled that community members who expressed even polite reservations regarding the introduction of CDC had their comments removed from local MP Keith Pitt's Facebook page:

> 'We went on there— there were people saying "oh, the cashless card is going to be perfect for the area", then we went under there, "but it's going to make [us] second-class citizen[s] … and it's going to make us feel unworthy of being a part of this community". Then that comment [was] deleted.' (Anthony, Hinkler)

Andrew (Ceduna), who has been a vocal opponent of the policy, recalled that he had been threatened with legal action: "I was very, very critical on Allan Suter, the [then] Mayor, and sort of engaged him. He was threatening to sue me and I just sort of called him out. Mate, I'm on fuckin' Centrelink, sue me [laughs]. What are you going to take [laughs]?".

As such, many interviewees felt that they had been denied a voice in CIM debate, and were sensitive to the risk of recrimination if they tried to speak up. Several Hinkler interviewees further explained that they had first heard about the CDC when they received a Centrelink letter advising that they would be placed on the card in a matter of weeks. These interviewees had not been consulted and described these letters as an unwelcome shock.

Depleted socio-emotional resources

In addition to these contextual factors, the socio-emotional impacts of CIM (described in detail in Chapter 4) also functioned to shape and constrain cardholder dissent. This was particularly evident in Australia, where – without the mediating effect of Youth Services mentoring – the deleterious impacts of CIM were felt most acutely. Numerous Australian cardholders told us of their support in principle for or desire to participate in collective action to oppose CIM, but they observed that the risks associated with public protest precluded their involvement. More specifically, these interviewees cited the investment of time and emotion that open resistance would entail and explained that CIM had left them with depleted resources in both areas.

As Chapter 4 described, the logistical challenges associated with CIM created significant work for many Australian cardholders, particularly those at CDC trial sites, whose time was increasingly spent negotiating spending restrictions, juggling funds, and chasing up payment failures. Dave in Hinkler, for example, explained that he had been less involved in collective resistance efforts since the card was introduced:

> 'Before the card actually came into Bundaberg, we did a protest where we'd actually go to the Bundaberg Council and we just protested outside about the card. But … since the card came in, I've been too busy with my daughters and been worrying about how I can spend the money, where I can spend it and everything, that I haven't been bothered to protest anything.' (Dave, Hinkler)

Other interviewees expressed similar sentiments, with single parents stressing that they had had little free time even before CIM was introduced.

The most common reason that interviewees cited regarding their abstinence from public protest, however, concerned the social and emotional costs of public visibility. As Chapter 4 again explored, interviewees already felt stigmatised and vilified by their inclusion in the programme. Cardholders were maligned in policy narratives regarding the cards, and consequently experienced considerable shame when using their cards in public. In this context, it is unsurprising that many interviewees were reticent to expose themselves to further scrutiny and potential ostracisation by publicly acknowledging their participation in the programme. Tahlia (Hinkler) explained:

> 'I don't go to [protests], simply because I am too embarrassed and it's back to that stigma thing. I don't want to put myself on show and be looked down upon. I know that's probably what people think when they see people on the card and protesters and all that. I don't want to do that to myself.' (Tahlia, Hinkler)

In Ceduna, Sue, who was involved in the local protest movement confirmed the validity of this concern, observing that members of the public assumed that protesters had dishonest reasons for opposing the scheme:

> '[E]veryone that sees you fight against it makes assumptions that you must want that because you're a drug addict, or you're a dealer, and you want people buying from you, who have no cash. So, you're instantly looked down on, just because you're like, "hang on, this is my human rights". They're like, "oh, look at that one there. I wonder what they want the money for?"' (Sue, Ceduna)

Accepting dominant political discourses surrounding the card, local supporters of the scheme assumed that cardholders who were not doing anything 'wrong' would have no reason to oppose the policy.

This prospect of further stigmatisation was particularly concerning for individuals with precarious mental health, many of whom already avoided community participation so as to minimise the chances of public humiliation and associated reductions in mental wellbeing. Even some interviewees who had been involved in past protest movements chose to avoid public dissent. As Andrew (Ceduna) explained, the emotional costs were just too great:

> '[T]here's a certain fatalism that's involved in not being an activist or not being vocal … I don't think it's right but I'm not going to be the scapegoat or I'm not going to be the fall guy. I've sort of already stepped into that position and I realised that society doesn't want change and there's no use burning out trying to create it. … Until there's enough community support, it's a little bit soul destroying I find. I haven't managed to be able to maintain [a] sort of equilibrium with activism, so I just keep out of it.' (Andrew, Ceduna)

Andrew also went on to point out:

> '[I]t is a thing of I didn't speak out when I could have. That thing where that's actually quite a confronting thought but by not speaking out then you're sort of— you are accepting it. That is quite heavy. … [There's a perception that] on Centrelink, like, what have you got to complain about? Like, you're getting this 'free ride' and these sort of ideas are really, really confronting for people to try and argue against when you feel like you're in a position of sub-class or you don't have the power to tell people "well, look, no I've got rights as well".' (Andrew, Ceduna)

Choosing not to actively protest could thus be confronting in its own right. Speaking out publicly in a stigmatising environment, however, was even harder. This confluence of sociopolitical and socio-emotional factors thus resulted in two clear trends vis-a-vis cardholder resistance. First, Australian cardholders were more likely than their New Zealand counterparts to resent and resist CIM policies. Second, as Scott's (1989) framework would predict, many interviewees from both countries chose to adopt safer and more clandestine forms of resistance, thus avoiding the socio-emotional risks associated with overt dissent.

Resisting by circumventing restrictions

While only a minority of interviewees had engaged in open forms of protest (as discussed in greater detail later), the vast majority had taken clandestine steps to resist CIM or mitigate its more harmful consequences. Efforts to circumvent the cards' restrictions were particularly common and comprised a key theme in both the Australia and New Zealand interviews.

As Chapter 4 foreshadowed with respect to cardholder (in)dependence, interviewees frequently explained that they had made arrangements with friends, family members and even landlords to minimise the cards' impacts on their budgetary choices. In Australia, for example, participants frequently used their cards to purchase groceries or other essential items for their landlords or housemates as a way to cover their rental contributions while avoiding the challenges associated with making electronic payments and using scarce cash for rent. In Playford, Kane even credited this circumvention strategy with helping him to quit marijuana, as it meant he had sufficient cash to purchase cigarettes: "[M]e personally, I believe you can't quit two things at once," he explained, "like you're going nutty in the head". Making his rental contribution in groceries rather than cash allowed him to tackle one addiction at a time and thus achieve what he hoped would be lasting results.

Cardholders also regularly purchased permissible items and exchanged them for cash or, in some cases, items from banned retailers. These transactions often took place in the context of trusting family relationships. For example, numerous interviewees explained that when they needed cash, they would organise to buy groceries or other needed items for a family member, who would then reimburse them. This was a common arrangement in both Australia and New Zealand: "If I need cash, mum uses my cashless card … she's not on the cash[less] card because she's 47, so I just get cash off mum and she uses my card" (Tania, Hinkler).

> 'I used to do it with my sister; like, when she needed something from the PAK'nSAVE [supermarket] she would be like, oh, can you get me like these things … and she was like, "I'll give you the cash back" because I was paying for them with my Payment Card and I would be, like, "sure".' (Aroha, New Zealand)

In New Zealand, some interviewees also used their Payment Cards to buy gift vouchers (a permissible purchase, unlike in Australia with the CDC) as a way of gaining access to a greater range of stores and products. While these strategies provided many interviewees with access to cash at relatively low risk, they were not equally available to all cardholders. As previous research on welfare recipients' social networks would predict (Peterie et al, 2019b), many interviewees did not have well-resourced friends or family members to whom they could turn; Australian cardholders were also banned from spending quarantined funds on gift vouchers. In this context, some cardholders turned to unscrupulous businesses or even members of the public in their efforts to access cash. As Anthony (Hinkler) stressed, this approach could leave cardholders out-of-pocket if the people providing this 'service' reimbursed them at a significantly lower rate: "[T]hey say, 'oh, I'll put $100 worth of fuel in' and they get only $50 back for it, so in the long run they're out of pocket for $50."

New Zealand interviewees shared similar examples. One young woman, for instance, frequented a shop where she could make an electronic payment of $240, and received $200 in cash. "I pay them $40", she explained (Sharmaine, New Zealand).

Numerous interviewees had also been personally approached by fellow cardholders – often outside major supermarkets – who wished to buy their groceries for them in exchange for cash:

> 'Someone asked me … if they could do my shopping and I give them the money, because then they could have money. I was like, sorry, no. … Even random people like me, they would come up to me and go "can you just do $20 worth of shopping off my BasicsCard and then can you give me the $20?"' (Marnie, Shepparton)

Other interviewees described strategies such as purchasing whitegoods or bottles of Coca-Cola using their cards and selling these (often at a loss) for cash.

In most instances, cardholders used these strategies simply as ways to make ends meet. As previous chapters have explored, it was difficult to survive without access to disposable cash:

> 'I don't know if you're allowed to do it, but people – I just get people to spend the money off my payment card because I don't know if you're actually allowed to do that but I don't care. You have to live … It's not like I'm getting— from doing that I'm not getting any more money. I'm still getting the same amount of money as my benefit, but yeah. … You have to, otherwise you're just going to— you actually can't live on $50 [the amount of cash permitted].' (Manaaki, New Zealand)

It was broadly recognised, however, that these techniques were sometimes also used by people with addictions to gain access to alcohol or illicit substances:

> '[My friend has] tried to quit [marijuana], and he turns mental. He's on the CDC and all he does is buy fuel for his dad or his neighbour for cash. He uses his card to pay for whatever they need, they give him cash, he goes and gets his drugs.' (Dawn, Hinkler)

As Drew from Shepparton told us, the reality that "your drug dealer is still a person" with expenses like grocery shopping also meant that some dealers were willing to accept goods as payment. "If you spent half your BasicsCard money buying him shopping, I'm sure you can arrange that with someone in the town", he explained (Drew, Shepparton). In some cases, interviewees observed, desperate cardholders even bartered the cards themselves, losing access to their entire quarantined income in the process.

Resisting by advancing counter-narratives

Everyday resistance involves marginalised groups expressing dissent through subtler and safer actions than those associated with open resistance. This might entail individuals taking action to obstruct or mitigate the effects of what they perceive to be an oppressive policy, as has been described in cardholder efforts to circumvent CIM's restrictions. It can also, however, involve the development of discourses that contest the 'denial of status (humiliation, disprivilege, assaults on dignity)' (Scott, 1989, p 56) associated with subjugation. As Scott posits, these counter-narratives are often hidden at first, but comprise an important aspect of more open resistance efforts if and when shifting power dynamics render such activities safe (Scott, 1989). 'Symbolic or ideological resistance', including 'gossip, slander, rejecting imposed categories, [and] the withdrawal of deference' (Scott, 1986, p 22), is thus recognised as a critical dimension of everyday resistance.

Government discourses surrounding CIM typically cast programme participants as irresponsible citizens who require heavy-handed intervention to become morally sound and financially independent members of society. In this context, Australian and New Zealand cardholders engaged in everyday resistance when they asserted their long-standing and enduring status as upstanding citizens. In New Zealand, these narratives remained largely hidden, and interviewees regularly professed their own worthiness for income support without drawing conclusions regarding the suitability (or otherwise) of CIM more broadly. In Australia, however, the existence of strong online activist and support groups provided cardholders with social validation of their dissenting emotions and experiences, and emboldened some to engage in public protest and the dissemination of these policy counter-narratives – for example, through televised media engagement, writing submissions to CDC parliamentary inquiries, and contacting politicians about their CDC experiences.

Asserting deservingness

Cardholders in both Australia and New Zealand asserted social identities that ran counter to those advanced in dominant discourse. Where popular portrayals of CIM constructed targeted welfare recipients as bad financial managers, irresponsible parents and/or people with drug, alcohol or gambling problems (Peterie et al, 2021), the majority of participants in this study declared themselves to be good citizens who were innocent of these charges.

Popular representations of Australian CIM participants as drug users, alcoholics and irresponsible parents were a cause of distress for many interviewees and stood in stark contrast to interviewees' perceptions of themselves. Participants in Ceduna, for instance, observed that CIM targeted Indigenous peoples, who were portrayed and treated as a homogenous group of 'problem citizens': "Basically, everyone is getting punished. Not every Aboriginal [person] has got a problem with pokies and drinking. … We're getting the card because of these few that have got the problem and it's just caused nothing but problems" (Ellen, Ceduna).

Interviewees in other Australian locations expressed similar sentiments, stressing that they did not personally struggle with drug, alcohol or gambling addictions, but were nonetheless subject to interventions to address them:

> 'I didn't gamble, I didn't drink, I didn't choose drugs. I lead a very clean lifestyle. I didn't do any of those things anyway. I think for the most part people don't. If you're busy running around with a kid, you're not exactly leading a party lifestyle for the most part. I mean, it's tiring – parenting is tiring.' (Tahlia, Hinkler)

The majority of interviewees reported that – notwithstanding the meagreness of Australia's social security benefits – they had managed their finances effectively prior to being placed on CIM: "I said, 'But I've never had any financial [problems] – a history of financial difficulties, a history of alcoholism, a history of gambling,' you know? I said, 'Check my background!' And they said, 'I'm sorry but you've got to go on it'" (Alistair, Playford).

CIM, these interviewees insisted, thus saw large numbers of Australians unduly stigmatised on the basis of their location, receipt of a social security payment and demographic details.

This theme of inaccurate representations was also present in the interviews with New Zealand participants, who refuted the assumption – implicit in Money Management's targeting of 16- to 19-year-olds – that young people lack the skills and experience necessary to responsibly manage their finances. Few New Zealand interviewees recognised themselves in stereotypes of naïve and financially reckless youths. Indeed, the stories interviewees shared frequently indicated an exceptional ability to manage tight finances; many participants spent the entirety of their benefit payments on household expenses and items for their children:

> 'I've got control of a life. I'm looking after a life, but you don't trust me with, like, $200, do you know what I mean? … I could understand if they're giving me thousands of dollars that you're sort of going to

> spend, but really they're only giving you enough just to live, so you can't really do much else anyway. But I don't know, it's just like, if you're letting me look after a child, come on, like can't I look after my own money?' (Manaaki, New Zealand)

As interviewees continuously described in both countries, most parents – including inexperienced ones – make these kinds of decisions, choosing their children's wellbeing over other purchases. Many parents consequently believed that they deserved a little independence and respect, including the freedom to occasionally spend money on items for themselves:

> 'I've always got food. I've always got power. My daughter's always got what she needs. My sister's always got what she needs. And on top of that I'm able to get them whatever they want. But all I want is a cigarette and a cup of tea in the morning.' (Tangaroa, New Zealand)

Tangaroa stressed, if "you're in full-time work, you're all good, you can do whatever you want"; only welfare recipients were held to a strict puritan standard.

Pushing back against assumptions that income support recipients were content to 'live off welfare', interviewees in both Australia and New Zealand also went to great lengths to explain *why* they required income support. Job shortages were a key theme in Australian accounts:

> 'How the hell are you meant to get a job? When you go to the interview, and there's 20 other people sitting there for the one job. Or you go for an interview and nobody sends you an email or a text or anything, to say sorry you've been unsuccessful, you're just left sitting here waiting. … The amount of jobs I went for that, other than disability work, I didn't get replies! I didn't get emails to say sorry you're unsuccessful. I couldn't even get a job at McDonald's.' (Pearl, Hinkler)

Some interviewees also pointed to the influence of other underlying factors, such as age discrimination, in determining who was and was not successful in securing paid employment. One interviewee in Playford, for example, observed that employers often preferred younger candidates: "My wife is on Newstart, she volunteers, because she's over 60 and has found it very hard to get jobs, a job. Being a woman and her age. No matter what anybody says, it's pretty obvious, because she is really highly qualified" (Alistair, Playford).

Racism can also present as a key barrier to finding employment (Paradies and Cunningham, 2009; Biddle et al, 2013; Houkamau et al, 2017). Thus, as numerous interviewees explained (and contrary to popular belief), the problem of unemployment was rarely a problem caused by some deficiency in the unemployed.

In sharing their stories, interviewees in both Australia and New Zealand also showed that they were *already* contributing members of their families and communities, despite their receipt of income support payments. This theme was particularly strong in interviews with single parents who worked long hours caring for children, yet nonetheless felt judged and chastised for not 'contributing' to society through paid work. As one young mother in Hinkler said:

> 'It's really hard when you're a mum and they say, "oh well, you can work as well". But I'm doing a full-time study course and working and then doing all sport and school and homework. It's too much for one person, for me to do. ... I don't have that energy and I've got so much to do already. I'm just focused on the study and then I can go work.' (Annie, Hinkler)

A New Zealand benefit advocate, Sharon, shared a similar reflection, observing that – in requiring YPP participants to meet educational obligations and prepare for future employment – the Youth Services model failed to appreciate the work involved in learning to be a first-time parent: "These are young women trying to learn to be a parent. To put that extra pressure on them at this point. ... At 16 and 17, their whole world has changed. To expect them to get motivated to get full employment [or education] at that age [is unreasonable]."

Many interviewees hoped to find paid employment eventually – as one young woman, Aroha (New Zealand), told us, "you just want to get out there and work for yourself" – but this was not an immediate possibility for most. This was not least because the New Zealand policy settings meant that Youth Payment and Young Parent Payment recipients were incentivised only into education and training. The rationale here was that young people who had completed further education would enjoy better long-term prospects than those who simply found unskilled employment or concentrated on raising children. Although comparing well with Australia's focus on paid work for all, this policy did not meet the needs of some young people who wished to work and be independent, or had no idea what they wished to train for in terms of a future vocation.

Parents of children with disabilities were particularly constrained in their ability to find employment. These interviewees expressed their hurt regarding stereotypes that simultaneously overlooked the difficult realities of their day-to-day lives and undervalued their extensive unpaid labour:

> 'If they've got a mother and father and they both work and can support their kids, that's great. But if you have a child with special needs and

that child can't communicate with you and you spend a lot of time and effort trying to figure out what they need – whether it's a drink, whether it's food, whether they want a cuddle or [to] go outside and play – that is a full-time job on its own.' (Pearl, Hinkler)

People who struggled to find appropriate employment due to illness or disability shared similar sentiments. The idea that a person's social value was in some way reducible to their participation in the labour market, these interviewees implied, was insensitive, ignorant, and unfair. In portraying CIM as an intervention to combat problem behaviour, they showed, official discourses ostracised and alienated people who were doing their best in sometimes difficult circumstances, and who had reasonably expected community and government support.

Educating others

In addition to presenting these identities and alternative policy narratives in the interview context, some study participants described their efforts to assert them at the micro level of their individual relationships. In Hinkler, for instance, Dawn recalled a confrontation with a high school friend who – in a discussion of Australia's social security system – had reproduced a popular trope regarding the non-deservingness of income support recipients:

'[H]e thinks that we have no right to free money anyway. I'm just like, "Do you understand what would happen if there was no welfare system? The economy would collapse, more people would lose their jobs. Then the problem would become worse and we'd end up in a recession or depression". He's just like, "No, that wouldn't happen". I'm like, "Honestly people need to stop looking at it as handouts and look at it for what it is. It helps keep the community alive. Without all the people on Centrelink putting the money back into the community, businesses would shut, people would lose their jobs". But no, they don't see that. They just see what the media and the stupid goddam politicians have put out there to win votes.' (Dawn, Hinkler)

Pearl (Hinkler) explained that she had made a concerted effort to respond to public stigma by educating people who might otherwise judge or look down on her. Instead of hiding her card or avoiding scrutiny in shopping contexts, she instead anticipated any judgement by sharing her story:

'[W]hen someone says "Do you want cash out?" I'm like, "It's the cashless debit card, I can't get no cash out". Making other people who work aware that it's costing taxpayers $12,000 to put people on this

> card, their hard-earned money, on to a card that I don't want to be on. … I tell people, "I don't like it, it's something I'm forced on to, I don't need to be on it. You can see my groceries, am I buying, am I not providing for my children?"' (Pearl, Hinkler)

Through interactions like these, cardholders subtly pushed back against their own vilification and presented an understanding of Australia's social security system that ran counter to public discourse.

Cardholders in New Zealand shared similar stories of everyday interactions where they experimented with alternative understandings of Money Management. One young woman, for instance, described an interaction between herself and members of her extended family at a supermarket checkout:

> 'I brought out my green card, went and did it, and they were like, "Oh, how come you pay with that?" His aunty had to explain to them … "Silly people have ruined it, so now everyone has to get paid through a green card". They're like, "Oh, but you don't smoke and you don't drink?"' (Manaaki, New Zealand)

While this interpretation of CIM as a valid response to the actions of an irresponsible minority fell short of critiquing CIM as a whole, it nonetheless provided the interviewee with social confirmation of her own deservingness. As the next section will explore, such validation could be important in galvanising cardholders in their opposition to CIM and, ultimately, facilitating more open forms of dissent.

Resisting through collective action

Up to this point, the experiences of Australian and New Zealand CIM participants have been relatively similar vis-a-vis their resistance efforts. A stark difference between these case studies, however, concerns the extent to which cardholders engage in open resistance and, more specifically, in collective action to oppose the policy.

Diverging paths

A number of contextual factors help to explain this trend. First, the focus on mentoring and youth development in New Zealand's Youth Service meant that things were not 'all bad' for many New Zealand cardholders, and that overall political opposition to the policy was thus weaker (see Chapter 2). Second, the New Zealand policy's targeting of young welfare recipients may have made open resistance less likely. Being new to the welfare system and having never received *non*-quarantined income support payments, many of the New Zealand interviewees accepted the current policy as the status quo. Third, given the eligibility criteria surrounding YP and YPP benefits, many of those effected by CIM had come from the care of the state, were disengaged from their families, and/or had come from otherwise disadvantaged backgrounds. Many of these young people thus had little social capital with which they could effectively contest their subjectification or claim a voice in the public sphere. Finally, where many Australian cardholders – as will be seen – were able to find strength in communities of fellow cardholders, fewer such networks (either formal or informal) existed in New Zealand.

In Australia, numerous grassroots groups have arisen as local responses to CIM. For instance, in August 2012, the highly active 'Stop Income Management in Playford' (SIMPla) (now renamed 'Stop Income Management SA') group was formed in opposition to the BasicsCard. In the Northern Territory, Alice Springs' 'Intervention Rollback Action Group' (IRAG) has repeatedly pushed back on everything connected with the Northern Territory Emergency Response, including CIM via the BasicsCard; they have organised protests in Alice Springs, presented evidence before Parliamentary committees, and formed a Facebook group after many years of having a separate website. On 18 October 2015, the 'Say NO to the Welfare Debit Card Ceduna' group arose in response to the proposal that Ceduna be the first CDC trial site. The 'No Cashless Debit Card/HINKLER REGION' Facebook group was similarly created prior to the roll out of the CDC in that area in 2019.

There have been national groups formed in response to the CDC, too, such as the 'Cashless Welfare Debit Card Australia National Support Group' (a closed Facebook group where CDC participants offer emotional and practical support to each other in relation to challenges presented by the card) and 'Say No Seven' (a public Facebook group focused on public activism). There is also the 'Accountable Income Management Network' (AIMN), which was formed in 2015 with a public Facebook site later created in 2019. AIMN includes NGOs, academics, policy workers, and some government income support recipients, and aims to hold the federal government accountable for its policies and to advance a dignified system of income support.

Research attests that social media can play a powerful role in organising communities and galvanising them into action. Social media and other online platforms have altered the shape of contemporary activism – allowing disparate community members to connect and maintain communication and providing spaces where people can express dissent (Cernison, 2019; Demirdis, 2019). Critically, these technologies are comparatively inexpensive and accessible, thus making them a valuable tool for resource-poor and marginalised individuals who may not otherwise have a voice in the public sphere. Many social media sites also allow the creation of private spaces (for example, closed Facebook groups) where members are shielded from the attacks that can occur on public pages. As Archer-Lean and Pavitt (2012, p 3) explain, social media has thus been a game-changer for marginalised communities:

> The accessibility of new media are [sic] part of their democratic impetus, facilitating some agency for voices previously outside the mainstream media and political discussion. … The freedom from face to face contact can enact a space where ordinary people feel comfortable to voice dissent and to discuss political issues in heated and politically productive and democratic ways. (Archer-Lean and Pavitt, 2012, p 3)

Social media platforms are also notable for their capacity to rapidly spread information to large groups of people to (for example) organise physical assemblies (Shirky, 2008). Indeed, social media platforms such as Facebook have been credited with facilitating uprisings such as those during the Arab Spring (Tufekci and Wilson, 2012; see also Demirdis, 2019).

Academic debate regarding these platforms, however, has not been uniformly optimistic in tone. Reviewing available research regarding the value of social media in social movements, Kidd and McIntosh (2016) observe that the democratic potentialities of these platforms may be overstated. While evidence exists of social media's political power, it is also true that most major platforms are owned by large corporations beholden to commercial imperatives, and that social media is utilised in surveillance efforts by governments and authorities (Kidd and McIntosh, 2016).

It is also clear that the democratisation of new media has resulted in the dissemination of misinformation and hate speech (DePaula et al, 2018), and that psychological preferences for information that conforms with pre-existing views together with social media algorithms have compounded existing social divisions through the creation of ideological 'echo-chambers' (Garimella et al, 2018). While these realities are concerning, they do not negate evidence concerning the value of social media in resistance efforts; rather, they recommend a more nuanced view. As Kidd and McIntosh (2016, p 793) conclude, '[t]he best empirical evidence is that revolutionary movements today will certainly include social media, and may even need it, but will also need much more than that'.

Building communities of support

In describing their involvement with online social media groups opposing CIM, many of the interviewees stressed the support they received within these spaces. Many of these groups had originally been created in attempts to 'organise' community members in their opposition to the cards, but they became important spaces for the provision of informational and emotional support. Interviewees in Hinkler, for example, explained that they and fellow cardholders regularly shared updates in Facebook groups to keep each other "in the loop" (Cindy, Hinkler). These include the No Cashless Debit Card/ HINKLER REGION group and the Cashless Welfare Debit Card Australia National Support Group. In the initial days of the CDC's introduction to the region, for instance, members posted tips "saying where it's being declined" (Anthony, Hinkler) to protect other group members from the shame and indignity of having their cards rejected. Group administrators, sensitive to impacts of cards being declined, amplified these reports:

> '[T]hey're socially isolating themselves from the stigma out there. They're anxious about going shopping with the card. They'll choose times when it's not busy for fear— just in case it doesn't work, in case it goes down. That's why, on our pages, if somebody says it's down somewhere, we make it very public very quickly, just so that that gives people a heads up.' (Administrators, support group)

Other group members posted about their rental transfer and online payment problems to alert fellow cardholders to the potential issue and ask for advice. Relevant media stories and memes were also regularly shared and discussed.

In Ceduna, a group administrator discussed how the Facebook pages provided cardholders with a central database for sharing or locating useful information. "[T]he beauty of it", he explained, "is the information just goes up there as I find it and as I see it". In making his posts, however, this interviewee was careful not only to inform, but also to encourage: "I put up how to get exemptions, we've got [one cardholder] off on the same exemption. You've got to put your successes, even though they're small, you put them up there so that other people know that there is hope. Because everybody's just shutting down."

For many of the participants in this study, this emotional bolstering was the most important component of their group participation. Facebook groups such as 'Say NO to the Welfare Debit Card Ceduna', 'No Cashless Debit Card/HINKLER REGION', and the 'Cashless Welfare Debit Card Australia National Support Group' provided their members with information but – more than this – they constituted a safe and sympathetic community where isolated cardholders could give and receive socio-emotional support.

As a number of interviewees reflected, sharing a personal experience in an online support group involved disclosing more than mere information. Members also gave voice to their anger and hurt, reclaimed their power by laughing at the expense of policy proponents, and ultimately ameliorated the isolation and shame that CIM produced:

> 'Being able to understand that other people are having just as much trouble as we are [is helpful]. I've got more support from that side of things [in the Facebook group] and obviously asking questions and being able to vent when need be. … It's not just a few of us having a whinge and bitch, … it's showing all the different problems that we've had. Yeah, it definitely has that bit of a back-up sort of thing.' (Mary, Hinkler)

Expressions of emotion have not traditionally been understood as forms of resistance, yet, as Hochschild (1979) has argued, dominant discourses frequently impose rules on how we feel in a particular social situation. In this context, the expression of emotions that *deviate* from these scripts can constitute a subtle form of everyday resistance, as doing so asserts a different explanation of the situation in question (Koefoed, 2017; Benesch, 2018; Peterie et al, 2019a). As Peterie et al (2019a, p 796) explain with respect to unemployment:

> [I]n the context of a socio-political landscape that pressures the unemployed to feel shame and an associated willingness to accept work of any kind … expressions of anger can be a form of 'everyday resistance'. When they reject shame and instead convey anger, unemployed people challenge the narrative that they are personally responsible for their circumstances, and assert identities as full and worthwhile members of society.

By providing a safe space where cardholders could give voice to and receive affirmation concerning their (non-conforming) emotions, online support groups therefore allowed members to begin the work of resistance by vocalising emotional dissent – first in closed support groups and later on public pages.

These expressions constituted a form of everyday resistance in their own right. Significantly, however, they also informed and facilitated more open forms of offline resistance. Shared emotions, after all, are notable for their capacity to bind disparate individuals together into more politically powerful collectives (Baaz et al, 2017). As such, the exchange of emotional disclosures and supportive affirmations on these social media platforms laid the groundwork for face-to-face collective action.

Protest and lobbying

While many Australian interviewees preferred everyday resistance to open activism and confrontation, a large minority described their involvement in more recognisable forms of political activism, including participation in public protests. Much of this public work occurred within the context of local groups, such as the highly active 'Stop Income Management in Playford' (SIMPla) (now the 'Stop Income Management SA') group.

SIMPla have employed a number of strategies to oppose IM, including: regularly releasing press statements; holding community forums, some of which have been addressed by visiting Aboriginal community leaders from the NT; distributing fliers outside the local Centrelink office; writing an open letter to the Australian government, signed by 50 non-government organisations, demanding the suspension of IM programmes; publicising the negative experiences of individual IM participants; and organising protest rallies at the SA State Administration Centre, the SA Labor Party Convention, and SA Parliament House (ABC News, 2014; Forgione, 2014, 2015).

Other groups have taken a comparable approach. Protests have been organised by the 'Intervention Rollback Action Group' (IRAG) in Alice Springs, by the 'Stop the Intervention Collective Sydney' in the Sydney Central Business District and Bankstown, by the 'Say NO to the Welfare Debit Card Ceduna' group in Ceduna, and by the 'No Cashless Debit Card/ HINKLER REGION' group in Hervey Bay and in Bundaberg. These rallies have attempted to raise public awareness concerning the problems associated with life on CIM. For example, one protestor at a Hinkler protest in May 2019 displayed a sign stating that they had received a breach notice from their real estate agent because Indue paid their rent late.

For some interviewees, participating in these collective actions was a way of both asserting and reclaiming their power as citizens. Participating in collective action meant making one's (literal) voice heard. As people who had been regularly disempowered and silenced through CIM's design and implementation, making "as much noise as possible" (Sue, Ceduna) afforded a valuable sense of agency. Interviewees who had confronted politicians directly to express opposition to the policy shared similar sentiments. In Hinkler, for instance, Dawn described meeting local MP Keith Pitt and giving voice to the anger and hurt that had bubbled within her for months:

> 'I was intending just to go there and listen. As soon as he opened his mouth I'm just like, "No. I'm going to let it all out". So, I walked up to him— he was like, "Oh, how are you?" I'm like, "Could be a lot better actually". "Oh, okay. What are you having problems with?" So, I was very dramatic [laughs]. I rolled up my sleeves, I walked in front of him, I was like, "Do I look like a junkie? Do my kids look like they are well looked after. ... You say this is what this is for, I'm not any of those things and yet you've pushed for something to come in that dictates what I can and can't do".' (Dawn, Hinkler)

While Dawn experienced this confrontation as a moment of release and empowerment ("it felt so good to have him standing in front of me and for me to tear strips off him", she told us), activities of this kind could also leave participants feeling deflated.

Back in Ceduna, local community organiser Mick shared his own memories of a protest march through the town's centre:

> 'Everyone just marched up the street. "No card, no card." ... But it just happened too quick, everybody charged and charged and [I'm] standing around the corner and down to the jetty and it was all over, yeah. ... Instead of staying there with pots and pans and making a fucking big din it just all— that's it.' (Mick, Caduna)

While the march had been successful, attracting a crowd of up to 200 Ceduna locals, it was ultimately anti-climactic. Kevin (Ceduna) shared Mick's view, noting that as important as it was to raise one's voice, protests to date had resulted in minimal impact, "because no one's been listening" (Kevin, Ceduna).

Echoing the concerns of numerous interviewees who chose not to participate in these actions, some protesters also observed that public activities could inflame community hostilities towards cardholders. For example, Desmond (Ceduna) experienced additional stigmatisation in the wake of his protest involvement. "[W]e just got called troublemakers, basically", he explained. "Yeah, 'you're all bad, you're all rotten'".

Yet the impacts of Australia's grassroots movement to combat CIM are arguably discernible in media coverage of the issue, which can play an important role in shaping public opinion (see Chapter 4). Where New Zealand's Money Management policy has been all but ignored by that nation's press (Humpage et al, 2020a), CIM has received relatively consistent attention in Australia's mainstream media. This has been driven, in part, by regular changes to and expansions of the scheme, which have been fiercely debated in the Australian parliament. Significantly, however, such media coverage has featured the stories of individual welfare recipients who – through their involvement in online support groups and grassroots community activism efforts – have developed connections with non-government organisations, advocacy bodies and members of the press.

As noted earlier, academic studies of contemporary activism have highlighted the democratic potential of social media, noting that new media allows marginalised individuals to bypass traditional media gatekeepers to have their voices heard in the public sphere:

> Politics has to do with the power to define what is right and wrong, what is legal and illegal, what is legitimate dissent or treason. Traditionally, it has used the mainstream media (newspapers, television, radio, film) to disseminate these discourses, with access (in terms of

> production) limited to a narrow elite, and with content subject to varying political and economic agendas. Social media have made possible the presentation of alternative discourses to local and global audiences, challenging the orthodoxies of those in power. (Christensen, 2009, np)

These stories demonstrate, however, that online communities and the activism they facilitate can help individuals to build strong social identities and public profiles, which can in turn bring them to the attention of the media elite.

In Playford, for example, Steph spoke with pride about sharing her own story with local and national journalists following her involvement with grassroots resistance efforts and the organisations that supported them:

> 'The Anti-Poverty Network. … They're the main people to kind of thrust me in the spotlight for a while … I did the Don Dunstan Foundation doco type thing that they did. I think three or four interviews on a newspaper. Got in a spot on *ABC News* on TV … I was on ABC radio. … I also got onto the little indie radio station that I did a really long, I think an hour-long, interview with them. I also did another radio interview for Radio Adelaide, which ended up getting Interview of the Year.' (Steph, Playford)

She had been given the option, she recalled, of doing these interviews anonymously, but had decided that disclosing her identity was important: "[T]hey were like, 'You don't have to say your name, you don't have to go into massive detail'. And I was like, 'You know what? I really don't care if someone notices'. … It needs to have a face. It needs to have a name" (Steph, Playford).

In choosing "to be loud and proud" rather than succumbing to stigma and shame, Steph and others like her posed a direct challenge to CIM by publicly refuting the narratives that underpinned them.

Conclusion

CIM has a profound and debilitating impact on many of the individuals subject to this policy. As the previous chapters have illuminated, the experience of being subject to welfare quarantining is frequently one of deprivation, isolation and stigmatisation. In this context, it is unsurprising that many programme participants express a reticence to engage in overt acts of resistance, which might place them under additional psychological strain or see them subjected to further public scrutiny.

As this chapter has revealed, however, many of the participants in this study nonetheless engaged in covert or 'everyday' forms of political dissent. In both Australia and New Zealand, participants resisted CIM by finding ways to circumvent the restrictions that were most corrosive to their quality of life, and by pushing back against dominant discourses that saw them (mis) characterised as lazy, immoral and financially irresponsible.

While these everyday forms of resistance were the only form of protest immediately available to New Zealand participants, some Australian cardholders ultimately *did* brave the risks associated with overt resistance by becoming involved in more recognisable forms of political action.

A significant social movement has developed around CIM in Australia, and a large minority of the interviewees were themselves members. These participants were active in online communities of resistance and support, where they shared information, told their stories, and reassured themselves and each other that they were not alone. These online communities helped members to mitigate the harshest social and emotional impacts of CIM, but they could also have a politicising effect. Numerous interviewees identified these groups as spaces where they and others organised to challenge CIM policies and expose their detrimental impacts. While it is essential to recognise the adverse impacts of CIM on those affected, it would be both inaccurate and unhelpful to portray programme participants as two-dimensional victims of state power. The participants in this study used a range of covert and overt strategies to assert their enduring social value, to express their opposition to CIM policies, and, ultimately, to lobby for a fairer and more humane approach to social security provision.

7

Voluntary Income Management and financial education

> 'I got put on it [IM] because I needed to learn financial responsibility. ... But yeah, we found being on it— it didn't really help. It actually restricted it a lot more.' (Tamsyn, Playford)

Introduction

A central conclusion of this comparative empirical study is that IM in Australia and New Zealand does more harm than good. Being placed on IM has made many feel infantilised, having been compelled into a system that was not of their choosing and which exacerbates rather than alleviates economic insecurity. Nevertheless, despite uncovering a general and strong aversion to compulsory IM schemes, this research has also found some support for voluntary IM. Some IM participants and community stakeholders in both countries saw voluntary IM as having potential to return an important sense of agency to welfare recipients while offering an avenue of support for those who find IM useful for budgeting. Nevertheless, many of the research participants also held the view that different approaches were needed to build financial capability and address poverty; that IM alone could not achieve this objective. Many touched on the need to raise the base rate of unemployment benefits to an amount that would alleviate (rather than create or exacerbate) poverty. Others described the potential benefit of financial counselling and education, which would align with the IM objectives of strengthening financial knowledge and behaviours while avoiding the hard paternalism associated with compulsory IM schemes.

In this chapter, the focus turns towards the possibility of voluntary IM and financial education as alternatives to compulsory IM. This discussion is placed in the foreground by drawing on public health literature to explore links between economic insecurity and mental and physical health and wellbeing, briefly reviewing the findings in relation to the impacts of compulsory IM on economic insecurity. A critical discussion of the question of voluntary IM follows, in which the empirical data are drawn on to consider the possible strengths and weaknesses of an entirely voluntary IM scheme. The latter part of the chapter explores other evidence-based means of building financial management skills, which could work alongside voluntary IM or alone. In particular, insights are drawn from the research literature on poverty reduction to assess the possible efficacy of financial education, before its use alongside IM is critically discussed.

In considering these alternatives to punitive forms of welfare conditionality, this chapter highlights some of the differences between New Zealand and Australia, identifying lessons that Australia could learn from New Zealand regarding the use of mentors and more empowering forms of budget support. It also argues, however, that voluntary IM and financial education schemes continue to depoliticise economic insecurity as something that can be 'fixed' via interventions in individual behaviours and human capital, while broader political, economic and social structures are ignored. Drawing on insights from a range of studies and disciplines, the chapter concludes with an argument for evidence-informed social policies, which would reframe questions of economic and social security.

Economic (in)security and Income Management

Economic insecurity involves experiences of uncertainty, anxiety and stress about financial (in)stability (Stiglitz et al, 2009; Bossert and D'Ambrosio, 2013; Rohde et al, 2016). Such insecurity is strongly correlated with a range of negative physical and mental health outcomes (Blakely et al, 2003; Booth and Carroll, 2008; Stiglitz et al, 2009; Rohde et al, 2016; Higashi et al, 2017; Kopasker et al, 2018; Hossain and Lamb, 2019). Economic insecurity can reduce food security, access to quality healthcare, and opportunities for secure and healthy housing, which influence physical health and safety as well as mental health and wellbeing (Catalano, 1991; Higashi et al, 2017; Bentley et al, 2019).

Causes of economic insecurity are multiple and varied (Stiglitz et al, 2009; Rohde et al, 2016). Job loss, relationship breakdown, and other significant changes in individual or household circumstances can act as triggers, while structural influences such as economic recession can also play a central role. Ultimately, Rohde et al (2016, p 256) suggested the need for a broad approach to understanding economic risk, showing that negative health impacts are observed across 'any risky situation that threatens the economic wellbeing of the individual'. Conversely, experiences of poor physical and/or mental health can also cause or exacerbate economic insecurity, including through job loss or high costs of medical care (Stiglitz et al, 2009).

As discussed in previous chapters, neoliberal renderings of the issue of economic insecurity tend towards individualising discourses that blame the predicament of disadvantaged populations on their behaviours and proclivities. IM is an excellent case study of how structural causes of poverty can be 'rendered technical' through a narrow and exclusive focus on perceived individual deficit (Li, 2007, p 46). Indeed, the core narrative that drives IM policies is that welfare recipients end up in dire economic circumstances because they cannot manage their money or they spend it unwisely, thereby justifying the logic of 'help and hassle' welfare conditionality to get them on track (Mead, 1997, p 24). However, while cashless welfare cards are proposed as a means of improving economic security and financial management behaviours, the reality for many IM participants is that they can instead trigger or exacerbate economic insecurity. As discussed in Chapter 4, this can occur when cashless card technologies fail, when individuals are unable to use their money in ways that reduce costs (such as using cash at fresh food markets to save money), and also as a result of extra financial burdens brought on by charges and fees accrued under IM (for example, due to fees on the cards, or fees related to missed or late bill payments arising from card processing errors). Rental payments being missed because of administrative errors (frequently reported) can also compromise housing security (Peterie et al, 2020).

Ultimately, many of the participants who had previously described themselves as "strong money manager[s]" (Jocelyn, Hinkler) have been thrust into significant financial turmoil and even "complete ruin" (Talika, Northern Territory) as a result of being compulsorily placed on IM. Insofar as IM can create or exacerbate economic insecurity, then, it also aggravates associated negative health and wellbeing impacts that arise from poor access to material needs (Momsen, 2021). Many of the research participants also reported direct impacts on their mental health, describing IM as having produced feelings of powerlessness, loss of control, and worthlessness. For example: "It is really stressful, I fear being homeless, it has been a big part in putting me on depression medication … I no longer have control of my money" (Carliha, Ceduna).

This sense of powerlessness was a recurring theme across the interviews, and 84 per cent of the Australian survey respondents also said that being on IM made them feel like they had 'less control' or 'far less control' over their lives. Conversely, only six per cent of survey respondents said IM gave them 'more control' or 'far more control'; the remaining ten per cent were undecided. This has the potential to produce further harms, since other studies have also shown that when people feel that events and outcomes are beyond their control (that is, when they exhibit an external 'locus of control'), they also tend to experience less financial wellbeing, worse health, greater stress, poorer eating and exercise habits, and lower intensity job-search behaviours (Sandler and Lakey, 1982; Lefcourt et al, 1984; Cvetanovski and Jex, 1994; Perry and Morris, 2005; Ryon and Gleason, 2013; Cobb-Clark et al, 2014; Caliendo et al, 2015; Prawitz and Cohart, 2016; Schnitzlein and Stephani, 2016). 'Locus of control' is a widely recognised concept with its origins in psychology. It is defined by Rotter (1966, p 1) as 'the degree to which the individual perceives that reward follows from, or is contingent upon, his own behaviour or attributes versus the degree to which he feels the reward is controlled by forces outside of himself and may occur independently of his own actions'. In sum, while IM is framed as a 'fix' for economic insecurity, it was generally experienced by the research participants as a malaise, triggering a cycle of worsening economic hardship and creating poorer health and wellbeing. In large part, and as these data bear out, this is because the primary cause of economic insecurity has been misdiagnosed under IM policies as poor money management behaviours rather than simply a lack of income.

Although a small number of research participants said that being placed on IM was helpful (especially those who had volunteered to be put on the scheme, as discussed later), the vast majority said it did not help alleviate their economic insecurity because that insecurity did not stem from financial mismanagement in the first place. Instead, for most of the Australian participants, the primary cause of their economic insecurity was difficulty in finding suitable employment in an increasingly precarious and unstable market, and thereby having to survive, often for long periods of time, on very low social security benefits. For the young New Zealand participants, many of whom had never been in paid work and none of whom faced work obligations as part of IM, economic insecurity was more strongly tied to lacking familial financial support, or the costs associated with pregnancy. But they similarly struggled to make ends meet on the low benefit rates available to YP and YPP recipients, especially when a large proportion of that income was quarantined.

In contrast with public narratives about 'dependent' recipients who are unable to budget, many participants saw themselves as very *good* money managers. Indeed, with such low social security payments, many were forced to be as a matter of sheer survival:

> 'I have been a single mum on Centrelink for almost 10 years and have lived on my own with my children for most of that time. I have always budgeted well and done whatever I can to make our money stretch to meet our needs for food, etc., such as shop at Aldi, buy second hand, etc., and have never had issues budgeting and paying bills. It is one of, if not my top, priority when it comes to my finances.' (Tina, Hinkler)

Tangaroa, a Māori New Zealand Money Management participant who had recently exited child protective care and was now caring for her sister as well as a young daughter, stressed that she alone could manage both her and her family's needs effectively:

> 'I'll go and buy my cigarettes, but I've always got food. I've always got power. My daughter's always got what she needs. My sister's always

> got what she needs, and on top of that I'm able to get them whatever they want. But all I want is a cigarette and a cup of tea in the morning.' (Tangaroa, a Māori New Zealand Money Management participant)

She contrasted this with her parents, who had lost custody of the participant and her siblings, and asked, "we're the ones on the money management, why didn't they experience it?" (Tangaroa, New Zealand). More generally, she felt the government used statistics on Māori benefit dependency, drug use and crime based on her *parents'* generation to punish young people like herself who were trying to overcome familial dysfunction.

Even where the research participants said that they did need to develop their budgeting and financial management skills, they still tended to see compulsory IM as being unable to provide the support needed and, in some cases, it made budgeting even harder. For example, Tamsyn (Playford), who is also a mother of five children, was interested in being placed on the BasicsCard after being told that she needed to "learn financial responsibility". However, the mother's initial enthusiasm about the potential for IM to help her financial situation quickly faded:

> 'I thought it was a good idea because I'd heard about it and I thought oh, no, this will be good. It will help us out. Then I think … it was after the first payment that I got on it, I was like this isn't really helping. Maybe it will get better. Then after a couple more payments, it was like no, this isn't helping. We're sick of it.' (Tamsyn, Playford)

She went on to talk about how the BasicsCard made it harder to budget because she was tied to shopping at major stores where the card was accepted, preventing her from going to smaller stores where she might otherwise find discounts on basic goods. As Chapter 4 showed, this was a consistent complaint among participants; most of the time, the cashless cards themselves were seen as a blunt, punitive and ineffective tool when it came to improving economic security and financial management – and often, they made things worse. Indeed, the New Zealand MSD evaluation of Money Management even acknowledged that it could cause debt, citing an instance where the Youth Service Support Unit would not allow an IM participant to use savings on their Payment Card to pay down credit card debt beyond the minimum payment (Momsen, 2021).

MSD data accessed through New Zealand's *Official Information Act 1982* also highlights that, between 2013 and 2018, 39,845 applications were made by YP and YPP recipients for hardship assistance (provided when someone cannot meet emergency costs), 95 per cent of which were granted. This suggests that even social security entitlement decision makers recognise that current benefit levels cannot meet all needs.

Although there was no difference in success rates across the two benefits, 55.4 per cent of hardship applications were made by YPP recipients, suggesting that parents struggle to cover emergency costs under IM more than people without dependants, which is in line with the findings of this study. Specific data were also available on Targeted Additional Support applications (to cover essential costs, most often food) for those on IM specifically; between 2012 and 2019, 37.5 per cent of 11,742 applications were granted (46 per cent among YPP recipients, even though 59 per cent of applications came from YP recipients). That Targeted Additional Support applications were much higher among YP/YPP recipients on IM than those who had exited suggests that quarantining essential costs on a Payment Card does *not* improve recipients' ability to meet all essential costs using their core benefit income.

Such issues with IM led to two recurring suggestions from interview participants in both countries. The first was the potential efficacy of making IM a voluntary-only scheme, so that those people who saw benefit in the policy could choose to participate, while the harms associated with compelled participation could be avoided. The second suggestion was that IM should be replaced with other ways of improving financial management, such as financial education programmes. The following sections first explore the potential for voluntary-only IM schemes, then discuss the evidence for and potential role of financial education programmes as a way of improving financial management skills.

Voluntary Income Management

Most people currently on IM in Australia and all in New Zealand were initially placed compulsorily on the schemes and, thus, voluntary participants generally represent only a small fraction of participants overall. In New Zealand, Money Management participants can choose whether or not to remain on IM after they have met their participation obligations, though the proportion of participants who choose to do so is unclear. Conversely, Australian IM enables people to voluntarily participate without the need for a social service referral. At 1 January 2021, of Australia's 35,400 IM participants, 3,083 (about 7.7 per cent) had volunteered to be part of the scheme (Australian Government, 2021a; 2021b).

People reported various reasons for volunteering to participate in IM. For some, incentive payments had encouraged them to participate. For instance, under New Income Management in the Northern Territory (implemented from 2010), individuals could receive a $250 incentive payment for each six-month period they spent on the scheme (Bray et al, 2014). Similar incentive payments were also made available elsewhere under broader Place Based IM initiatives until mid-2015. These payments were often useful for supplementing very low social security incomes. As voluntary Australian participant, Trent (Shepparton), explained:

> 'I think it was a woman we spoke to at Centrelink, [she] just gave us a basic rundown of what the card's about and part of our payments go to Income Management for rent and electricity and all that. Yeah, we thought it was quite a good idea and at the time, every six months, you'd – and that was a good bit of an incentive to go on it. That's $500 a year for nothing really. That went straight onto your BasicsCard and that would help with groceries and Christmas and all that sort of thing.' (Trent, Shepparton)

While an early evaluation of Place Based IM found that the receipt of incentive payments likely had little effect on participants' decisions to remain on voluntary IM (Deloitte Access Economics, 2014, p 40), their subsequent removal has nevertheless been subject to criticism on the basis that it has increased material poverty, placing some at 'greater risk of financial hardship, domestic violence, social alienation and housing stress' (Banks and Tennant, 2016, pp 427). However, as helpful as the incentive payments were for some, reliance on ad hoc incentive schemes to alleviate risk of financial hardship provides little security for recipients. It also distracts from the bigger issue of inadequate social security payment rates, as elaborated on later, while simultaneously drawing even more people into the IM system where they are subject to increased government surveillance.

Notwithstanding these accounts, other Australian participants were primarily interested in volunteering to be on IM in the hope that it might assist them to manage their finances. In these instances, people were more likely to talk about having experienced financial or budgeting issues in the past, which had triggered their interest in IM. For example, voluntary IM participant, Grace (Playford) explained: "When I lost my second husband, he didn't teach me, or my first husband didn't even teach me how to pay bills or do that type of thing. So, what I was doing when he died, I was just spending the money."

Ultimately, it was found that those who had volunteered to participate in Australian IM were more likely to see it as being helpful for staying on top of regular bills and expenses than those who were forced onto compulsory IM. This reflects other studies, including an evaluation of Northern Territory IM undertaken by Bray et al (2014, pp 171), which found that voluntary participants were far more likely to report that IM had made things 'better' for them overall, and that they were also less likely to want to exit IM. In the present study, some voluntary IM participants reported that it had reduced the stress involved in managing their financial affairs:

Trent (Shepparton):	Yeah, I reckon it's a big help. A few people I know say, "Oh, it's rubbish". I reckon it's one of the best

	ideas. … Just having the extra cash there to buy— top up the groceries. We know that every fortnight the rent's paid and bills are paid. It's a big help.
Facilitator:	Do you find that that makes life easier?
Trent:	Yeah. A lot easier, not having to worry about, "Oh shit, we've spent $400 on groceries and we're $150 short on rent". It takes that worry out and the stress level.
Facilitator:	Do you think it improves your ability to manage money?
Trent:	Yep.
Facilitator:	Why is that?
Trent:	Just gets— when you know your payments are going into the bank and, right, I know I can use this much and if we do have to— if something comes up we've got that little bit extra there to pay for what we need like kids' medication or something like that … I think it just gives you a bit more security and peace of mind.

Rose (Shepparton) explained that having her bills paid automatically in advance "is such a relief for me by knowing that they've dealt with it". Indeed, a core benefit of IM for most voluntary participants was the assurance it provided that a pool of money was safely stored away for bills, and that those participants would then not need to think about making payments:

Facilitator:	How has it helped you?
Grace (Playford):	Because I can do what I want. I don't have to worry about the bills.
Facilitator:	So, all those bills are sorted out for you and you know you're not going to get in arrears and things like that?
Grace:	That's right, because that's what I was doing.
Facilitator:	Does that make you feel a bit happier?
Grace:	Oh, it makes me a lot happier.

Still, for others, Centrepay – a direct debiting facility available through Centrelink for payment of recurring bills – already served this purpose. Voluntary participant, Stephanie, stated: "I said it's not going to change much from what I was actually originally doing. Because it already had all my bills coming out of Centrepay. I had all the necessary items being managed by them, so it wasn't going to make any major difference."

It is questionable whether voluntary IM, used in this manner, simply externalises control of finances rather than building financial capability. As compulsory IM participant, Drew (Shepparton), asked: "If you're used to this system of your money gets managed for you then you don't really learn how to dig your way out of that [financial] hole and work it out." A New Zealand participant gave evidence of the lack of agency IM encourages; she chose to return voluntarily to Money Management because "I jumped off it for a few [weeks] but I couldn't— didn't know how to budget properly, so I jumped back on it" (Tui, New Zealand). It is also possible that other financial products might hold similar or greater benefit than voluntarily participating in IM. For instance, John, a Playford resident on voluntary IM, described how he had previously used a Christmas savings account, opened through his bank, to put away funds before going on to voluntary IM: "I'd put $50 or $60 from that $130 or whatever it was back in those days, probably near enough the same, for electricity. Then, a couple of years ago, I got a letter from them [the bank] saying 'You are $1,140 in advance'." Other products may also offer better interest on savings, which does not accrue on the Australian BasicsCard or New Zealand's Money Management, but is accrued at a 'standard industry rate' on the Cashless Debit Card (Australian Government, 2019; see also Fletcher, 2019). However, this was a later change in CDC policy introduced because people on the card complained about earning no interest on their Indue account balances for many years.

Further, while volunteering to be placed on IM has been positive for some, it does not preclude them from experiencing some of the same challenges as compulsory IM participants. For instance, Bray et al (2014) showed that about 23.5 per cent of their Australian survey respondents on voluntary IM reported paying more money for basic goods because of having to use the BasicsCard (Bray et al, 2014, p 135). Given the limited number of shops where the Payment Card can be used, this was also an issue in New Zealand. In this sense, the benefit of volunteering to be on IM likely depends on how the individual plans to use it. Having a pool of funds 'locked away' for recurring household bills (paid, for example, through direct debit) is useful for some, but it may be less effective for others who wish to use the quarantined amount of their income to shop around for discounts (requiring cash or the ability to use the cards in a wider range of stores). In New Zealand, the difficulties that sole parents had in accessing baby items through the Payment Card meant that only YP recipients reported voluntarily staying on IM. Nevertheless, the advantage of a voluntary scheme is that it is up to the individual to decide what best suits their circumstances, while also enabling others to avoid the harmful impacts of being compelled onto IM.

The notion of choice was central to the support for voluntary IM that some of the participants articulated. As discussed in earlier chapters, compulsory IM strips away individual choice and treats participants as spectators to defining their own needs (Sennett, 2003). Carliha (Ceduna) explained that being compulsorily placed on IM meant "I no longer have control of my money"; another went further, "I am not in control of my life" (Travis, Goldfields). Conversely, voluntary IM, at least in theory, returns agency and control to the individual. This has practical implications for peoples' health and wellbeing; as the literature clearly shows, an internal locus of control is correlated with a range of positive health and wellbeing outcomes. Returning peoples' agency over IM participation also removes the impetus to circumvent it, the act of which can place people in difficult situations and, in extreme cases, have the effect of extending 'zones of criminality' (von Sturmer and Le Marseny, 2012, p 21; Scott et al, 2018). As Damian (Hinkler) put it: "If it's voluntary then people *want* help so they can sign up and ask to be put on it. … People have to want the help because otherwise they will just find a workaround. And we see a lot of that."

New Zealand participants also reported many of these 'workarounds', notably buying vouchers or products with their Payment Card that they could on-sell, allowing family members to use their card in return for cash, or frequenting shops that (illegally) allowed them to buy cigarettes or alcohol, or withdraw cash using their Payment Card.

Voluntary IM also has ethical implications, signalling a level of trust and respect for welfare recipients that is noticeably absent under the hard paternalism of compulsory IM. Bridget, who is a community service provider in Playford, explained that this could have positive flow-on effects for people's overall sense of dignity: "To have a choice … [about going on IM] just immediately improves dignity, and so it improves self-image and enables people to be an adult, to take on that adult role rather than being treated as infants who can't make decisions for themselves."

Voluntary IM schemes also have potential to be less polarising than compulsory ones. For instance, only a very small minority of the Australian interviewees, and a mere 21 per cent of the survey respondents, said they would support the continuation of compulsory IM. Conversely, a larger proportion of Australian IM interview participants and 39 per cent of survey respondents said they would support voluntary-only IM. The survey showed that, when it came to the question of voluntary IM, there was far greater alignment between the views of those who had directly experienced IM and those who had not. An MSD survey found that around 35 per cent of current and former IM participants in New Zealand wanted to maintain compulsory IM, but also wanted Youth Service providers to have the discretion to decide which young people needed it; only 18 per cent preferred a voluntary option. However, 58 per cent said that if they had a choice themselves, they would opt to have their payment managed, while 79 per cent of these same IM participants said they would choose to complete a budgeting course if it was voluntary, and 81 per cent said they would choose to talk to a youth coach about their budget (Momsen, 2021). This highlights that the punitive management of income is far less popular than general budgeting assistance, a finding corroborated by the New Zealand interviewees in this study, who felt that keeping a voluntary option would enable those who needed/wanted help to receive it.

Nevertheless, while some research participants expressed support for voluntary IM, such a scheme would also have clear limits. Indeed, if improved economic security – and the health and wellbeing benefits that flow from it – is the purported objective of the Australian and New Zealand governments, then voluntary IM alone cannot produce that. Thus, it would be crucially important to consider how a voluntary IM scheme might also interact with broader changes to produce a fairer social security system that can better address and alleviate economic insecurity. This would demand a shift away from concentrating solely on technical, individually focused "band-aid fix[es]" (Candice, Playford stakeholder) such as IM and towards addressing structural causes of poverty, as discussed in Chapter 8. The decision to continue supporting a voluntary IM scheme would also carry financial and opportunity costs. If mainstream financial products, such as high-interest savings accounts, provide as much or more benefit, then continuing to invest in voluntary IM may not be worthwhile for participants. Continued government investment in voluntary IM may also redirect funding away from other, evidence-based social support measures that could have greater chance of addressing economic insecurity and improving health and wellbeing. As Terri (Hinkler) explained, "education, preventative healthcare measures and harm minimisation are way more cost effective and can be targeted to specific individuals who need help". Similarly, a social security advocate in New Zealand summed things up like this:

> 'I think you're talking about ultimately a system where you have a universal basic income where people are guaranteed the ability to survive with a degree of dignity. You start from an assumption that problems don't exist where people have the capacity to address those problems. There then should be an array of supports that can be accessed for people who have individual health-related problems, like substance abuse, gambling. They need to be framed as [a] health-related issue.' (Social security advocate, New Zealand)

This kind of multifaceted approach would align with international research on poverty reduction, which has shown that holistic interventions across education, health and housing, coupled with a supportive social security system, are crucial (see, for example, Edelman, 2013; Page and Pande, 2018).

Ultimately, whether or not there is broader community support for voluntary IM versus alternative measures needs to be more thoroughly studied. The fact that the total number of Australians volunteering for IM has decreased in recent years – by about ten per cent between November 2019 and January 2021 (that is, from 3,427 to 3,083) – raises questions about how satisfied voluntary participants are in general. However, while the question of voluntary IM remains open, it was not the only potential alternative put forward by research participants. Many also highlighted the potential efficacy of increasing funding to financial literacy schemes as an additional (or replacement) social support. "Early intervention in financial education" was described by some participants in Australia as potentially going "deeper" than IM (Karina, Shepparton stakeholder). As one Australian stakeholder explained:

> 'I would say that Income Management would never be the best option. … But certainly, for me, I think that education is critical, and teaching families about financial capability, financial literacy, and supporting them in a way that shows them the benefit, that's not punitive in any way. … So, I think government's gone completely the wrong way around Income Management. I think that it teaches families nothing at all about financial competence. In actual fact, it probably is the opposite. So, yeah, anything but Income Management, in my view.' (Stakeholder Australia 4)

Now, the chapter turns to the issue of financial education. It describes how it has been integrated, to some extent, under IM in both Australia and New Zealand, as well as drawing out some potential lessons from these experiences. It then considers the research evidence for financial literacy education before critically examining its normative assumptions.

A role for financial education?

Australian and New Zealand 15-year-olds have high levels of financial literacy compared to their international peers (OECD, 2012). However, using 2016 Household, Income and Labour Dynamics in Australia (HILDA) survey data, Preston (2020) argued that about 45 per cent of Australian adults could still be considered financially illiterate against the threshold of 'understanding … at least three basic financial literacy concepts', referred to as the 'Big 3': interest rates, inflation, diversification. In New Zealand, the Commission for Financial Capability reported findings from a recent survey of the financial knowledge of 3,132 adult New Zealanders, which showed that only 66 per cent of respondents reached the minimum threshold for demonstrating financial literacy, and only 22 per cent achieved a score that demonstrated strong financial literacy (Galicki, 2020, p 4). Financial literacy also differs between demographic groups, with women, Indigenous peoples, and young people tending to have the lowest financial literacy rates in Australia and New Zealand (Brimble and Blue, 2013; Rohde et al, 2015; Galicki, 2020; Preston, 2020, p 5). Similarly low levels of financial literacy have been found in other liberal democracies (OECD, 2020), resulting in an increasingly strong focus in recent decades on delivering financial literacy education (Pinto, 2012), including in combination with IM.

Financial education under Income Management

Financial counselling is now offered in coordination with most IM schemes in Australia and forms a central aspect of New Zealand's Money Management policy, where IM participants are required to attend budgeting courses, set financial goals and engage with mentors when making financial decisions. In New Zealand, participants who attend budgeting programmes are eligible for a $10 per week incentive payment; if they do not attend, they can have financial sanctions imposed and will not be allowed to exit IM. Conversely, Australian financial education schemes tend to be voluntary, though in some cases incentives are also used to encourage engagement.

In the Northern Territory, for example, a one-to-one matched savings scheme (up to a maximum of $500 per person) was initially used to incentivise completion of financial education, after which individuals would become eligible for the matched savings (Bray et al, 2014, 2016). Ultimately, however, fewer than one per cent of Australian IM participants took up the Northern Territory Matched Savings financial education incentive scheme and, when considered alongside other evidence about the ways in which people used the BasicsCard, Bray et al (2016, p 385) reported that the scheme 'had little impact on improving the financial management capabilities of participants'. Overall, they described the matched savings programme as being 'ineffective' (Bray et al, 2016, p 391). Nevertheless, among recipients in the Northern Territory who did take up financial counselling, it tended to be those on voluntary IM who found most benefit (Bray et al, 2014, p 92). Conversely, under Cape York IM, a statutory authority – the Family Responsibilities Commission – can compel individuals to attend financial counselling as part of their 'family responsibilities agreement', which they must abide by if they hope to exit IM (Section 68, *Family Responsibilities Commission Act 2008* [Qld]). They can choose not to follow their agreement, but if they do so they will likely remain on IM (Scott et al, 2018).

Under IM elsewhere in Australia, some exemption applications also require individuals to pass a 'financial vulnerability test', one aspect of which is to show they have attended an 'approved money management course' to support them to 'learn or update financial skills', 'develop a personal budget' and 'stick to the budget or achieve any financial goals' (Australian Government, 2021d). In some Australian IM schemes, there may also be a perception that financial counselling is compulsory, even where it is not. In Bray and colleagues' (2014, p 92) study of IM in the Northern Territory, for example, those who attended financial counselling reported most commonly that they had done so 'because someone had told them to', and nearly 30 per cent said they were instructed to do so by Centrelink. Aside from this, there is very little evaluative evidence of the efficacy of financial education as a supplement to IM in Australia.

In New Zealand, interviews with Youth Service provider employees indicated that some participants demonstrated an improved ability to budget after completing Money Management financial education courses, but others did not show improvement, even after receiving mentoring for several months. A small number of young people subject to New Zealand's IM scheme told us they found value in the financial counselling and support provided through Money Management, despite the mandatory requirements, which many of them disliked. Nevertheless, the reasons given did not necessarily suggest that financial capability had been enhanced. For instance, some participants said that the budgeting course and mentoring that they had undertaken enabled them to better distinguish between 'needs' and 'wants', but several indicated they would still give into their wants if they got the chance. For instance: "[W]e've got to do the six-month of school plus the budgeting course and then the parenting course to jump off [Money Management] … [I] lasted like a couple of days [off Money Management] … I was like, 'nah I can't do this' – because I'm a smoker" (Tui, New Zealand).

The MSD's 2021 evaluation of Money Management reported similar findings, suggesting that *requiring* young people to engage in financial literacy education does not necessarily lead to improved knowledge and skills (Momsen, 2021). Such mandatory requirements have also been found to be an impediment to positive outcomes elsewhere (Kaiser and Menkhoff, 2017). Indeed, many New Zealand IM participants instead came to depend on their Youth Service mentors for assistance in monitoring their quarantined funds. Card balances could not be checked via ATM, and internet access was often unavailable or unaffordable for participants. This lack of access to real-time account details made it difficult for many to manage their money independently and saw some regularly calling their mentors for basic account balance information. As noted, some New Zealand participants said that having redirections in place meant they did not have to worry or think about paying bills, while some mentors spent considerable time ensuring young people subject to Money Management met their obligations to avoid financial sanctions and to gain the financial incentives available in the New Zealand system. This likely did little to improve participants' financial literacy, and in fact led some to become reliant on others to manage their financial matters (as also noted earlier in relation to Australian IM).

Although there is evidence that financial education has been useful for a small number of Australian and New Zealand IM participants, the evidence is clearly very mixed. As discussed later, this accords with the wider evidence concerning financial education, which indicates that education can be helpful for some people while being unhelpful or even counterproductive for others (O'Connell, 2009). Non-attendance at financial literacy courses may also, however, be a result of poor delivery. In both Australia and New Zealand, financial education that occurs alongside IM was initially delivered through third parties, generally not-for-profit service providers. Whether or not service providers are community embedded and led is important in terms of their relevance, but also for establishing the trust and rapport necessary to attract clients. However, despite the disproportionate overrepresentation of Indigenous peoples among those placed on IM, there is no explicit commitment to engaging Indigenous service providers to deliver financial counselling services alongside IM in Australia. The use of Indigenous providers has nevertheless been identified elsewhere as an important way to engage clients and ensure that services are culturally appropriate – see, for example, Moodie and colleagues' (2014) evaluation of an Indigenous-led Australian financial literacy programme. Although some New Zealand Youth Service providers have created in-house budgeting programmes to better meet their clients' needs – most notably by focusing lessons on experiences relevant to young people, and incorporating Māori concepts and cultural protocols – there is no evidence that Māori service providers have been contracted to deliver financial counselling services.

Despite this, the experience of Money Management mentoring in New Zealand was valued by many of the Money Management participants interviewed for this study, and the MSD's evaluation found that providers and participants agreed that budgeting mentoring was far more useful than the management of income and that, if IM was maintained, Youth Service mentors should decide who should be subject to management (Momsen, 2021). In the study presented in this book, Youth Services staff noted how they tried to engage with and to case manage Money Management participants in a non-punitive way – for example, by calling them to remind them about obligations they needed to meet to avoid financial sanctions. This represented a contrast to the compliance-focused and disjointed engagement Australian welfare beneficiaries tend to have with numerous members of Centrelink staff.

In this regard, the New Zealand model presents potential lessons for Australia. Indeed, as street-level bureaucrats, social workers can either maintain or erode the social stigma associated with welfare receipt, and thereby either exacerbate or repair the cultural injury produced through misrecognition (Lipsky, 1980; Lovell, 2007). However, it is this deeper, emancipatory potential of social work which continues to be constrained by the profession's capture by neoliberal objectives and the associated undermining of social workers' access to the time and space they need to develop and sustain meaningful relationships with their clients (Rush and Keenan, 2014). As noted earlier, there is also a need to go beyond thinking of financial literacy as a panacea to economic or social wellbeing:

> 'I've never seen anybody [say] that money is just the problem … most of the time, it's mental health, domestic violence, children with disabilities, disabilities themselves. It's all the other stuff that makes it really difficult for them in their life, not just in their financial life, in their life. The financial part is just a symptom of the rest of it. So you've got to do the holistic— there you go there's a good word.' (Barbara, Playford stakeholder)

In this sense, while financial education may provide benefit to some, there is a continued need for additional holistic, wrap-around supports, as well as broader structural change that would see, for example, higher social security benefit rates (see Chapter 8). As Pollard and colleagues (2020) argue, while financial counsellors can provide assistance, establishing adequate income support payments is a far more effective way to achieve economic security and related wellbeing outcomes. Others have also recognised the importance of integrating financial counselling into broader and multidimensional networks of support, but also the importance of placing social security recipients' experiences in historical and social context – particularly for Indigenous peoples, sole parents and people with a disability (see, for example, Moodie et al, 2014). This would better align with Indigenous wellbeing frameworks, such as 'social and emotional wellbeing', which sees wellbeing as an outcome of health across multiple interrelated domains: body, culture, country (Dudgeon et al, 2017). However, non-Western ontologies tend to run up against financial literacy education schemes, as the following section touches on. The broader evidence base for financial education is also mixed, which raises further questions about the efficacy of such approaches.

The evidence base for, and normative assumptions of, financial literacy education

The integration of financial education alongside IM policies presupposes that it can have beneficial impacts on participants' financial literacy. However, financial literacy is complex, and people likely respond in different ways to educational interventions (O'Connell, 2009, p 4). Overall, the evidence base for financial literacy programmes suggests that their impacts are weak, and it is yet to be exhaustively proven that such education is effective at enhancing financial management outcomes (Williams, 2007; Mandell and

Klein, 2009; O'Connell, 2009; Crossan et al, 2011; Brimble and Blue, 2013; Fernandes et al, 2014; Frijns et al, 2014; Miller et al, 2015; Kaiser and Menkhoff, 2017). For instance, high school financial literacy courses have been found to leave students no more financially literate and with similar financial behaviours to their non-participating peers (Mandell and Klein, 2009). Furthermore, in a systematic review of the literature on financial literacy education programmes for children and adolescents, Amagir et al (2018) found that while programmes can improve financial attitudes and knowledge, there is very little known about whether this results in changed behaviour; overall, the evidence suggests little or no effect.

Meta-analyses of financial education programmes for adults have also shown they tend to have few positive impacts on financial behaviours, and that, at best, highly targeted education aimed at specific behaviours might have a small benefit (Fernandes et al, 2014). Another meta-analysis by Miller et al (2015) found that financial education can positively impact some aspects of financial behaviour, such as saving, but has no effect on others, such as by reducing loan defaults. More recently, Kaiser and Menkhoff (2017) found that financial education had a significant effect on financial literacy and behaviours. However, they also found that *mandatory* education is less effective, and that financial education is least effective for those on low incomes (Fernandes et al, 2014; Kaiser and Menkhoff, 2017). While these results are mixed, even less is known about the efficacy of financial literacy education for minority populations, such as Indigenous Australians and New Zealand Māori, though smaller studies have shown some potential for successful outcomes when culturally appropriate approaches are taken (for example, Moodie et al, 2014).

Willis (2009, p 419) argued that overall, 'the necessary predicate belief in the efficacy of FLE [Financial Literacy Education] is largely based on ideology rather than evidence', ideology whereby individuals are framed as poor money managers while access to sufficient incomes or jobs is ignored (see also Willis, 2008). The targeting and pedagogy of financial education may provide a partial explanation for these mixed results, but there are also other factors, such as cognitive biases that are relatively resistant to change, a rapidly changing financial marketplace which can quickly render financial knowledge outdated and obsolete, and the influences of different social norms amongst family members and peers (Willis, 2008; Arnold and Rhyne, 2016). It is also the case that, in contrast to continued characterisations of humans as *homo economicus*, 'most individuals do not behave rationally and predictably when it comes to spending money, undermining efforts to educate them', or at least undermining the assumed link between *knowledge* and *behaviour* (Williams, 2007; Brimble and Blue, 2013, p 208). Additionally, and perhaps even more importantly, financial decision-making is merely one factor that influences overall economic security; it is also critical to consider structural factors that shape individual economic outcomes. The normative assumptions embedded in financial literacy education can also render it more or less useful for some groups, though these assumptions are rarely problematised in public discourse.

Arthur (2016, p 115) argues that strong and growing public emphasis on financial literacy education shifts attention away from structural impediments to poverty alleviation, teaching 'the populace that financial insecurity is an individual problem requiring individuals to work harder and invest their financial and human capital better'. Similarly, Pinto and Coulson (2011, p 75) warn that financial literacy education tends to be promoted as a 'gender-blind, neutral construct … [insinuating] that individual economic prosperity simply boils down to choice'. However, the economic insecurity that is disproportionately experienced by some groups (for example, indigenous populations, women), arises from structural factors such as the ongoing effects of colonisation, institutional discrimination, and others (as also described in Chapters 1 and 2).

Narrowly framing economic insecurity as being a result of financial illiteracy is not only incorrect, but perpetuates the myth of meritocracy while distracting attention from the need for collective, structural responses to poverty (Arthur, 2016). As Willis (2009, p 419) argued, the pursuit of financial literacy education, as opposed to alternative public policies that 'might improve consumer financial conditions', represents an important potential opportunity cost that demands more careful and critical consideration. There are also ethical and moral implications that arise from (what is often) an ahistorical and decontextualised focus on human capital development in financial literacy schemes. In Australia, for example, there is deep irony in a settler state which demands that Indigenous peoples find their own way out of poverty through financial literacy; a poverty that has its roots in the theft of Indigenous lands, from which settlers continue to extract significant and disproportionate wealth in the absence of treaty and/or compensation. In addition, however, financial literacy education contains embedded normative assumptions that may render it at least partly, or even entirely, obsolete, and counterproductive for some.

Arguing that 'literacy' (financial, educational, health, and so on) has become a significant recent trope in policy making, Bacchi and Goodwin (2016, p 92) call for critically questioning its social construction and impacts: 'While the term 'literacy' may sound benign and indeed worthwhile, it is important to reflect on what goes into its making and with what effects.' Indeed, the notion of financial literacy carries implicit value propositions, reifying lives that are governed by the market, while rendering other ways of being as holding deficit value, as markers of 'illiteracy'. Financial literacy is frequently linked with 'empowerment' discourses (Williams, 2007). The OECD (2017, p 23), for example, claims that 'addressing women's financial literacy [is] … a way to improve their financial empowerment, opportunities and wellbeing'. Empowerment, as the OECD understands it, narrowly refers to the erosion of knowledge and skill barriers that might prevent market participation (Williams, 2007) and, thus, financial literacy promises to empower individuals to pursue freedom within and through the market, while delegitimising freedom *from* the market (Rose, 1999). However, the reality for many women is that the market itself is often a *dis*empowering domain, frequently experienced as a site of discrimination and still regularly failing to recognise and value non-market care work that continues to be disproportionately undertaken by women worldwide. This situation has worsened under COVID-19, especially where schools and child care centres have temporarily closed (Gausman, 2020; Power, 2020). Thus, an alternative to empowering women towards economic participation through financial literacy 'upskilling' would be to ensure a fairer marketplace that properly values women's work and addresses structural barriers to their engagement, or otherwise reconfigures the capitalist market structure itself to suit (rather than ignore) women's needs (Bacchi, 1999; Fraser, 2013). A similar argument can be made with regard to people living with disability, for whom a combination of factors – such as high costs of medical care and barriers to employment – mean that they also experience poverty disproportionately. Similarly, however, no amount of financial upskilling will 'solve' this issue without concomitant attention being paid to methods of removing barriers to employment and ensuring adequate social supports are in place.

The reification of capitalist market engagement under financial literacy discourses is also highly problematic in settler colonial contexts, such as Australia and New Zealand, where settler norms typically run counter to Indigenous ontologies. For instance, prior to colonisation, Māori and Indigenous Australians participated in economies that were 'non-monetary, subsistence and collectivist … [depending] entirely on the land and the natural environment' (Houkamau et al, 2019, p 143; see also Brimble and Blue, 2013). In many cases, Indigenous Australians and New Zealanders still exist and live in intercultural domains, straddling hybridised economies that mix both market and customary ways of living (Altman, 2011). Like people in many other non-Western cultures, Māori consider that 'monetary obligations to the *whānau* [extended family] … at times take precedence over household obligations' (Houkamau et al, nd, p 3). Furthermore, cultural demands for reciprocity, where 'people tend to share their money with their families and communities, rather than save it, and rely on reciprocity when they are in need', also tends to be highly prioritised (Galicki, 2020, p 23). As Galicki (2020) reports, this can mean that Māori and Pasifika people are less likely to set funds aside for an emergency. But this is not 'poor budgeting' or 'poor financial literacy', instead it reflects obligations based in cultural practice – *tikānga Māori* (Wood, 2016), or for Indigenous Australians, a 'moral economy' where the sharing of resources with extended families and kin is crucial to upholding social norms (Altman, 2011; Brimble and Blue, 2013).

Culturally determined demand sharing can also be a vital form of resistance for Indigenous peoples – a means of reasserting the importance of collectivist ontologies against a backdrop of hegemonic individualism (Altman, 2018). Communitarian objectives such as these are, however, incompatible with policy narratives about financial literacy, including those that position IM as supporting the ends of improved literacy (and behaviour), as a route out of poverty. In this sense, financial literacy education itself may not only be incommensurate with non-Western ontologies, but it may also be counterproductive and harmful – an argument that has also been made about IM itself (see, for example, Bielefeld, 2015; Humpage, 2016). Overall, therefore, even if financial education is beneficial to some, either as a supplement to voluntary IM or on its own, it is by no means a panacea for economic insecurity.

Conclusion

While these research data show that there is significant benefit in moving away from compulsory IM schemes, whether voluntary IM and/or greater investment in financial education offer good alternatives is debatable. A core benefit of voluntary IM is that it returns at least some agency to welfare recipients, enabling them to decide whether IM would or would not be useful to them. This would also mean that the harmful impacts of compulsory IM schemes would be removed. Nevertheless, continuing to invest in any IM scheme, whether voluntary or not, may mean missing opportunities to fund other evidence-based social support strategies that could offer greater chance of alleviating economic insecurity (as discussed in the final chapter).

Investment in financial education may also provide benefit to some, though the evidence base regarding financial education schemes shows that they can be of limited use, or they can even be harmful and counterproductive. This potential is particularly high for Indigenous peoples, who are overrepresented in IM, but whose ontological positioning tends not to align with individualistic Western understandings of wealth accumulation, which are embedded in both IM policy and financial education programming. The potential is also high for other groups who tend to disproportionately experience economic insecurity, such as sole mothers and people with disability. In such circumstances, those who do not conform are regularly labelled financially 'illiterate', which can then be mobilised as a justification for further paternalism to encourage obedience to the market.

A recurrent theme in this chapter and, indeed, throughout this book, is the tension between structure and agency that is so well exemplified in IM policy and practice. Indeed, a key thread that also links the two alternative options explored in this chapter is that both perpetuate a focus on individual knowledge and behaviour, without addressing structure as a key cause of economic insecurity. If we are serious about alleviating economic insecurity, however, then equal attention must be given to both structure and agency. For instance, as Arthur (2016, p 121) explained in his essay on financial literacy education:

> Any ethical response to economic insecurity would not teach how to improve one's individual position within a system that privileges economic growth over individual security but would stress that our ethical obligations to others extend beyond what the market deems possible, support critical reflection on our implication in the reproduction of capitalism's structural insecurity and enable us to create with others a more just, secure world. (Arthur, 2016, p 121)

This argument is becoming even more relevant, as experiences of economic insecurity continue to worsen in Australia, New Zealand and elsewhere. The continued rise of insecure work and growth of a global precariat class affects both material and psychological wellbeing, making it increasingly difficult to find a stable income and reap the psychological benefits often associated with work (Standing, 2011; New Zealand Council of Trade Unions, 2013; Carney and Stanford, 2018). Other global trends, such as the job-displacement impacts of climate change and the far-reaching economic impacts of the COVID-19 pandemic, have also worsened economic insecurity for many; especially for groups who already suffer from entrenched labour market inequalities.

Rather than devising technical fixes that operate within the parameters of the economic and social structures that have caused severe poverty in the first place, there is instead a need to critically engage with and challenge those structures. This would mean, for example, resisting discourses and practices that depoliticise poverty as something that occurs because of poor individual decision-making or behaviours, as is so often the case under highly conditional welfare policies such as IM. Turning greater attention towards ensuring adequate income support payments, decent employment and training opportunities, and accessible social services would be a better starting point for creating healthy, economically secure and socially inclusive communities. The next chapter builds on these ideas, considering how the role of social policy might be recalibrated from the current conditionality paradigm to instead produce more ethical and effective responses to economic insecurity.

8

Recalibrating social security and reimagining work

Introduction

As social uncertainty and economic precarity grow, it is time to rethink the obligations of governments, particularly in regard to the ends and means of social security policy and meaningful employment. The global COVID-19 pandemic has given impetus to the 'utopian demand' (Weeks, 2011) for a fundamental reset of societal and economic goals. Addressing the inadequacy of income support payments, ensuring decent employment and training opportunities, valuing all forms of work, and ensuring affordable housing and accessible social services is arguably a better starting point for cultivating healthy and economically secure communities than persisting with punitive conditionality.

The final chapter in the book has three key aims. First, the chapter emphasises the key lessons from the rollout of CIM in Australia and New Zealand, from both an empirical and ethical point of view. Second, the chapter connects these findings with the broader social, economic and environmental context that is providing the catalyst for a reset of social security policy and practice. Third, the chapter points a way forward on social security policy, based on first principles, which would help reorientate policy settings and the public discourse around income security and the markers of social citizenship.

Bottom-up perspectives on the conditionality narrative

There are strong views on all sides of the CIM policy debate in Australia and New Zealand. There is little disagreement across the political spectrum about having a social security system focused on alleviating poverty and promoting participation in social and economic activities. There is, however, a great deal of disagreement about the best ways to achieve this goal. The extent to which the state should intervene to limit the freedoms of its citizenry is particularly contentious – especially if those limitations are not universally applied, if the reported benefits are contested, or where there is clear evidence that the policies are in fact causing material and psycho-social harm.

Chapters 4 to 7 of this book have illustrated that the evidence in support of continuing with CIM is weak. The research presented in this book is certainly not the first to suggest that this set of policy measures requires a fundamental rethink. What this study has attempted to ensure, however, is that the voices of those targeted by CIM are prominent in what is reported about the material effects and the lived impacts of the policy. The hope is that amplifying these voices will unsettle the dominant 'truths' about people on income support payments and by extension the political rationale for CIM.

Chapters 4 to 7 highlighted the hidden costs of CIM for individuals and communities in Australia and New Zealand. The deep sense of shame and stigma, the daily anxiety of not knowing whether the CIM card will work, the administrative bungles that leave people with their rights and needs unmet, and the restrictions on basic financial freedoms and rights that most citizens take for granted all add up to a heavy individual burden, with few benefits. The costs of conditional welfare are not just economic and practical, they are also personal and social, getting to the very core of how people see themselves. CIM is a policy that, for the most part, renders welfare recipients as 'failed subjects' – mere spectators to defining their own needs (Sennett, 2003). These symbolic costs must be recognised in formal evaluations of CIM, as policy design and testing is never a simple technical exercise in ascertaining 'what works'.

Policy evaluation requires nuance and a willingness to listen to what people convey about what works and for whom, under what circumstances. It is also necessary to give due consideration to alternative policy ideas, especially those put forward from people living in these communities, who are the real experts on how to address the challenges faced. Not providing genuine feedback loops and bottom-up perspectives means the mistakes of the past will be repeated and harms will go unchecked. Policymakers have an ethical obligation to engage in high quality listening and reflection if they want to act in ways that are genuinely in the interests of meeting individual and community needs (Miller, 2012).

In a distributional sense, social justice is not simply about how fairly economic resources are distributed across different groups in the wider polity; it is also about how the burden of active citizenship is calibrated across civil society. In her study of welfare conditionality, Patrick (2017) makes the point that more should be done to consider the burden of welfare reform on wider social security infrastructure in the mixed economy of welfare, including the pressure placed on non-profits, state and local governments to mitigate the 'tough love' approach of national governments.

We need an approach to policy design that is informed by the best available evidence. As Chapter 7 highlighted, there are many factors that contribute to financial wellbeing, such as having an ability to save, and low levels of personal debt. Psychological and emotional factors also have an impact, with research indicating that those with responsibility for day-to-day management of their money have higher levels of mental health and wellbeing (Kempson et al, 2017). This finding is not surprising, so it is disappointing that these recognised connections between mental health and social identity, self-determination and financial wellbeing, are missing from the dominant policy debate about the merits of CIM in Australia and New Zealand.

What these arguments about policy evaluation highlight is that there are multiple ways in which we might determine whether conditionality achieves its goals, depending, of course, on how these goals are defined. The goals of CIM have shifted over time from preventing child abuse and neglect, to promoting better financial management, to reducing community crime and opening pathways to employment. On any one of these measures there is very little demonstrable evidence that the policy has achieved its ends. In addition to these instrumental goals there are also normative frameworks that provide a benchmark against which we can judge whether extreme forms of welfare conditionality are ultimately beneficial for individuals, communities and society as a whole.

As shown in Chapter 5, it is possible to assess CIM within a rights-based framework and determine that CIM undermines economic, social, individual and procedural rights. From a utilitarian perspective, these individual rights-based concerns could – at least theoretically – be set aside if we collectively determined that the policy ultimately achieved societal benefits such as reduced poverty, better school retention, or improved population health and community wellbeing. However, there is no compelling evidence that CIM has delivered such benefits. A more fundamental question is whether individual and societal benefits might be achieved through unconditional forms of income support. The second part of this chapter returns to this question, as government responses to COVID-19 in Australia and New Zealand have provided a natural experiment on the benefits of more adequate levels of income support combined with less conditionality. For now, the focus turns to how we might determine whether welfare conditionality is ethical.

At the lower end of an ethical standard, the sort of 'hassle and help' approach envisaged by Lawrence Mead (1997) – which follows the logic that receiving state income support by definition generates obligations for the citizen – could be said to have moral virtue. According to this line of thinking, the state fulfils its end of the social citizenship bargain by providing material benefit in the form of income support; it is therefore only fair that citizens must be subjected to some level of accountability through pre-defined actions that demonstrate personal effort and moral worth. A middle ground on the ethics of conditionality would expect that coercive state interventions should generally have positive social or individual outcomes. The moral obligation in this scenario is on the state to demonstrate that its interventions do more good than harm, or do no harm. A higher ethical standard would insist that economic and social rights are inalienable and should not be compromised by state actions that unduly restrict self-determination and autonomy.

While many western countries have accepted the premise that political and civil rights are non-negotiable, there are very few countries (if any) that treat social, economic and cultural rights with the same ethical reverence. Ultimately, all national governments must grapple with political and policy choices about what they consider to be ethically responsible and publicly legitimate. As such, there is no universally accepted ethical standard for determining whether conditionality is justifiable. In short, context matters.

With respect to CIM in Australia and New Zealand, it is clear that the ethical standard on whether conditionality is warranted needs to be interrogated. There is an interdependence between ethical reasoning and empirical evidence, which pertains directly to the political justifiability of conditionality: if no added value can be shown to be associated with the conditional element of a given intervention then it can be considered neither efficacious nor ethical (Watts and Fitzpatrick, 2018). Further, as Watts and Fitzpatrick (2018, p 152) write, unless there are compelling answers to the following questions in relation to the design of a given welfare conditionality programme then it is hard to justify moving to implementation:

1. Does the behaviour change incentivised by the proposed conditionality *align with the ultimate societal goals* sought?
2. Is the conditional approach underpinned by a *plausible theory of change*?
3. Is there compelling evidence of the *effectiveness in practice* of the conditional approach in bringing about the desired behavioural changes?
4. Does the conditional element of the programme bring *added value* over and above alternative, non-coercive means of seeking the desired change?
5. Are the techniques of conditionality *proportionate*, in other words, do they deploy the minimum level of 'power over' people commensurate with achieving the relevant goals?
6. Is the conditional intervention *cost-effective* relative to the available alternatives?

In the case of Australia and New Zealand's CIM policies, the answers to these questions would indicate that CIM is not cost-effective or ethical.

It is important to acknowledge that this book is not advocating an all or nothing approach in assessing the legitimacy of welfare conditionality from an ethical perspective. Where citizens have had a genuine opportunity to exercise agency and informed consent, certain forms of income restriction can theoretically be justified. If some form of IM is to continue in Australia or New Zealand, the findings of this research suggest there is sufficient support among participants and community stakeholders for exploring ways to implement a voluntary scheme, dovetailed with wrap-around social services and evidence-based financial capability education and training. Such a scheme would need to be co-designed with people on income support and reflect the social context of their lives, including their varying contexts and communities – particularly for people living in remote Aboriginal and Torres Strait Islander communities. A voluntary-only IM policy would undoubtedly be less polarising and problematic than the compulsory catch-all scheme in operation now.

It is important to recognise other pressing systemic issues integral to assessing the ethical foundations of a social security system, such as the adequacy of income support payments. In both Australia and New Zealand, the standard rate of payment for unemployment benefits leaves many people below the poverty line, even when rent assistance and other supplementary payments are added to household income (Welfare Expert Advisory Group, 2019; Child Poverty Action Group, 2021; Whiteford and Bradbury, 2021). Maintaining benefits at low levels in relatively rich countries makes a mockery of the public discourse of a 'social safety net', given that a large proportion of working age adults on income support payments are left in poverty. A 2019 OECD analysis found that, when rent assistance was included, the rate of payment for someone on unemployment benefit in Australia was the lowest in the OECD, coming in at 39 per cent of the previous wage compared to the OECD average of 68 per cent. New Zealand was not far behind, placing third lowest and well behind France, Germany and the UK (Whiteford, 2019). Whiteford and Bradbury (2021) has argued that the small increase in the unemployment benefit of $50 per fortnight from April 2021 will move Australia's position compared with other OECD countries from the lowest to the second lowest, just ahead of Greece. It seems unlikely New Zealand's position will radically change either, leaving both countries less generous than most in the OECD group.

A spotlight was thrown on the inadequacy of income support payments in the early stages of the COVID-19 pandemic, and for the first time in decades some governments responded by lifting the rate through temporary supplements. Not only did this expenditure provide a real lift in people's living standards, it also served as a natural experiment on whether there could be benefits for individuals and communities without resorting to coercive conditional means of welfare provisioning. For these reasons, it is worth reflecting on the path-breaking possibilities arising from government responses to the pandemic, as well as the material impacts of a significant increase in social security spending and the suspension of various forms of welfare conditionality, as evidenced in Australia, New Zealand and other advanced economies.

Rethinking social security, value and the drivers of change

Global pandemics reveal much about the resilience of supply chains, labour markets, national health care and the adequacy of the social security system. Put under pressure, systems, markets and institutions can falter or break down completely. In these situations, citizens invariably turn to governments as the ultimate risk managers. During the COVID-19 pandemic, some national governments have been found wanting in their response, while others have stepped up and demonstrated real leadership and a genuine commitment to protecting vulnerable workers, households, and others at the margins of society.

In order to understand the profound impacts that income support levels have on the wellbeing of individuals and societies, it is worth briefly reviewing Australia and New Zealand's markedly different responses to COVID-19. As Arundhati Roy (2020, np) eloquently argues in an essay on the pandemic, it is important to exercise moral imagination in the midst of a global crisis:

> Our minds are still racing back and forth, longing for a return to 'normality', trying to stitch our future to our past and refusing to acknowledge the rupture. But the rupture exists. And in the midst of this terrible despair, it offers us a chance to rethink the doomsday machine we have built for ourselves. Nothing could be worse than a return to normality. Historically, pandemics have forced humans to break with the past and imagine their world anew. This one is no different. It is a portal, a gateway between one world and the next.

The revaluation Arundhati Roy proposes seeks to stimulate new objectifications of our subjective activity both in our social security systems and in how work is valued, organised and remunerated. The pandemic and the ensuing health, social and economic crisis it sparked have begun a reconsideration of the value of forms of work that were previously underpaid and neglected, and have been newly revealed as central to society's subsistence and reproduction. The struggle going forward is for our forms of value to accurately capture the new status of those workers classed as 'essential' in the crisis, spanning everything from retail to waste, elderly care to education (Pitts, 2021, np). This revaluation can also be extended to those reliant on social security payments for their income, as income support recipients are also parents, volunteers, employees. The dominant frame in media and political discourse about social security recipients is that they demonstrate flawed decision-making, irresponsibility, and a deficit of active agency (Wright, 2016). The COVID-19 pandemic presents an opportunity to challenge this discourse.

Unfortunately, New Zealand did not take up this challenge. The Labour-led government permanently increased main benefit rates by NZ$25 per week in April 2020 in response to COVID-19 but few recipients received the full amount because this increased income saw supplementary assistance decrease or public housing rent increase (Humpage and Moore, 2021). The Winter Energy Payment was temporarily doubled and work obligations and medical certificate requirements for those experiencing disability or illness were also paused. However, the Labour-led government's main response to growing unemployment and underemployment was to introduce a new COVID-19 Income Relief Payment for those who lost their jobs due to Covid-19 between March and October 2020. This untaxed benefit was paid at NZ$490 per week (if previously working full-time – or $250 per week part-time) for 12 weeks, making it considerably higher than the existing Job Seeker Support ($250 per week after tax). Moreover, recipients of the COVID-19 Income Relief Payment were not subject to work or other obligations (which can lead to financial sanctions) and had more generous eligibility conditions, such as a partner being able to earn up to $2,000 a week before the payment is reduced (Work and Income, 2020d). New employment centres and online employment tools were also available to COVID-19 Income Relief Payment recipients, while main benefit recipients could access only those available through Work and Income (RNZ, 2020). Thus, the timing and cause of their joblessness resulted in benefit recipients potentially having very different experiences depending on which type of income support they could access. These moves enhanced, rather than weakened discourses of social security benefits as being less 'deserving' than others and there is evidence that the introduction of this 'two-tier' system, which the government regarded as a step towards developing an unemployment insurance system in New Zealand for the first time, had a negative impact on the mental health of existing benefit recipients (Humpage and Moore, 2021).

In Australia, conditionality requirements were suspended during 2020, and income support recipients were provided with an additional lift in their rate of payment, which is similar to how a number of other countries responded. The increase in payments was substantial. In early 2020, the Australian Government moved to limit the spread of COVID-19, which caused unemployment and underemployment and led to an increase in the number of income support recipients. In March 2020, the Australian Government announced two packages of measures to support those needing assistance which included two $750 lump sum Economic Support payments to some social security and veterans' payment recipients and a Coronavirus Supplement of $550 per fortnight to nearly all income support recipients. Improved access to income support through changed eligibility criteria and a waiver of the asset tests and some waiting periods for certain payments were also introduced. The full supplement remained in place until September 2020, which is when the supplement was reduced to $250 per fortnight, eventually being phased out in February 2021.

The economic impact of COVID-19, combined with the measures to expand eligibility for social security, saw the number of people in receipt of the main income support payments for the unemployed (JobSeeker Payment and Youth Allowance) double from around 820,000 in December

2019 to around 1.64 million at the end of May 2020 (Klapdor and Giuliano, 2020). At the end of June 2020, a total of around 2.2 million social security payment recipients were receiving the Coronavirus Supplement (Klapdor and Giuliano, 2020). The total cost saw the social security budget increase by about 20 per cent. Despite calls from the business sector, economic think tanks and welfare peak bodies for a significant permanent increase in the rate of unemployment benefits, the Australian Government settled on a permanent increase of only $50 a fortnight from 1 April 2020, well below the amount needed to lift income support recipients out of poverty. In the end, this is somewhat similar to New Zealand's May 2021 benefit payment increases of up to NZ$55 per week to be implemented across two years, with those with children receiving an extra $15 per adult per week. While projected to lift between 19,000 and 33,000 children out of poverty on the after-housing costs measure in 2022/23 as a cost NZ$3.3 billion over four years (Robson, 2021), there is general consensus that these changes are insufficient to provide a liveable income for those living on benefits (Fletcher, 2019; Welfare Expert Advisory Group, 2019; Humpage and Moore, 2021; Child Poverty Action Group, 2021).

Attention also needs to be paid to how people used the additional income and what it meant for their overall wellbeing, as this provides an indication of what can be achieved without resort to coercive and punitive conditional welfare measures. Here, there is more data available in Australia than New Zealand. In terms of reducing poverty, an important goal of any social security system, the Coronavirus Supplement reduced the number of households in poverty by about 32 per cent in Australia as of June 2020 (Phillips et al, 2020). An ACOSS (2020) study of the impact of the Coronavirus Supplement reported that, of 955 respondents, 65 per cent said it was easier to pay rent or move to safer accommodation, 69 per cent said they could pay for medication, 75 per cent said they could pay their bills, and 83 per cent said they were eating healthier and not skipping meals. In a separate survey of 744 service providers, 81 per cent stated that the Coronavirus Supplement had had a positive effect on service users, and 72 per cent reported a positive effect from the suspension of mutual obligations (ACOSS, 2020). Such research highlights the importance of providing adequate income support and removing strict mutual obligations.

In other research that has mapped the economic benefits of the Coronavirus Supplement, Deloitte Access Economics (2020) estimates that returning the unemployment benefit to the pre-pandemic rate would bleed $31.3 billion from the Australian economy and cost the equivalent of 145,000 full-time jobs over the next two years. The report claimed that removing the Coronavirus Supplement would not make a material difference to the future path of Australian debt, but doing so without a plan to address the reduction in incomes would make a material difference to the economy

(Deloitte Access Economics, 2020). The Coronavirus Supplement also led to the sorts of beneficial behavioural outcome in individuals that are frequently attributed to conditional welfare measures. Academics at the Australian National University and Swinburne University undertook an online survey of 146 social security recipients in Australia to determine how people were spending the additional supplement, how they were using their time, and what the impact was on their subjective wellbeing. The key findings from this study included that:

1. The Coronavirus Supplement and suspension of mutual obligations improved respondents' physical and mental health and contributed to their overall wellbeing.
2. The changes enabled people to turn their attention away from day-to-day survival and towards envisioning and working towards a more economically secure future for themselves and their dependants.
3. The supplement and suspension of mutual obligations increased respondents' engagement in other economic activities.
4. The supplement and suspension of mutual obligations allowed people to better engage in many forms of unpaid productive work, including care work and community support.
5. These policy changes meant that the pandemic was a period of reprieve for many people receiving social security payments due to the easing of financial stress, scrutiny, and uncertainty. This is very different from normative characterisations of the pandemic and its associated lockdowns, which were experienced as a period of great stress and uncertainty by many people. (Klein et al, 2021, p 6)

In an extension of the kinds of crime metaphors used to stigmatise social benefit recipients under IM discourses, some politicians and other public figures claimed that greater influxes of cash with the Coronavirus Supplement had increased crime in some remote Indigenous communities because of presumed greater expenditure on alcohol (Roberts, 2020; Pearson in Taylor, 2020). To the contrary, however, emerging studies show that crime has either remained stable or reduced in these communities, at least in part due to the alleviation of general strain brought about by the relaxation of mutual obligations and increases in income, which has enabled greater expenditure on food and basic goods (Markham and Kerins, 2020; Staines and Zahnow, 2021).

New Zealand research based on a national survey and interviews with Sole Parent Support and Supported Living Payment recipients found similar findings in terms of improved food security, financial wellbeing and greater autonomy (Humpage and Neuwelt-Kearns, 2020; Humpage and Moore, 2021). Such research presents a counter-narrative to the government's dominant discourse that a low rate of payment and conditions are necessary to compel people to engage in job-seeking behaviours and spending on essential goods and services for improved physical health and wellbeing. As Klein et al (2021, p 40) note:

> Punitive welfare and mutual obligation settings are particularly problematic because they not only overlook unpaid care work and social reproduction more broadly, but punish people for engaging in this work. … This goes to a major and enduring flaw in Australian social security; its inability to recognize various productive activities people undertake – including unpaid care work which is largely undertaken by women. People receiving social security are accused of being dependent on welfare, but actually the economy and society are dependent on their unpaid labour. During the COVID-19 pandemic, they worked to educate their children when the schools were closed, looked after other people in the community, and participated in self-care and advocacy.

Findings from studies on the impact of additional income also illustrate what improvements are possible in the lives of income support recipients when there is a political will to act decisively and effectively. In contrast to the evidence from the multiple evaluations of CIM the increase in payments associated with the COVID-19 response and the temporary suspension of mutual obligation has meant that people have been able to exercise self-determination and make responsible choices. For instance, New Zealand social security recipients told how the doubling of the Winter Energy Payment (an extra weekly cash payment over the winter months that aims to assist with heating costs) enabled them to live with less stress because they could use this money how they wished, with some opting to pay down debt or pay outstanding expenses unrelated to heating (Humpage and Moore, 2021). We can conclude that, if governments want people to be responsible and make the right choices, they need to extend both trust and responsibility. The social experiment enabled by temporarily increasing benefit incomes shows that most people want to improve their lives. Part of what holds them back from doing so is insufficient income and income volatility and a social security system that frames unemployment in terms of personal deficiencies, rather than a structural problem of demand and supply where there are not enough jobs for everyone.

The reset required would take an alternative framing and policy direction, one that advances social security as a fundamental economic right, builds capabilities and addresses systemic drivers of disadvantage (Klein et al, 2021). Major reform is necessary to ensure social security systems are fit for purpose in the twenty-first century, particularly in a world where employment has become a less reliable source of rights, income and belonging. There is still time to ensure we don't collectively waste the opportunity presented by the crisis, but that time is running out and there are increasing signs national governments are favouring a reboot, rather than a reset. Most major social policy developments in Australia and elsewhere result from a crisis of one form or another (Esping-Andersen, 2002). Exogenous shocks, such as war and depression, led to welfare state expansion in the twentieth century and a fundamental recognition that unemployment was not the result of individual failing. This sentiment was again being expressed in the context of the COVID-19 global pandemic. However, the acknowledgement that unemployment can be structurally determined remains situated firmly within the 'unprecedented' nature of the pandemic, meaning the policy response is also seen as 'extreme' and by definition temporary by the national government.

In May 2020, for example, the Australian Prime Minister, in his National Press Club address, warned against the COVID-19 budgetary measures lasting too long, since they served as an "emergency response" and that eventually "you've got to get your economy out of ICU [the intensive care unit]", lest the economy get "too accustomed" to the "medication" (Office of the Prime Minister [OPM], 2020). Such metaphors situate the government's Keynesian intervention within the public health discourse and outside the usual fiscal management. Even in April 2020 there were public statements being made about workers refusing to work while on wage subsidies, and the Prime Minister invoked anecdotal evidence that the unemployed were inhibited from engaging in job search because the payment was too high (Kehoe, 2020; Waters, 2020), stating: "Getting the JobKeeper [wage subsidy] phase-out correctly balanced with JobSeeker (Coronavirus Supplement) is critical because the objective must be for Australians to see the value in earning a livelihood" (Kehoe, 2020). This echoed the New Zealand government's 'deserving versus undeserving' trope, found in the persistent distinction between existing benefit recipients and the 'newly jobless' who 'had little or no previous interaction with MSD services who may be experiencing significant economic hardship for the first time' (MSD, 2020, p 24) to justify the COVID-19 Income Relief Payment.

Rather than presenting an opportunity to imagine other relations between work and welfare, the Australian government has categorised the policy response to COVID-19 as extraordinary and unsustainable (Morrison, 2020), while New Zealand plans to build an unemployment insurance system that privileges those with marketable skills and social capital by paying them at a higher rate than other unemployed people. In both cases, the assumptions about unemployment as a problem of the individual, irrespective of labour market conditions and social and political factors, has been a persistent feature of the political discourse during the pandemic. However, there is still a degree of hope among many in the relevant research and policy communities that what has been exposed about the inadequacy of social security payments, as well as the uneven labour market and economic recovery will lead to a new normal – a future state better than the present state.

What would a fundamental reset look like?

The COVID-19 pandemic has exposed the weaknesses and imitations of the labour market in Australia and New Zealand and reignited debates about the future of work and whether it is politically possible and technically feasible to loosen the tight coupling between income and labour. The way the labour market distributes rewards and recognition to people depends on a whole range of arbitrary arrangements, including occupational barriers and the sorts of work that receive compensation. Being a parent is usually unpaid, yet it is vital to the operation of the system. Coronavirus has highlighted the arbitrariness of these arrangements. Entire industries, such as tourism and hospitality, have been devastated. The idea that workers get what they deserve has again been exposed as misguided. All of these factors highlight the need for a rethink of labourist attitudes and the professed sanctity of human labour.

In Australia and New Zealand, as in other OECD countries, there have been calls for more far-reaching reforms to provide greater economic security and real freedoms. Some of the more prominent proposals include universal basic income (UBI) and universal basic services (UBS). A UBI consists of regular payments made to individuals to provide an economic floor to alleviate poverty, spur economic growth and generate entrepreneurial activity. A UBI conceptualises risk and security as two sides of the same coin. If we want people to experiment with new forms of income generation in a changing labour market and undertake all forms of work (both paid and unpaid), then we need to provide them with a basic level of economic security so they can take calculated risks and combine economic activities without facing a price premium on how they use their time. UBI proposals encourage a public discussion about the need for a new politics of time in which we collectively see money and time as a matter of social justice in the sense of a good that is unevenly distributed. Some households have considerable temporal autonomy, and other households, particularly those with sole parents, have very little discretionary time to pursue activities that are personally valued, or activities that contribute to community wellbeing, such as volunteering. A UBI recognises all forms of work, not just labour.

National and global advocacy for UBI has intensified in the context of the pandemic. Some countries have implemented basic income schemes in the face of COVID-19. The largest scheme in terms of scope and coverage is the basic income introduced in Spain in 2020, which came amid the growing economic hardship experienced by households. The measure, which is expected to cost an annual three billion euros is aimed at ending extreme poverty, which affects about 1.6 million adults in Spain. The scheme will guarantee an income of €462 a month for an adult living alone, while for families there would be an additional €139 per person, whether adult or child, up to a maximum of €1,015 euros per household. The scheme is not universal, and carries conditions in the form of job search, so it falls short of a more fully fledged, unconditional UBI. What is important about the initiative is that it is permanent and it is national (Donaghy, 2020). There is a lot to learn from these social policy experiments. It is interesting to note, however, that governments in Australia and New Zealand remain largely uninterested in the lessons of these trials and experiments. Australia instead continues to pour millions into extending conditional IM trials and evaluations of those trials, and New Zealand has ignored research indicating IM does not work (Humpage, 2018; Momsen, 2021).

Based on the same principle of universalism as a UBI, UBS provides access to de-commodified forms of health, education and other services to meet social needs. A UK proposal on UBS includes access to health care, education, democracy, legal services, shelter, food, transport and information (Social Prosperity Network, 2017). The UK report suggests that a UBS and a UBI could co-exist, though they also acknowledge that a UBS is a cheaper option than a full UBI. The academic literature also points to the tension between UBS and UBI. On one hand, some libertarian proponents of UBI are strongly critical of UBS on the basis that they believe it is paternalistic and that decisions about what constitutes basic and essential needs should be left to individuals themselves, not the government (Ackerman and Alstott, 2006). On the other hand, some of the most prominent advocates for UBS, such as Coote (2019), are critical of UBI because they think that it will, in practice, reinforce individualistic consumerism and reliance on the market.

A discussion about what constitutes UBS is also warranted, as is the need to be careful to distinguish the aspiration for collective provisioning and the implementation of universal services. Public services are frequently described as collective, but they do not necessarily feel collective to those who use them. We need to remember that universal public services can mask exclusionary practices, as many classic and contemporary studies of street-level bureaucracy have shown (Lipsky, 2010). Whether front-line public servants see themselves as agents of the state or agents of the citizen can depend on many factors, with some of these variables being as fickle as whether someone is well mannered or has the right appearance in their interactions with front-line public servants (Maynard-Moody and Musheno, 2003). We also need to guard against paternalism when it comes to thinking about solutions to poverty. Poverty is primarily a problem of insufficient cash, not a problem of character (Bregman, 2016).

In New Zealand, the Welfare Expert Advisory Group (2019) has also highlighted the importance of considering housing and adequate social services when rethinking how best to support social security recipients. Drawing on Māori values, it further argued that the New Zealand welfare system should be underpinned by "manaakitanga – caring with dignity and respect; ōhanga – economics; whanaungatanga – treasuring kinship ties and relationships; kotahitanga – unity; takatūtanga – preparedness; kaitiakitanga – guardianship" (WEAG, 2019, p 19). This would require that the design and operation of welfare system, amongst other things, "be person-centred and wellbeing focused", "value whānau and families" and "treat people with dignity, respect, compassion" (WEAG, 2019, p 19) alongside ensuring income adequacy. Our research shows that, without these ethical values driving social security, disrespectful policies like IM can actually diminish wellbeing, challenge family functioning and ignore the person who is affected by the policy.

Other ethical foundations for economic security and real freedom go beyond individual rights to consider the merits of the argument for a rightful share that is divorced from any moral or legal obligation to contribute something in return. Such arguments are based on the idea that the distribution of wealth and other resources is not a result of the efforts of individuals in any one generation. Ferguson (2015) claims that this form of redistribution is a kind of claims-making that involves neither compensation for work, nor an appeal for 'help', but rather a sense of rightful entitlement to an income that is tied neither to labour nor to any sort of disability or incapacity; this claim is based on a due and proper share grounded in nothing more than membership in a national collective. Needless to say, there are still questions about who gets to be included in this national collective. Mays et al (2016) define membership for the purposes of receiving a basic income in terms of permanent residency rather than citizenship, though they also acknowledge that some form of temporary social security payment would need to be retained for asylum seekers and refugees.

The sorts of economic security offered by UBI proposals can also be justified on the basis of resilience, not only in the face of the current pandemic, but also against the increased frequency of extreme weather events linked to climate change, such as floods, droughts and bushfires. There are a host of problems in ensuring money gets to households and individuals in a timely fashion following these catastrophes. These sorts of rationales and policy proposals would take national policy settings in a new direction in a post-COVID recovery. The crisis would this become a catalyst for a reset of our social and cultural norms, as well as our social security policy settings.

In terms of implementation, reputable modelling has shown how countries could afford a UBI, with a mix of carefully calibrated tax reforms (including some temporary taxes such as eco-taxes or automation taxes, and a modest wealth tax), changes to income tax scales, and cashing out of some of the questionable tax benefits that primarily flow to high-income earners (Ingles et al, 2019). Nations could also start with a stepping-stone approach, focusing on introducing a basic income for some sections of the population, such as those in increasingly difficult transitions, including school leavers or older citizens of pre-retirement age, many of whom face discrimination in the labour market. In settler colonial contexts, such as Australia and New Zealand, there are also strong ethical arguments for extending a basic income to Indigenous populations as a first port of call and precursor or complement to fuller reparation packages, which acknowledge and pay some restitution for the ongoing violence and innumerable harms of settler colonialism, including theft of Indigenous lands (Altman and Markham, 2016). Governments could then incrementally expand the coverage. This stepping-stone approach would emphasise the unconditional rather than the universal features of a basic income. The evaluations from the initial rollout could inform additional changes to the scheme as its coverage is expanded. This evidence-informed approach to social security policy would stand in direct contrast to the millions that have now been spent on CIM schemes and which have not proven effective.

A UBI interlocked with UBS may not be the best solution to addressing poverty and precarity. However, these kinds of bold policy concepts are at least getting citizens and experts asking the right questions about redistribution and respectful recognition; about what it would take to design a social security system where there was a high degree of accountability and transparency in decision-making, where the rules were simple and clear, and where the payments provided were adequate to provide genuine security and real freedom in the face of growing uncertainty and precarity. What we have now is a complex, opaque and patchy system of categorial payments that create gaps and poverty traps.

Big policy ideas provide the citizenry with a vision of a better future that can be used to critique the present set of institutional arrangements that are unable to adequately protect against old and new risks communities and individuals face. There are a host of new and emerging risks that income support systems must respond to in the twentieth century, including shifting demographics of age and household formation, increased geographical mobility, income volatility, and new forms of precarious labour associated with changes in technology and environmental risks resulting from climate change. These new risks combined with a traditional set of social security needs to do with sickness, unemployment, disability and care provide a strong moral and practical justification for rethinking the role of social security to ensure it is fit for purpose.

In responding to material poverty and economic uncertainty what is also clear is the need to get past an impoverished moral imagination about what is possible. One of the consequences of the highly conditional turn in social security policy, for example, has been a hollowing out of the meaning of reciprocity and mutual respect. The notion of 'activation' in welfare discourse has come to be defined almost exclusively in terms of citizens' responsibilities, rather than the activation of the nation state (Esping-Andersen, 2002). The extent to which government action is visible has been through controlling and cajoling citizens at the bottom rung of the income scale. Governments have become experts in setting out the obligations of citizens if they are to receive meagre income support payments, while remaining silent on governments' obligations towards citizens, particularly in terms of social and economic rights. This silence has been temporarily interrupted by the COVID-19 pandemic as we have reawakened the seemingly forgotten proposition that, in many areas of need, governments could in fact be the risk managers of first rather than last resort.

Conclusion

In the final analysis, the research presented in this book has shown that CIM undermines rather than supports the stated policy objectives of creating more autonomous, healthy, financially independent individuals who are able to transition into employment. As has been argued elsewhere, and is again highlighted in the present study, the core challenge for those arbitrarily placed on CIM is not managing money, but instead a lack of cash to pay for essential goods and services. This deprivation is a product of comparatively low social security allowance payments in Australia and New Zealand, as well as the restrictions of CIM itself. As Klein et al (2021, p 40) argue in their analysis:

> Current social security policy is operating contrary to the outcomes government are purportedly trying to achieve by creating barriers to work, compromising physical and mental health, reducing self-worth and wellbeing, providing inadequate financial resources for basic living needs, reducing capacity to focus on anything other than survival and compliance, and disregarding people's unpaid caring responsibilities, community contributions and long-term goals.

Constructing a vision of a social security system that recognises all forms of work requires acknowledging the contradictions of the present, such as the way in which the welfare state is both an enabling and disabling force. We also need to acknowledge that inequality and competition are integral features of capitalist economies. These structural dynamics cannot be wished away by market integration talk that distorts certain truths, such as the fact that markets are, by definition, discriminatory. Addressing discrimination, reducing income inequality and providing income security are political, ethical and economic challenges that will require imagination, deliberation and reason to overcome. The democratic public sphere in many countries is struggling to embody these qualities. Prejudice, pre-conceived ideas and political tribalism make it difficult to advance and sustain reasoned debate and points of connection on social security policy. Structural problems of demand and supply, for example, continue to be misinterpreted as problems of character or individual morality, with citizens seen as consumers or as entrepreneurs seeking advancement through competitive markets of mobility and self-improvement (Marston et al, 2019).

The process of refurbishing a connected and embedded model of social citizenship will need to build on the dialectical relationship between political and social rights. Addressing inequality and poverty requires clarity of values, mobilising a diverse coalition of support, and expanding opportunities for the voices of ordinary citizens to be listened to and respected in the public sphere. This, in turn, will help to define and shape a form of citizenship that is authentically connected to social, cultural and economic modes of participation, not a model whereby people are positioned as 'responsibilised risk managers' in a narrowly defined 'job holder' society. The social citizenship and social justice envisaged here is, as Tilly (1999, p 56) notes, 'thick' in terms of rights and equal status – as opposed to 'thin' citizenship, which is loaded up with responsibilities and unevenly distributed forms of punitive conditionality.

To transform the present state, we need policy metaphors and social policy research that is able to sharpen rather than blunt social realities in order to envision what Olin Wright (2010, p 4) refers to as 'real utopias'. This will mean articulating the design principles and architecture for a fairer future, while at the same time developing a more fully fledged diagnosis of social problems in the present. As the leader of the Australian Labor Party, Anthony Albanese (2020, np), recently remarked: 'We have a once-in-a-century moment to rethink and renew. To propose and to listen. To continue what works and change what doesn't. To look at the big picture.' Social policy scholars have a role to play in listening to diverse voices and interpreting what this big picture could look like – leaving behind the intellectual confines and real harms of unethical forms of welfare conditionality.

References

ABC News (2014) 'Cashless welfare payments proposal sparks protest outside Adelaide ALP convention', *ABC News*, [online] 15 November, Available from: https://www.abc.net.au/news/2014-11-15/cashless-welfare-protest-outside-alp-conference-adelaide/5893936 [Accessed 23 March 2021].

Abeyta, A.A., Routledge, C., Kersten, M. and Cox, C.R. (2017) 'The existential cost of economic insecurity: threatened financial security undercuts meaning', *The Journal of Social Psychology*, 157(6): 692–702.

Ackerman, B. and Alstott, A. (2006) 'Why stakeholding?' in B. Ackerman, A. Alstott and P. Van Parijs (eds) *Redesigning Distribution: Basic Income and Stakeholder Grants as Cornerstones for an Egalitarian Capitalism*, London/New York: Verso, pp 43–65.

ACOSS (2020) *'I can finally eat fresh fruit and vegetables' Survey of 955 People Receiving the New Rate of JobSeeker and Other Allowances*, Sydney: ACOSS.

Adler, M. (2013) 'Challenging workfare practices: conditionality, sanctions and the weakness of redress mechanisms in the British New Deal', in E. Brodkin and G. Marston (eds) *Work and the Welfare State: Street Level Organisations and the Welfare State*, Washington: Georgetown University Press, pp 234–46.

Adler, M. (2016) 'A new leviathan: benefit sanctions in the twenty-first century', *Law and Society*, 43(2): 195–227.

Albanese, A. (2020) 'Australia beyond the coronavirus', *Sharon Bird MP*, [media release, online] 11 May, Available from: https://www.sharonbird.com.au/australia_beyond_the_coronavirus [Accessed 14 April 2021].

Allam, L. (2020) 'Power outages leave Aboriginal people on NT islands with no food, fuel or phones for three days', *The Guardian*, [online] 4 March, Available from: https://www.theguardian.com/australia-news/2020/mar/04/power-outages-leave-aboriginal-people-on-nt-islands-with-no-food-fuel-or-phones-for-three-days [Accessed 1 February 2021].

Alston, P. (2019) 'World stumbling zombie-like into a digital welfare dystopia, warns UN human rights expert', *United Nations Human Rights: Office of the High Commissioner*, [online], Available from: https://www.ohchr.org/EN/NewsEvents/Pages/DisplayNews.aspx?NewsID=25156 [Accessed 30 December 2020].

Altman, J. (2008) *Submission to The Northern Territory Emergency Response Review, Centre for Aboriginal Economic Policy Research Topical Issue No. 10/2008*, Canberra: Australian National University.

Altman, J. (2011) 'A genealogy of 'demand sharing': from pure anthropology to public policy', in Y. Musharbash and M. Barber (eds) *Ethnography & the Production of Anthropological Knowledge: Essays in Honour of Nicolas Peterson*, Canberra: Australian National University Press, pp 187–200.

Altman, J. (2018) '"The main thing is to have enough food": Kuninjku precarity and neoliberal reason', in C. Gregory and J. Altman (eds) *The Quest for a Good Life in Precarious Times*, Canberra: ANU Press, pp 163–96.

Altman, J. and Markham, F. (2016) 'Basic income and cultural participation for remote-living Indigenous Australians', in E. Klein, J. Mays and T. Dunlop (eds) *Implementing a basic income in Australia,* Cham: Palgrave Macmillan, pp 87–109.

Amagir, A., Groot, W., Maasen van de Brink, H. and Wilschut, A. (2018) 'A review of financial-literacy education programs for children and adolescents', *Citizenship, Social and Economics Education,* 17(1): 56–80.

Anaya, J. (2010) 'Observations on the Northern Territory Emergency Response in Australia', *National Council of Churches in Australia,* [online] February, Available from: http://www.ncca.org.au/files/Natsiec/NTER_Observations_FINAL_by_SR_Anaya_.pdf [Accessed 19 December 2020].

Anderson, J. and Honneth, A. (2005) 'Autonomy, vulnerability, recognition, and justice', in J. Christman and J. Anderson (eds) *Autonomy and the Challenges to Liberalism: New Essays*, Cambridge and New York: Cambridge University Press, pp 127–49.

Anderson, P. (2011) *Research for a better future, keynote address to the Third Aboriginal Health Research Conference, Coalition for Research to improve Aboriginal Health*, Sydney, 5–6 May, Available from: https://www.lowitja.org.au/content/Document/PDF/Pat_Anderson-CRIAH-27_04_2011.pdf [Accessed 23 March 2021].

Archer-Lean, C. and Pavitt, H. (2012) 'Politics and ethics in social media', *Social Alternatives*, 31(2): 3–5.

Ardern, J. (2016) 'Social Security (Extension of Young Persons Services and Remedial Matters) Amendment Bill – In Committee', *New Zealand Parliament*, [online] 5 July, Available from: https://www.parliament.nz/en/pb/hansard-debates/rhr/combined/HansDeb_20160705_20160705_16 [Accessed 21 December 2020].

Arnold, J. and Rhyne, E. (2016) *A Change in Behaviour: Innovations in Financial Capability*, [online] Available from: https://content.centerforfinancialinclusion.org/wp-content/uploads/sites/2/2018/09/a-change-in-behavior-final-2.pdf [Accessed 15 February 2021].

Arthur, C. (2016) 'Financial literacy education as a public pedagogy: consumerizing economic insecurity, ethics and democracy', in C. Aprea, E. Wuttke, K. Breuer, N.K. Koh, P. Davies, B. Greimel-Fuhrmann and J.S. Lopus (eds) *International Handbook of Financial Literacy,* New York: Springer, pp 113–25.

Arthur, D. (2015) 'Income management: a quick guide', *Parliament of Australia*, [online] 15 July, Available from: https://www.aph.gov.au/About_Parliament/Parliamentary_Departments/Parliamentary_Library/pubs/rp/rp1516/Quick_Guides/IncomeManagement [Accessed 23 January 2021].

Arthur, D. and Ayoub, J. (2020) 'Social Security (Administration) Amendment (Continuation of Cashless Welfare) Bill', *New Zealand Parliament*, [online] 2 December, Available from: https://parlinfo.aph.gov.au/parlInfo/download/legislation/billsdgs/7669864/upload_binary/7669864.pdf;fileType=application%2Fpdf#search=%22WX2%22 [Accessed 30 January 2021].

Australian Bureau of Statistics (2018) 'Estimates of Aboriginal and Torres Strait Islander Australians', *Australian Bureau of Statistics*, [online] 18 September, Available from: https://www.abs.gov.au/ausstats/abs@.nsf/mf/3238.0.55.001 [Accessed 14 April 2021].

Australian Bureau of Statistics (2019) *Census of Population and Housing 2016 and 2011 Customised Report*, Canberra: ABS.

Australian Bureau of Statistics (2020) 'Gender Indicators Australia', [online] Available from: https://www.abs.gov.au/statistics/people/people-and-communities/gender-indicators-australia/latest-release [Accessed 18 December 2020].

Australian Government (2009a) *Report on the Northern Territory Emergency Response Redesign Consultations*, Canberra: Commonwealth of Australia.

Australian Government (2009b) *Future Directions for the Northern Territory Emergency Response*, Canberra: Commonwealth of Australia.

Australian Government (2011) Stronger Futures in the Northern Territory: Report on Consultations, Canberra: Australian Government.

Australian Government (2019) 'Cashless debit card – further extension and expansion, 2019 budget fact sheet', *Department of Social Services*, [online] Available from: https://www.dss.gov.au/sites/default/files/documents/04_2019/pbs-fact-sheet-cashless-debit-cardfzlfexz_0.docx [Accessed 12 February 2021].

Australian Government (2020) 'Youth and long term payment recipients', *Services Australia*, [online] 18 November, Available from: https://www.servicesaustralia.gov.au/individuals/services/centrelink/income-management/who-can-get-it/youth-and-long-term-payment-recipients [Accessed 6 February 2021].

Australian Government (2021a) 'Australian Government Cashless Debit Card program data', *Data.gov.au*, [online] Available from: https://data.gov.au/data/dataset/australian-government-cashless-debit-card-program [Accessed 12 February 2021].

Australian Government (2021b) 'Australian Government Income Management program data', *Data.gov.au*, [online] Available from: https://data.gov.au/data/dataset/australian-government-income-management-program [Accessed 10 February 2021].

Australian Government (2021c) 'Cashless Debit Card data summary January 2021', *Australian Government Cashless Debit Card Program*, [online] 1 January, Available from: https://data.gov.au/dataset/ds-dga-e5a6ca38-b17c-4e65-af70-84e7759a0ffa/details?q= [Accessed 1 February 2021].

Australian Government (2021d) 'Guides to social policy law: Social security guide, version 1.277, 11.1.14.30 Principal carer exemptions from income management – financial vulnerability test', *Department of Social Services*, [online] Available from: https://guides.dss.gov.au/guide-social-security-law/11/1/14/30 [Accessed 12 February 2021].

Australian Government (2021e) 'Income management data summary January 2021', *Australian Government Income Management Program*, [online] 1 January, Available from: https://data.gov.au/dataset/ds-dga-fd464dd1-0031-4e4a-abdd-c08282192d86/details?q= [Accessed 1 February 2021].

Australian Indigenous Doctors' Association and Centre for Health Equity Training, Research and Evaluation UNSW (2010) *Health impact assessment of the Northern Territory Emergency Response*, Canberra: Australian Indigenous Doctors' Association.

Australian Law Reform Commission (2015) *Traditional Rights and Freedoms – Encroachments by Commonwealth Laws: Final Report*, ALRC Report 129, Sydney: Australian Law Reform Commission.

Australian National Audit Office (2018) 'The implementation and performance of the cashless debit card trial (Auditor-General Report No.1 2018–19)', *Australian National Audit Office*, [online] 17 July, Available from: https://www.anao.gov.au/work/performance-audit/implementation-and-performance-cashless-debit-card-trial [Accessed 22 December 2020].

Baaz, M., Heikkinen, S. and Lilja, M. (2017) 'Editorial', *Journal of Political Power*, 10(2): 127–32.

Bacchi, C. (1999) *Women, Policy and Politics: The Construction of Policy Problems*, London: SAGE Publications.

Bacchi, C. (2009) *Analysing Policy: What's the Problem Represented to Be?*, Melbourne: Pearson Education.

Bacchi, C. and Goodwin, S. (2016) *Poststructural Policy Analysis*, New York: Palgrave Macmillan.

Bailey, C., Powell, M. and Brubacher, S. (2017) 'Reporting rates of child sexual abuse in Indigenous communities in two Australian jurisdictions', *Child Abuse and Neglect*, 68: 74–80.

Banks, M. and Tennant, D. (2016) 'Community worker perceptions of the income management regime in Shepparton', *Australian Journal of Social Issues*, 51(4): 419–32.

Baumberg, B., Bell, K., Gaffney, D., Deacon, R., Hood, C. and Sage, D. (2012) *Benefits Stigma in Britain*, London: Turn2Us.

Béland, D. and Cox, R. (2016) 'Ideas as coalition magnets: coalition building, policy entrepreneurs, and power relations', *Journal of European Public Policy*, 23(3): 428–45.

Benesch, S. (2018) 'Emotions as agency: feeling rules, emotion labor, and English language teachers' decision-making', *System*, 79: 60–9.

Bennett, P. (2012a) 'Social Security (Youth Support and Work Focus) Amendment Bill second reading', *New Zealand Parliament*, [online] 12 June, Available from: https://www.parliament.nz/en/pb/hansard-debates/rhr/document/50HansD_20120612_00000028/social-security-youth-support-and-work-focus-amendment [Accessed 20 December 2020].

Bennett, P. (2012b). 'Social Security (Youth Support and Work Focus) Amendment Bill first reading', *New Zealand Parliament*, [online] 27 March, Available from: https://www.parliament.nz/resource/en-NZ/50HansD_20120327/2e9750df6a57cf1a86e47b7d172d7ccad0d4821c [Accessed 16 December 2020].

Bentley, R., Baker, E. and Aitken, Z. (2019), 'The 'double precarity' of employment insecurity and unaffordable housing and its impact on mental health', *Social Science & Medicine*, 225: 9–16.

Beresford, P. (2013) *Towards Inclusive User Involvement: Beyond the Usual Suspects*, London: Shaping Our Lives.

Berlant, L. (2004) 'Introduction: compassion (and withholding)', in L. Berlant (ed) *Compassion: The Culture and Politics of an Emotion*, New York: Routledge, pp 1–13.

Biddle, N., Howlett, M., Hunter, B. and Paradies, Y. (2013) 'Labour market and other discrimination facing Indigenous Australians', *Australian Journal of Labour Economics*, 16(1): 91–113.

Bielefeld, S. (2012) 'Compulsory income management and Indigenous Australians – delivering social justice or furthering colonial domination?', *University of New South Wales Law Journal*, 35(2): 522–62.

Bielefeld, S. (2013) 'Compulsory income management under the Stronger Futures Laws – providing "flexibility" or overturning freedom of contract?', *Indigenous Law Bulletin*, 8(5): 18–21.

Bielefeld, S. (2014a) 'Compulsory income management – exploring counter narratives amidst colonial constructions of vulnerability', *Sydney Law Review*, 36(4): 695–726.

Bielefeld, S. (2014b) 'Income management and Indigenous peoples – nudged into a Stronger Future?', *Griffith Law Review*, 23(2): 285–317.

Bielefeld, S. (2015) 'Compulsory income management, Indigenous peoples and structural violence: implications for citizenship and autonomy', *Australian Indigenous Law Review*, 18(1): 99–118.

Bielefeld, S. (2018b) 'Government mythology on income management, alcohol, addiction and Indigenous communities', *Critical Social Policy*, 38 (4): 749–70.

Bielefeld, S. and Beaupert, F. (2019) 'Income management and intersectionality: analysing compulsory income management through the lenses of critical race theory and critical disability studies ('DisCrit')', *Sydney Law Review*, 41(3): 327–57.

Bielefeld, S., Marston, G., Peterie, M. and Staines, Z. (2020) 'Submission No 118 to the Senate Standing Committee on Community Affairs', *Inquiry into the Social Security (Administration) Amendment (Continuation of Cashless Welfare) Bill 2020*, 23 October, 1–34.

Billings, P. (2010) 'Social welfare experiments in Australia: more trials for Aboriginal communities', *Journal of Social Security Law*, 17(3): 164–95.

Bissell, K. and Parrott, S. (2013) 'Prejudice: the role of the media in the development of social bias', *Journalism and Communication Monographs*, 15(4): 219–70.

Blakely, T., Collings, S. and Atkinson, J. (2003) 'Unemployment and suicide: evidence for a causal association?', *Journal of Epidemiology & Community Health*, 57(8): 594–600.

Booth, A. and Carroll, N. (2008) 'Economic status and the Indigenous/non-Indigenous health gap', *Economics Letters*, 99(3): 604–6.

Bossert, W. and D'Ambrosio, C. (2013) 'Measuring economic insecurity', *International Economic Review*, 54(3): 1017–30.

Boyle, D., Coote, A., Sherwood, C. and Slay, J. (2010) *Right Here, Right Now: Taking Co-production into the Mainstream*, London: New Economics Foundation.

Bray, J.R. (2015) 'Presentation to Community Affairs Legislation Committee', *Hansard*, 11 September: 6–11.

Bray, J.R., Gray, M., Hand, K. and Katz, I. (2014) *Evaluating New Income Management in the Northern Territory: Final Evaluation Report. Social Policy Research Centre Report 25/2014*, Sydney: Social Policy Research Centre.

Bray, J.R., Gray, M., Hand, K. and Katz, I. (2016) 'Compulsory income management in the Northern Territory – evaluating its impact', *Australian Journal of Social Issues*, 50(4): 373–96.

Bregman, R. (2016) *Utopia for Realists: The Case for Universal Basic Income, Open Borders and a 15-hour workweek*, Amsterdam: De Correspondent.

Briggs, C. and Buchanan, J. (2000) 'Australian labour market deregulation: a critical assessment', *Parliament of Australia*, [online] Available from: https://www.aph.gov.au/About_Parliament/Parliamentary_Departments/Parliamentary_Library/pubs/rp/rp9900/2000RP21#current [Accessed 18 December 2020].

Brimble, M. and Blue, L. (2013) 'Tailored financial literacy education: an Indigenous perspective', *Journal of Financial Services Marketing*, 18(3): 207–19.

Brough, M. (2006a) 'Speech: social innovations dialogue', *Parliament of Australia*, [online] 29 April, Available from: https://parlinfo.aph.gov.au/parlInfo/download/media/pressrel/OIIK6/upload_binary/oiik66.pdf;fileType=application%2Fpdf#search=%22media/pressrel/OIIK6%22 [Accessed 18 December 2020].

Brough, M. (2006b) 'ACOSS National Congress', *Department of Social Services*, [online] 23 November, Available from: https://formerministers.dss.gov.au/2912/acoss-national-congress/ [Accessed 17 December 2020].

Brough, M. (2007) 'National emergency response to protect Aboriginal children in the NT', *Department of Social Services*, [press release] 21 June, Available from: https://formerministers.dss.gov.au/3581/emergency_21june07/ [Accessed 14 December 2020].

Bryson, L. (1992) *Welfare and the State: Who Benefits?*, New York: Macmillan Education.

Bryson, L. and Verity, F. (2009) 'Australia: from wage-earners to neo-liberal welfare state', in P. Alcock and G. Craig (eds) *International Social Policy*, Houndmills: Palgrave Macmillan, pp 66–87.

Buckmaster, L. and Ey, C. (2012) 'Is income management working?', *Parliament of Australia*, [online] 5 June, Available from: https://parlinfo.aph.gov.au/parlInfo/download/library/prspub/1603602/upload_binary/1603602.pdf;fileType=application%2Fpdf#search=%22library/prspub/1603602%22 [Accessed 12 December 2020].

Buckmaster, L., Ey, C. and Klapdor, M. (2012) 'Income management: an overview', *Parliament of Australia*, [online] 21 June, Available from: https://parlinfo.aph.gov.au/parlInfo/download/library/prspub/1727168/upload_binary/1727168.pdf;fileType=application/pdf [Accessed 10 December 2020].

Bush, G.W. (2002) *Fact Sheet: Compassionate Conservatism*, Washington: White House.

Calavita, K. (2016) *Invitation to Law & Society: An Introduction to the Real Study of Law* (2nd edn), Chicago and London: The University of Chicago Press.

Caliendo, M., Cobb-Clark, D. and Uhlendorff, A. (2015) 'Locus of control and job search strategies', *The Review of Economics and Statistics*, 97(1): 88–103.

Canavan, M. (2019) *Speech to the Senate*, 2 December: 94–5.

Cantwell, K. (2015) 'PBIM engagement'. Paper presented to *Examining Income Management programs in Australia Conference*, Melbourne: Monash University, 16 July.

Cape York Institute for Policy & Leadership (2007) *From Handout to Hand Up: Welfare Reform Report: Design Recommendations*, Cairns: Cape York Institute for Policy & Leadership.

Carcasson, M. (2006) 'Ending welfare as we know it: President Clinton and the rhetorical transformation of the anti-welfare culture', *Rhetoric and Public Affairs*, 9(4): 655–92.

Carney, T. and Stanford, J. (2018) *The Dimensions of Insecure Work: A Factbook*, Canberra: The Australia Institute.

Carter, J.W. (2012) *Cases and Materials on Contract Law in Australia* (6th edn), Sydney: LexisNexis Butterworths.

Castles, F. (1985), *The Working Class and Welfare: Reflections on the Political Development of the Welfare State in Australia and New Zealand, 1890–1980*, Sydney: Allen & Unwin.

Castles, F. and Mitchell, D. (1992) 'Identifying welfare states regimes: the links between politics, instruments and outcomes', *Governance*, 5: 1–26.

Castles, F., Curtin, J. and Vowles, J. (2006) 'Public policy in Australia and New Zealand: the new global context', *Australian Journal of Political Science*, 41(2): 131–43.

Catalano, R. (1991) 'The health effects of economic insecurity', *American Journal of Public Health*, 81(9): 1148–52.

Cernison, M. (2019) *Social Media Activism*, Amsterdam: Amsterdam University Press.

Child Poverty Action Group (2021) *CPAG Budget Analysis 2021*, [online] Available from: https://www.cpag.org.nz/assets/Budget/CPAG-Budget-2021-AnalysisSummary.pdf [Accessed 22 March 2021].

Christensen, C. (2009) 'Iran: networked dissent?', *Le Monde Dipliomatique*, [online] Available from: http://www.mondediplo.com/blogs/iran-networked-dissent [Accessed 23 March 2021].

Clague, M. (1997) 'Thirty turbulent years: community development and the organisation of health and social services in British Columbia', in B. Wharf and M. Clague (eds) Community Organizing: Canadian Experiences, Toronto: Oxford University Press, pp 91–112.

Clasen, J and Siegel, D. (2007) 'Levels and levers of conditionality: measuring change within welfare states', in J. Clasen and D. Siegel (eds) *Investigating Welfare State Change*, Cheltenham: Edward Elgar Publishing, pp 166–97.

Closing the Gap Refresh (2018) *Special Gathering Statement: Closing the Gap Refresh: Building Pathways for Future Prosperity, February 2018*, Canberra: National Indigenous Australians Agency, [online] Available from https://closingthegap.niaa.gov.au/sites/defa ult/files/special-gathering-statementcoag.pdf [Accessed 10 February 2021].

Cobb-Clark, D., Kassenboehmer, S. and Schurer, S. (2014) 'Healthy habits: the connection between diet, exercise and locus of control', *Journal of Economic Behaviour & Organisation*, 98: 1–28.

Collier, R.B. and Collier, D. (1991) *Shaping the Political Arena: Critical Junctures, the Labor Movement, and Regime Dynamics in Latin America*, Princeton: Princeton University Press.

Commonwealth of Australia (2007) 'Parliamentary debates', *House of Representatives*, 7 August.

Commonwealth of Australia (2020) *Indigenous Voice Co-design Process: Interim Report to the Australian Government October 2020*, Canberra: National Indigenous Australians Agency.

Commonwealth Ombudsman (2012) *Review of Centrelink Income Management Decisions in the Northern Territory: Financial Vulnerability Exemption and Vulnerable Welfare Payment Recipient Decisions (Report No 4/2012)*, Canberra: Commonwealth Ombudsman.

Commonwealth Ombudsman (2013) *Commonwealth Ombudsman 2012–2013 Annual Report*, Canberra: Commonwealth Ombudsman.

Commonwealth Ombudsman (2014) *Commonwealth Ombudsman 2013–2014 Annual Report*, Canberra: Commonwealth Ombudsman.

Commonwealth Ombudsman (2015) *Commonwealth Ombudsman Annual Report 2014–2015*, Canberra: Commonwealth Ombudsman.

Commonwealth Ombudsman (2017) *Commonwealth Ombudsman Annual Report 2016–2017*, Canberra: Commonwealth Ombudsman.

Community Affairs Legislation Committee (CALC) (2012) *Stronger Futures in the Northern Territory Bill 2011 (Provisions)*, Canberra: Commonwealth of Australia.

CALC (2015) *Social Security Legislation Amendment (Debit Card Trial) Bill 2015 (Provisions)*, Canberra: Commonwealth of Australia.

CALC (2017) *Social Services Legislation Amendment (Cashless Debit Card) Bill 2017 Provisions)*, Canberra: Commonwealth of Australia.

CALC (2019a) *Social Security (Administration) Amendment (Income Management and Cashless Welfare) Bill 2019*, Canberra: Commonwealth of Australia.

CALC (2019b) *Social Security (Administration) Amendment (Income Management to Cashless Debit Card Transition) Bill 2019 (Provisions)*, Canberra: Commonwealth of Australia.

CALC (2020) *Social Security (Administration) Amendment (Continuation of Cashless Welfare) Bill 2020 (Provisions)*, Canberra: Commonwealth of Australia.

Contini, D. and Richiardi, M.G. (2010) 'Reconsidering the effect of welfare stigma on unemployment', *Journal of Economic Behavior and Organization*, 84: 229–44.

Cooley, C. (1902) *Human Nature and the Social Order*, New York: Scribner.

Coote, A. (2015) *People, Planet, Power: Towards a New Social Settlement*, London: New Economics Foundation.

Coote, A. (2019) 'Universal Basic Services and Sustainable Consumption', *Sustainability, Science, Practice and Policy*, 17(1): 32–46.

Crossan, D., Feslier, D. and Hurnard, R. (2011) 'Financial literacy and retirement planning in New Zealand', *Netspar Discussion Paper, no. 1/2011–015*, [online] Available from: https://ssrn.com/abstract=1809680 [Accessed 10 February 2021].

Cunneen, C., Allison, F. and Schwartz, M. (2014) 'Access to justice for Aboriginal people in the Northern Territory', *Australian Journal of Social Issues*, 49(2): 219–40.

Cvetanovski, J. and Jex, S. (1994) 'Locus of control of unemployed people and its relationship to psychological and physical wellbeing', *Work & Stress: An International Journal of Work, Health & Organisations*, 8(1): 60–7.

Dalley, B. and Tennant, M. (eds). (2004) *Past Judgement: Social Policy in New Zealand History*, Dunedin: University of Otago Press.

Dean, M. (2009) *Governmentality: Power and Rule in Modern Society* (2nd edn), London: Sage Publications.

Deloitte Access Economics (2014) *Place Based Income Management – Process and Short Term Outcomes Evaluation*, Canberra: Deloitte Access Economics and Department of Social Services.

Deloitte Access Economics (2015) *Consolidated Place Based Income Management Evaluation Report 2012–2015*, [online] Available from: https://www.dss.gov.au/sites/default/files/documents/11_2015/deloitte_access_economics_consolidated_evaluation_report_201115.pdf [Accessed 20 December 2020].

Deloitte Access Economics (2020) *Estimating the Impacts of Lowering Current Levels of Income Support Payments*, Sydney: ACOSS.

Demirdis, S. (2019) 'The role of Facebook and Twitter in social movements: a study on the July 15 coup attempt in Turkey', *Türkiye İletişim Araştırmaları Dergisi*: 32–49, DOI: 10.17829/turcom.477180.

Department of Social Services (2016) *Cashless Debit Card Trial Progress Report*, Canberra: Australian Government.

Department of Social Services (2017) *Cashless Debit Card Trial Evaluation: Final Report*, [online] Available from: https://www.dss.gov.au/sites/default/files/documents/10_2018/cashless-debit-card-trial-final-evaluation-report_2.pdf [Accessed 20 December 2020].

Department of Social Services (2018) 'Cashless Debit Card (CDC) and Income Management (IM) summary', *Department of Social Services*, [online] 30 March, Available from: https://data.gov.au/dataset/ds-dga-3b1f1fb7-adb5-48ea-8305-9205df 0a298c/distribution/dist-dga-986ef7fe-1ba8-460e-b1c4-2cf00145a948/details?q= [Accessed 30 March 2018].

DePaula, N., Fietkiewicz, K.J., Froehlich, T.J., Million, A.J., Dorsch, I. and Ilhan, A. (2018) 'Challenges for social media: misinformation, civic engagement, and data regulations', *Computer Science*, 55(1): 665–8.

Dillon, M.C. (2021) *Codesign in the Indigenous Policy Domain: Risks and Opportunities*, Canberra: Centre for Aboriginal Economic Policy Research, Australian National University.

Dobson, R. (2015) 'Power, agency, relationality and welfare practices', *Journal of Social Policy*, 44(4): 687–705.

Dolowitz, D. and D. Marsh. (2000) 'Learning from abroad: the role of policy transfer in contemporary policy-making.' *Governance*, 13(1): 5–24.

Donaghy, B. (2020) *A Basic Income for Australia: A Fair Go For All, How it Works, How to Pay For It*, Adelaide: Griffin Press.

Doocey, M. (2016) 'Social Security (Youth Support and Work Focus) Amendment Bill – Second Reading', *New Zealand Parliament*, [online] 12 June, Available from: https://www.parliament.nz/en/pb/hansard-debates/rhr/document/50HansD_20120612_00000028/social-security-youth-support-and-work-focus-amendment [Accessed 9 December 2020].

Dougherty, D.S., Rick, J.M. and Moore, P. (2017) 'Unemployment and social class stigmas', *Journal of Applied Communication Research*, 45(5): 495–516.

Dudgeon, P., Bray, A., D'Costa, B. and Walker, R. (2017) 'Decolonising psychology: validating social and emotional wellbeing', *Australian Psychologist*, 52(4): 316–25.

Dwyer, P. (ed) (2019) *Dealing with Welfare Conditionality: Implementation and Effects*, Bristol: Policy Press.

Edelman, M. (1988) *Constructing the Political Spectacle*, Chicago: The University of Chicago Press.

Edelman, P. (2013) *So Rich, So Poor: Why It's So Hard to End Poverty in America*, New York: The New Press.

Esping-Andersen, G. (1990) *The Three Worlds of Welfare Capitalism*. Princeton: Princeton University Press.

Esping-Andersen, G. (2002) 'Towards the good society, once again?', in G. Esping-Andersen (ed), *Why We Need a New Welfare State*, Oxford: Oxford University Press, pp 5–34.

Eubanks, V. (2018) *Automating Inequality: How High Tech Tools Profile, Police and Punish the Poor*, New York: St Martin's Press.

Ferguson, J. (2015) *Give a Man a Fish: Reflections on the New Politics of Distribution*, Durham: Duke University Press.

Fernandes, D., Lynch, J. and Netemeyer, R. (2014) 'Financial literacy, financial education and downstream financial behaviors', *Management Science*, 60(8): 1861–83.

Fletcher, M., Hanna, K. and Anderson, D. (2013) 'The introduction of compulsory income management into New Zealand's social security system: the case of the Youth Service Package', paper presented at the *Labour, Employment and Work in New Zealand Conference*, 27–8 November, Wellington: Victoria University of Wellington.

Fletcher, P. (2019) 'Morrison Government extends successful Cashless Debit Card', *Parliament of Australia*, [media release, online] 25 March, Available from: https://parlinfo.aph.gov.au/parlInfo/download/media/pressrel/6579549/upload_binary/6579549.pdf;fileType=application%2Fpdf#search=%22media/pressrel/6579549%22 [Accessed 12 February 2021].

Forgione, P. (2014) 'Income management: Centrelink forgot to pay my rent', *Green Left Weekly*, [online] 4 July, Available from: https://www.greenleft.org.au/content/income-management-centrelink-forgot-pay-my-rent [Accessed 23 March 2021].

Forgione, P. (2015) 'Life on compulsory income management', *Green Left Weekly*, [online] 3 July, Available from: https://www.greenleft.org.au/content/life-compulsory-income-management [Accessed 23 March 2021].

Forrest, A. (2014) 'The Forrest review: creating parity', *National Indigenous Australians Agency*, [online] Available from: https://www.niaa.gov.au/sites/default/files/publications/Forrest-Review.pdf [Accessed 8 December 2020].

Foucault, M. (1978) *The History of Sexuality*, New York: Pantheon Books.

Fox, M. (2016) Social Security (Extension of Young Persons Services and Remedial Matters) Amendment Bill – In Committee, *Parliament of New Zealand*, [online] 14 June, Available from: https://www.parliament.nz/en/pb/hansard-debates/rhr/combined/HansDeb_20160614_20160614_28 [Accessed 7 December 2020].

Fraser, N. (2013) *Fortunes of Feminism: From State-managed Capitalism to Neoliberal Crisis*, New York: Verso.

Fraser, N. and Gordon, L. (1994) 'A genealogy of "dependency": tracing a keyword of the US welfare state', *Signs: A Journal of Women in Culture and Society*, 19(2): 309–36.

Frijns, B., Gilbert, A. and Tourani-Rad, A. (2014) 'Learning by doing: the role of financial experience in financial literacy', *Journal of Public Policy*, 34(1): 123–54.

Future Social Service Institute (2018) *What is Co-design?*, Melbourne: FSSI.

Galicki, C. (2020) *Financial Capability Barometer, 2018–19*, Wellington: Commission for Financial Capability.

Garimella, K., De Francisci Morales, G., Gionis, A. and Mathioudakis, M. (2018) 'Political discourses on social media: echo chambers, gatekeepers, and the price of bipartisanship', *World Wide Web Conference 2018*, [online] Available at: https://arxiv.org/abs/1801.01665 [Accessed 23 March 2021].

Garland, D. (2001) *The Culture of Control: Crime and Social Order in Contemporary Society*, Oxford: Oxford University Press.

Gausman, J. (2020) 'Sex and gender disparities in the COVID-19 pandemic', *Journal of Women's Health*, 29(4): 465–6.

Gibson, P. (2009) *Return to the Ration Days – The NT Intervention: Grass-roots Experience and Resistance*, Sydney: Jumbunna Indigenous House of Learning, University of Technology Sydney.

Goffman, E. (1963) *Stigma: Notes on the Management of Spoiled Identity*, London: Penguin.

Goldfinch, S. and V. Roberts. (2013) 'New public management and public sector reform in Victoria and New Zealand: policy transfer, elite networks and legislative copying', *Australian Journal of Politics & History*, 59(1): 80–96.

Grahame, T. and Marston, G. (2010) 'Welfare-to-work policies and the experience of employed single mothers on income support in Australia: where are the benefits?', *Australian Social Work* 65(1): 73–86.

Gregoire, P. (2019) 'The best form of welfare is a job: PM refuses to raise welfare payments', *Sydney Criminal Lawyers*, [blog] Available from: https://www.sydneycriminallawyers.com.au/blog/the-best-form-of-welfare-is-a-job-pm-refuses-to-raise-welfare-payments/ [Accessed 15 December 2020].

Gustafson, K. (2011) *Cheating Welfare: Public Assistance and the Criminalization of Poverty*, New York: New York University Press.

Hacker, J. (2006) *The Great Risk Shift: Assault on American Jobs, Families, Health Care and Retirement and How You Can Fight Back*, Oxford: Oxford University Press.

Haidt, J. (2012) *The Righteous Mind: Why Good People Are Divided by Politics and Religion*, New York: Pantheon Books.

Haidt, J. (2013) 'Moral psychology for the twenty-first century', *Journal of Moral Education* 42(3): 281–97.

Hatcher, D. (2015) *The Poverty Industry: The Exploitation of America's Most Vulnerable Citizens*, New York: NYU Press.

Henman, P. (2004) 'Targeted! Population Segmentation, electronic surveillance and governing the unemployed in Australia', *International Sociology*, 19(2): 173–91.

Herman, E.S. and Chomsky, N. (1988) *Manufacturing Consent: The Political Economy of the Mass Media*, New York: Pantheon Books.

Heshmat, S. (2015) 'What is confirmation bias', *Psychology Today*, [online] 23 April, Available from: https://www.psychologytoday.com/au/blog/science-choice/201504/what-is-confirmation-bias [Accessed 23 March 2021].

Higashi, R., Lee, S., Pezzia, C., Quirk, L., Leonard, T. and Pruitt, S. (2017) 'Family and social context contributes to the interplay of economic insecurity, food insecurity and health', *Annals of Anthropological Practice*, 41(2): 67–77.

Hiswals, A., Marttila, A., Malstam, E. and Macassa, G. (2017) 'Experiences of unemployment and well-being after job loss during economic recession: results of a qualitative study in east central Sweden', *Journal of Public Health Research*, 6(995): 135–41.

Hochschild, A.R. (1979) 'Emotion work, feeling rules, and social structure', *American Journal of Social Structure*, 85(3): 551–75.

Hockey, J. (2012) 'The end of the age of entitlement', *The Sydney Morning Herald*, [online] 19 April, Available from: https://www.smh.com.au/national/the-end-of-the-age-of-entitlement-20120419-1x8vj.html [Accessed 14 January 2021].

Hollander, J.A. and Einwohner, R.L. (2004) 'Conceptualizing resistance', *Sociological Forum*, 19(4): 533–54.

Hossain, B. and Lamb, L. (2019) 'Economic insecurity and psychological distress among Indigenous Canadians', *The Journal of Developing Areas*, 53(1): 109–25.

Houkamau, C.A., Stronge, S. and Sibley, C.G. (2017) 'The prevalence and impact of racism towards Indigenous Maori in New Zealand', *International Perspectives in Psychology: Research, Practice, Consultation*, 6(2): 61–80.

Houkamau, C., Sibley, C. and Henare, M. (2019) 'The Māori Identity and Financial Attitudes Study (MIFAS)', *New Zealand Journal of Indigenous Scholarship*, 8(2): 142–58.

Houkamau, C., Stevens, A., Oakes, D. and Blank, M. (nd) 'Taking control: Maori responses to money management wealth and saving', *University of Auckland Business School*, [online] Available from: http://www.maramatanga.co.nz/sites/default/files/project-reports/Taking%20Control_M%C4%81ori%20Responses%20to%20Money%2C%20Wealth%20and%20Savings.pdf [Accessed 10 February 2021].

Howard, J. (2007) 'Address to the Sydney Institute', *Pandora: Australia's Web Archive*, [online] 25 June, Available from: http://pandora.nla.gov.au/pan/10052/20080118-1528/pm.gov.au/media/Speech/2007/Speech24394.html%3E [Accessed 2 March 2020].

Howard, J. and Brough, M. (2007) 'Transcript of Prime Minister Hon John Howard MP joint press conference with Hon Mal Brough, Minister for Families, Community Services and Indigenous Affairs', *PM Transcripts: Transcripts from the Prime Ministers of Australia*, [online] 10 July, Available from: https://pmtranscripts.pmc.gov.au/release/transcript-15599 [Accessed 12 December 2020].

Howe, L. (1998) 'Scrounger, worker, beggarman, cheat: the dynamics of unemployment and the politics of resistance in Belfast', *The Journal of the Royal Anthropological Institute*, 4(3): 531–50.

Huang, J., Kim, Y. and Birkenmaier, J. (2016) 'Unemployment and household food hardship in the economic recession', *Public Health Nutrition*, 19(3): 511–9.

Humpage, L. (2015) *Policy Change, Public Attitudes and Social Citizenship: Does Neoliberalism Matter?*, Bristol: The Policy Press.

Humpage, L. (2016) 'Income management in New Zealand and Australia: differently framed but similarly problematic for Indigenous peoples', *Critical Social Policy*, 36(4): 551–71.

Humpage, L. (2018) *Youth Service and Money Management in New Zealand: Preliminary Research Findings*, Auckland: University of Auckland, [online] Available from: http://cdn.auckland.ac.nz/assets/arts/documents/youth-service-and-money-management-in-new-zealand-preliminary-research-findings.pdf [Accessed 18 December 2020].

Humpage, L. and Neuwelt-Kearns, C. (2020) 'Income support in the wake of Covid-19: Survey', [online] Available from: https://www.cpag.org.nz/assets/Covid%2019%20survey%20report%2012%20October%20final.pdf [Accessed 3 February 2021].

Humpage, L. and Moore, C. (2021) *Income Support in the Wake of COVID-19: Interviews*, [online] Available from: https://www.cpag.org.nz/assets/Covid-19%2520INTERVIEW%2520report%2520FINAL%252012%2520April%25202021.docx%2520%25281%2529.pdf [Accessed 20 March 2021].

Humpage, L., Peterie, M., Marston, G., Mendes, P., Bielefeld, S. and Staines, Z. (2020a) *Helping or Harming? Compulsory Income Management in Australia and New Zealand – Summary Report*, Brisbane: School of Social Science, The University of Queensland.

Humpage, L., Staines, Z., Marston, G., Peterie, M., Bielefeld, S. and Mendes, P. (2020b) 'The complexity of convergence: a multi-dimensional analysis of compulsory income management and social investment in New Zealand and Australia', *Policy Studies* [online first], https://doi.org/10.1080/01442872.2020.1783439

Hunter, S. (2015) *Power, Politics and the Emotions: Impossible Governance?*, London: Routledge.

Hynes, M. (2013) 'Reconceptualizing resistance: sociology and the affective dimension of resistance', *The British Journal of Sociology*, 64(4): 559–77.

Hynes, N. (2020) 'Basics Card outage leaves Northern Territory welfare recipients unable to buy food', *ABC News*, [online] 29 December, Available from: https://www.abc.net.au/news/2020-12-29/system-outage-affects-nt-basics-card/13018000 [Accessed 1 February 2021].

Ife, J. (2016) *Community Development in an Uncertain World*, Melbourne: Cambridge University Press.

Immervoll, H. and Scarpetta, S. (2012) 'Activation and employment support policies in OECD countries: an overview of current approaches', *IZA Journal of Labor Policy*, 1(9): 1–20.

Ingles, D., Philips, B. and Stewart, M. (2019) 'A Basic Income for Australia? Exploring Rationale, Design, Distribution and Benefits', *Hawthorn: Analysis and Policy Observatory*, [online] Available from: https://apo.org.au/node/270176?utm_source=APO-view&utm_medium=more-like-this&utm_campaign=resource-mlt [Accessed 12 March 2021].

Jahoda, M., Lazarsfeld, P.F. and Zeisel, H. (1972) *Marienthal: The Sociography of an Unemployed Community*, London: Tavistock.

Jahoda, M. (1981) 'Work, employment, and unemployment: values, theories, and approaches in social research', *American Psychologist*, 36(2): 184–91.

Jahoda, M. (1982) *Employment and Unemployment: A Social-Psychological Analysis*, London: Cambridge University Press.

Jensen, T. (2014) 'Welfare commonsense, poverty porn and doxosophy', *Sociological Research Online*, 19(3), https://journals.sagepub.com/doi/10.5153/sro.3441

Johansson, A. and Vinthagen, S. (2016) 'Dimensions of everyday resistance: an analytical framework', *Critical Sociology*, 42(3): 417–35.

John, P. (2003) 'Is there life after policy streams, advocacy coalitions, and punctuations: using evolutionary theory to explain policy change?', *Policy Studies Journal*, 31(4): 481–98.

Johnston, M. (2015) *Ceduna – How Was It Selected, Who Is in Scope, What Was the Nature of Consultation*, Canberra: Department of Social Services.

Kaiser, T. and Menkhoff, L. (2017), 'Does financial education impact financial literacy and financial behaviour, and if so, when? Policy Research Working Paper, no. 8161', *World Bank Group*, [online] Available from: https://elibrary.worldbank.org/doi/pdf/10.1596/1813-9450-8161 [Accessed 28 October 2020].

Kehoe, J. (2020) 'JobSeeker 'disincentives' for jobless to seek work face review', *Australian Financial Review*, 21 May: 5.

Kempson, E. Finney, A. and Poppe, E. (2017) 'Financial wellbeing: a conceptual model and preliminary analysis', *Oslo and Akershus University College of Applied Sciences*, [online] Available from: https://www.bristol.ac.uk/media-library/sites/geography/pfrc/pfrc1705-financial-well-being-conceptual-model.pdf [Accessed 23 March 2021].

Kidd, D. and McIntosh, K. (2016) 'Social media and social movements', *Sociology Compass*, 10(9): 785–94.

Klapdor, M. and Giuliano, C. (2020) The *Impact* of COVID-19 on JobSeeker Payment *Recipient Numbers* by *Electorate, Research paper series, 2020–21*, Canberra: Parliamentary Library.

Klein, E. (2014) 'Submission by Dr Elise Klein, CAEPR', in E. Klein (ed), *Academic Perspectives on the Forrest Review: Creating Parity*, CAEPR Topic Issue No. 2/2014, Canberra: Centre for Aboriginal Economic Policy Research, [online] Available from: https://openresearch-repository.anu.edu.au/bitstream/1885/114088/1/Topical%20Issue-2_2014.pdf [Accessed 12 December 20].

Klein, E. (2020) 'Settler colonialism in Australia and the Cashless Debit Card', *Social Policy and Administration*, 29 January 2020 [online first], https://doi-org.ezproxy.auckland.ac.nz/10.1111/spol.12576

Klein, E., Cook, K., Maury, M. and Bowey, K. (2021) *Social Security and Time Use During COVID-19*, Melbourne: Swinburne University of Technology & Centre for Excellence in Child and Family Welfare.

Klocker, N. (2004) 'Community antagonism towards asylum seekers in Port Augusta, South Australia', *Australian Geographical Studies*, 42(1): 1–17.

Koefoed, M. (2017) 'Martyrdom and emotional resistance in the case of Northern Kurdistan: hidden and public emotional resistance', *Journal of Political Power*, 10(2): 184–99.

Kokko, K., Pulkkinen, L. and Puustinen, M. (2000) 'Selection into long-term unemployment and its psychological consequences', *International Journal of Behavioral Development*, 24(3): 310–20.

Kopasker, D., Montagna, C. and Bender, K. (2018) 'Economic insecurity: a socioeconomic determinant of mental health', *SSM-Population Health*, 6: 184–94.

Lakoff, G. (2004) *Don't Think of an Elephant; Progressive Values and the Framing Wars: The Progressive Guide to Action*, Vermont: Chelsea Publishing.

Langton, M. (2015) 'Presentation to Community Affairs Legislation Committee', *Hansard*, 11 September: 1–5.

Lattas, A. and Morris, B. (2010) 'The politics of suffering and the politics of anthropology', in J. Altman and M. Hinkson (eds) *Culture Crisis: Anthropology and Politics in Aboriginal Australia*, Sydney: University of New South Wales Press, pp 61–87.

Lea, T. (2008) *Bureaucrats and Bleeding Hearts: Indigenous Health in Northern Australia*, Sydney: UNSW Press.

Lefcourt, H., Martin, R. and Saleh, W. (1984) 'Locus of control and social support: interactive moderators of stress', *Journal of Personality and Social Psychology*, 47(2): 378–89.

Li, T. (2007) *The Will to Improve: Governmentality, Development, and the Practice of Politics*, Durham: Duke University Press.

Lipsky, M. (1980) *Street-level Bureaucracy: Dilemmas of the Individual in Public Services*, New York: Russell Sage Foundation.

Lipsky, M. (2010) *Street-level Bureaucracy, 30th Anniversary Edition: Dilemmas of the Individual in Public Service*, New York: Russell Sage Foundation.

Lister, R. (2004) *Poverty*, Cambridge: Polity Press.

Logie, J. (2012) 'Social Security (Youth Support and Work Focus) Amendment Bill second reading', *New Zealand Parliament*, [online] 13 June, Available from: https://www.parliament.nz/en/pb/hansard-debates/rhr/document/50HansD_20120612_00000028/social-security-youth-support-and-work-focus-amendment [Accessed 2 December 2020].

Logie, J. (2015) 'Social Security (Extension of Young Persons Services and Remedial Matters) Amendment Bill – Second Reading', *Parliament of New Zealand*, [online] Available from: https://www.parliament.nz/en/pb/hansard-debates/rhr/document/51HansD_20160601_00000012/social-security-extension-of-young-persons-services-and [Accessed 10 December 2020].

Logie, J. (2016) Social Security (Extension of Young Persons Services and Remedial Matters) Amendment Bill – In Committee, *New Zealand Parliament*, [online] 14 June, Available from: https://www.parliament.nz/en/pb/hansard-debates/rhr/combined/HansDeb_20160614_20160614_28 [Accessed 14 December 2020].

Lovell, T. (ed) (2007) *(Mis)recognition, Social Inequality and Social Justice: Nancy Fraser and Pierre Bourdieu*, Oxon: Routledge.

Macklin, J. (2009a) 'Social Security and Other Legislation Amendment (Welfare Reform and Reinstatement of Racial Discrimination Act) Bill 2009 second reading', *Parliament of Australia*, [online] 25 November, Available from: http://parlinfo.aph.gov.au/parlInfo/genpdf/chamber/hansardr/2009-11-25/0046/hansard_frag.pdf;fileType=application%2Fpdf [Accessed 14 December 2020].

Macklin, J. (2009b) 'Speech to House of Representatives', *Hansard*, 25 November: 12783–8.

Malenfant, R., LaRue, A. and Vezina, M. (2007) 'Intermittent work and well-being: one foot in the door, one foot out', *Current Sociology*, 55(6): 814–35.

Mandell, L. and Klein, L. (2009) 'The impact of financial literacy education on subsequent financial behaviour', *Journal of Financial Counseling and Planning*, 20(1): 15–24.

Markham, F. and Kerins, S. (2020) *Policy responses to food insecurity in remote Indigenous communities: social security, store pricing and Indigenous food sovereignty*, Canberra: The Australian National University.

Marston, G. and Watts, R. (2003) 'Evidence based policy', *Just Policy: A Journal of Australian Social Policy*, 29: 32–48.

Marston, G. and McDonald, C. (2007) 'Assessing the policy trajectory of welfare reform in Australia', *Benefits*, 15(3): 233–45.

Marston, G. and Zhang, J. (2019) 'Limitations of the Australian social security system', in P. Saunders (ed), *Revisiting Henderson: Poverty, Social Security and Basic Income*, Melbourne: Melbourne University Press, pp 141–162.

Marston, G., McDonald, C. and Bryson, L. (2014) *The Australian Welfare State: Who Benefits Now?*, Melbourne: Palgrave Macmillan Australia.

Marston, G., Zhang, J., Peterie, M., Ramia, G., Patulny, R. and Cooke, E. (2019) 'To move or not to move: mobility decision-making in the context of welfare conditionality and paid employment', *Mobilities*, 14(5): 596–611.

Marston, G., Mendes, P., Bielefeld, S., Peterie, M., Staines, Z. and Roche, S. (2020) *Hidden Costs: An Independent Study into Income Management in Australia*, Brisbane: School of Social Science, The University of Queensland.

Mavromaras, K. Moskos, M. Isherwood, L.M. and Mahuteau, S. (2019a), *Cashless Debit Card Baseline Data Collection in the Goldfields Region: Qualitative Findings*, Canberra: Australian Government Department of Social Services, [online] Available from: https://www.dss.gov.au/sites/default/files/documents/02_2019/cdc_baseline_qualitative_data_collection_-_goldfields_region.pdf [Accessed 3 May 2021].

Mavromaras, K. Moskos, M., Isherwood, L. and Mahuteau, S. (2019b) *Cashless Debit Card Baseline Data Collection in the Bundaberg and Hervey Bay Region: Qualitative Findings*, Adelaide: University of Adelaide.

Mavromaras, K., Moskos, M., Mahuteau, S. and Isherwood, L. (2021) *Evaluation of the Cashless Debit Card in Ceduna, East Kimberley and the Goldfields Region: Consolidated Report*, Adelaide: University of Adelaide.

Maynard-Moody, S. and Musheno, M. (2003) *Cops, Teachers and Counsellors: Stories from the Front Line of Public Service*, Ann Arbor: University of Michigan Press.

Mayors Taskforce for Jobs (2021) 'Youth to Work', *Mayors Taskforce for Jobs*, [online] Available from: https://www.mtfj.co.nz/resources-and-useful-links/youth-to-work/ [Accessed 8 February 2021].

Mays, J., Marston, G. and Tomlinson, J. (eds) (2016) *Prospect for a Basic Income: Perspectives from the Neo-liberal Frontier*, Melbourne: Palgrave MacMillan.

McDonald, C. and Marston, G. (2005) 'Workfare as welfare: governing unemployment in the advanced liberal state', *Critical Social Policy*, 25(3): 374–401.

Mead, L. (ed) (1997) *The New Paternalism: Supervisory Approaches to Poverty*, Washington, DC: Brookings Institution Press.

Mendes, P. (2013) 'Compulsory income management: a critical examination of the emergence of conditional welfare in Australia', *Australian Social Work*, 66(4): 495–510.

Mendes, P. (2018) 'Community as a spray-on solution: a case study of community engagement within the income management programme in Australia', *Community Development Journal*, 53(2): 210–27.

Mendes, P. (2019) 'Top-down paternalism versus bottom-up community development: a case study of compulsory income management programs in Australia', *The International Journal of Community and Social Development*, 1(1): 42–57.

Mendes, P. (2020a) 'Conditionalising the unemployed: why have consecutive Australian governments refused to increase the inadequate Newstart Allowance?', *Australian Journal of Social Issues*, 56(1), DOI: 10.1002/ajs4.140.

Mendes, P. (2020b) 'The Australian Labor Party and compulsory income management: how and why did they reverse their position?', *Social Alternatives*, 39(1): 47–53.

Mendes, P., Waugh, J. and Flynn, C. (2014) 'Income management in Australia: a critical examination of the evidence', *International Journal of Social Welfare*, 23(4): 362–72.

Mendes, P., Roche, S., Marston, G., Peterie, M., Staines, Z. and Humpage, L. (2020) 'The social harms outweigh the benefits: a study of compulsory income management in Greater Shepparton and Playford', *Australian Social Work*, DOI: 10.1080/0312407X.2020.1820536.

Millan, T., Barham, T., Macours, K., Maluccio, J. and Stampani, M. (2019), 'Long-term impacts of conditional cash transfers: review of the evidence', *The World Bank Research Observer*, 34(1): 119–59.

Miller, M., Reichelstein, J., Salas, C. and Zia, B. (2015) 'Can you help someone become financially capable? A meta-analysis of the literature', *World Bank Research Observer*, 30(2): 220–46.

Miller, S.C. (2012) *The Ethics of Need: Agency, Dignity and Obligation*, New York: Routledge.

Ministry of Health (2018) 'Healthy homes initiative – Auckland co-design: testing ideas to make homes warmer and drier: Report on stage two', *New Zealand Ministry of Health*, [online] Available from: https://www.health.govt.nz/publication/healthy-homes-initiative-auckland-codesign-stage2 [Accessed 12 February 2021].

Ministry of Social Development (MSD) (2005) *Youth Transition Services: Lessons for Service Development*, Wellington: Ministry of Social Development.

MSD (2008) *Youth Transition Services: Process and Outcomes Evaluation Final Report*, Wellington: Ministry of Social Development.

MSD (2012a) *Departmental Report: Social Security (Youth Support and Work Focus) Amendment Bill*, 1 May.

MSD (2012b) *Social Security (Youth Support and Work Focus) Amendment Bill – Initial Briefing to Social Services Committee*, 28 March.

MSD (2012c) *Regulatory Impact Statement: Youth Package: Policy Decisions on the Youth Package*, Mackwell, S., nd.

MSD (2015) *Departmental Report to Social Services Committee – Social Security (Extension of Young Persons Services and Remedial Matters) Amendment Bill*, November.

MSD (2017) *Provider – Operational Guidelines Youth Service. Wellington: Ministry of Social Development*, November.

MSD (2019a) *Update on the Review of the Youth Service*, 26 June.

MSD (2019b) *Youth Service Review: Auckland North Workshop*, 28 September.

MSD (2020) 'National benefits', *Parliament of New Zealand*, [online] December, Available from: https://www.msd.govt.nz/about-msd-and-our-work/publications-resources/statistics/benefit/index.html [Accessed 8 December 2020].

MSD (2021a) *Experiences of Money Management in the Youth Service*, Wellington: New Zealand.

MSD (2021b) *Response to Inquiry under the Official Information Act 1982*, unpublished email correspondence with Dr Bielefeld, 12 March.

Moffatt, K. (2018) General Manager, Service and Contracts Management, Ministry of Social Development, unpublished email correspondence, 11 October.

Momsen, K. (2021) *Experiences of Money Management in the Youth Service*, Wellington: Ministry of Social Development.

Moodie, N., Roost, F. and Dommers, E. (2014) *My Moola: Report from the Evaluation of an Indigenous Financial Literacy Program*, Melbourne: First Nations Foundation.

Moreton-Robinson, A. (2000) *Talking Up to the White Woman: Indigenous Women and Feminism*, Brisbane: University of Queensland Press.

Moreton-Robinson, A. (2015) *The White Possessive: Property, Power, and Indigenous Sovereignty*, Minnesota: University of Minnesota Press.

Morris, A. and Wilson, S. (2014) 'Struggling on the Newstart unemployment benefit in Australia: the experience of a neoliberal form of employment assistance', *The Economic and Labour Relations Review*, 25(2): 202–21.

Morrison, S. (2020) Address, National Press Club, [online] Available from: https://www.pm.gov.au/media/address-national-press-club-260520 [Accessed 10 March 2021].

Mules, R., Pekepo, C. and Beaton, S. (2017) 'Co-design and community development: kōrero and insights from Māori co-designers', *Community Research*, [online] 19 October, http://www.communityresearch.org.nz/webinar-codesign-community-development-korero-insightsmaori-co-designers/ [Accessed 2 February 2021].

National Congress of Australia's First Peoples (2011) 'Statement to the Australian Government on the Northern Territory Intervention', *National Congress of Australia's First Peoples*, [online] Available from: http://www.nationalcongress.com.au/wpcontent/uploads/2011/10/CongressStatementNTER.pdf [Accessed 12 December 2020].

National Party and ACT Party (2011) 'Confidence and Supply Agreement', *Scoop: Independent News*, [online] Available from: https://img.scoop.co.nz/media/pdfs/1112/NationalACT_Confidence_and_Supply_Agreement.pdf [Accessed 9 December 2020].

National Rural Health Alliance (2017) *Poverty in Rural and Remote Australia*, Deakin: National Rural Health Alliance.

Neuwelt-Kearns, C. and Asher, I. (2020) *What Happened to 'Welfare Overhaul'? A Stocktake of Implementation of the Welfare Expert Advisory Group's 2019 Recommendations*, Auckland: Child Poverty Action Group.

New Economics Foundation (2008) *Co-production: A Manifesto for Growing the Core Economy*, London: NEF.

New Zealand Council of Trade Unions (NZCTU) (2013) *Under Pressure: A Detailed Report into Insecure Work in New Zealand*, Wellington: NZCTU.

Ngā Puhi Iwi Social Services (2019) 'Maharu: Ngā Puhi Iwi Social Services', *YouTube*, [video] Available from: https://www.youtube.com/watch?v=B4Ziond_zQ0 [Accessed 23 April 2021].

Ngāi Tūhoe Service Management Plan (2012) *Ngāi Tūhoe Service Management Plan*, Wellington: Ministry of Social Development, Ministry of Business, Innovation and Employment and Ministry of Education, [online] Available from: https://issuu.com/teurutaumatua/docs/tuhoe_-_smp_publication?e=18309847/31075420 [Accessed 19 May 2021].

Northern Territory Board of Inquiry into the Protection of Aboriginal Children from Sexual Abuse (2007) *Ampe akelyernemane meke mekarle: 'Little Children are Sacred'*, Darwin: Northern Territory Government.

O'Connell, A. (2009) 'Evaluating the effectiveness of financial education programmes', *OECD Journal*, 2008(3): 9–51.

OECD (2012) 'Programme for International Student Assessment (PISA): results from PISA 2012 Financial Literacy', *OECD*, [online] Available from: https://www.oecd.org/newzealand/PISA%202012%20country%20note%20FINLIT_NZ.pdf [Accessed 15 October 2020].

OECD (2017) 'G20/OECD INFE report on adult financial literacy in G20 countries', *OECD*, [online] Available from: http://www.oecd.org/daf/fin/financial-education/G20-OECD-INFE-report-adult-financial-literacy-in-G20-countries.pdf [Accessed 14 April 2021].

OECD (2020) 'OECD/INFE 2020 international survey of adult financial literacy', *OECD*, [online] Available from: https://www.oecd.org/financial/education/oecd-infe-2020-international-survey-of-adult-financial-literacy.pdf [Accessed 10 April 2021].

Office of the Minister of Social Development (2011) 'Policy decisions on the youth package', *Cabinet paper*, 15 December.

Office of the Prime Minister (OPM) (2020) *Ministerial Statement*, 8 April, Canberra: Attorney General.

Olin Wright, E. (2010) *Envisioning Real Utopias*, London: Verso.

Orima Research (2017) *Cashless Debit Card Trial Evaluation Final Report*, Canberra: Australian Government Department of Social Services.

Page, L. and Pande, R. (2018) 'Ending global poverty: why money isn't enough', *The Journal of Economic Perspectives*, 32(4): 173–200.

Paradies, Y. and Cunningham, J. (2009) 'Experiences of racism among urban Indigenous Australians: findings from the DRUID study', *Ethnic and Racial Studies*, 32(3): 548–73.

Parliament of Australia (2016) *Senate Standing Committee on Legal and Constitutional Affairs, Inquiry into Stolen Wages*, Canberra: Parliament of Australia.

Parliament of Australia (2019) *Explanatory Memorandum for the Social Security (Administration) Amendment (Income Management to Cashless Debit Card Transition) Bill 2019*, Canberra: Parliament of Australia.

Parliament of Queensland (2008) Family Responsibilities Commission Act 2008 [Qld], Parliament of Queensland: Brisbane, [online] Available from: https://www.legislation.qld.gov.au/view/pdf/inforce/2014-07-01/act-2008-009 [Accessed 12 December 2021]

Parliamentary Joint Committee on Human Rights (2013) 'Examination of Legislation in Accordance with the Human Rights (Parliamentary Scrutiny) Act 2011: Stronger Futures in the Northern Territory Act 2012 and Related Legislation', Canberra: Parliament of Australia.

Parliamentary Joint Committee on Human Rights (2016) *2016 Review of Stronger Futures measures*, Canberra: Commonwealth of Australia.

Parmjeet P. (2015) 'Social Security (Extension of Young Persons Services and Remedial Matters) Amendment Bill – First Reading', *Parliament of New Zealand*, [online] 21 July, Available from: https://www.parliament.nz/en/pb/hansard-debates/rhr/document/51HansD_20150723_00000024/social-security-extension-of-young-persons-services-and [Accessed 12 December 2020].

Parsons, C. (2002) 'Showing ideas as causes: the origins of the European Union', *International Organization,* 56(1): 47–84.

Patrick, R. (2016) 'Living with and responding to the 'scrounger' narrative in the UK: exploring everyday strategies of acceptance, resistance and deflection', *Journal of Poverty and Social Justice*, 24(3): 245–59.

Patrick, R. (2017) *For Whose Benefit? The Everyday Realities of Welfare Reform*, Bristol: Policy Press.

Paul, K.I., Geithner, E. and Moser, K. (2009) 'Latent deprivation among people who are employed, unemployed, or out of the labor force', *Journal of Psychology*, 143(5): 477–91.

Pearson, N. (2000) *Our Right to Take Responsibility*, Cairns: Noel Pearson and Associates.

Pearson, N. (2008) 'Feed the children', *The Australian*, 28 April: 8.

Peck, J. and Theodore, N. (2015) *Fast Policy: Experimental Statecraft at the Thresholds of Neoliberalism*, Minneapolis: University of Minnesota Press.

Pedersen, A., Watt, S. and Hansen, S. (2006) 'The role of false beliefs in the community's and the federal government's attitudes towards Australian asylum seekers', *Australian Journal of Social Issues*, 41(1): 105–24.

Peel, M. (2003) *The Lowest Rung: Voices of Australian Poverty*, Melbourne: Cambridge University Press.

Perry, V. and Morris, M. (2005) 'Who is in control? The role of self-perception, knowledge and income in explaining consumer financial behaviour', *The Journal of Consumer Affairs*, 39(2): 299–313.

Peterie, M. (2017) 'Docility and desert: government discourses of compassion in Australia's asylum seeker debate', *Journal of Sociology*, 53(2): 351–66.

Peterie, M. (2019) 'Compassion and power: (emotional) reflexivity in asylum seeker friendship programmes', in R. Patulny, A. Bellocchi, R.E. Olson, S. Khorana, J. McKenzie and M. Peterie (eds) *Emotions in Late Modernity*, Oxford: Routledge, pp 282–96.

Peterie, M., Ramia, G., Marston, G. and Patulny, R. (2019a) 'Emotional compliance and emotion as resistance: shame and anger among the long-term unemployed', *Work, Employment and Society*, 33(5): 794–811.

Peterie, M., Ramia, G., Marston, G. and Patulny, R. (2019b) 'Social isolation as stigma-management: explaining long-term unemployed people's "failure" to network', *Sociology*, 53(6): 1043–60.

Peterie, M., Bielefeld, S., Marston, G., Mendes, P. and Humpage, L. (2020) 'Compulsory income management: combatting or compounding the underlying causes of homelessness?', *Australian Journal of Social Issues*, 55(1): 61–72.

Peterie, M., Marston, G., Humpage, L., Mendes, P., Bielefeld, S. and Staines, Z. (2021) 'The trope of the vulnerable child in conditional welfare discourses: a comparative study of Australia and New Zealand', *Journal of Sociology*, [online first], https://journals.sagepub.com/doi/10.1177/14407833211008984

Phillips, B. Gray. M. & Biddle (2020) *COVID-19 JobKeeper and JobSeeker Impacts on Poverty and Housing Stress Under Current and Alternative Economic and Policy Scenarios*, Canberra: Australian National University, Centre for Social Research and Methods, [online] Available from: https://csrm.cass.anu.edu.au/sites/default/files/docs/2020/8/Impact_of_Covid19_JobKeeper_and_Jobeeker_measures_on_Poverty_and_Financial_Stress_FINAL.pdf [Accessed 12 March 2021].

Pinto, L. (2012), 'One size does not fit all: conceptual concerns and moral imperatives surrounding gender-inclusive financial literacy education', *Citizenship, Social and Economics Education*, 11(3): 177–88.

Pinto, L. and Coulson, E. (2011) 'Social justice and the gender politics of financial literacy education', *Canadian Journal of the Association for Curriculum Studies*, 9(2): 54–85.

Pitts, H. (2021) *A Revaluation of Value: The Politics of Value Between Populism and Pandemic*, Bristol: Bristol University Press, [online] Available from: https://futuresofwork.co.uk/2021/03/16/a-revaluation-of-value-the-politics-of-value-between-populism-and-pandemic/ [Accessed 14 March 2021].

Pollard, C., Booth, S., Louth, J., Mackenzie, C. and Goodwin-Smith, I. (2020) '"I'd be sleeping in the park, I reckon": lived experience of using financial counselling services in South Australia', *Economic Papers*, 39(4): 353–66.

Porter, C. and Tudge, A. (2017) 'Cashless Debit Card extended following positive independent evaluation', [media release] 14 March, Available from: https://formerministers.dss.gov.au/17390/cashless-debit-card-extended-following-positive-independent-evaluation/ [Accessed 12 February 2021].

Power, K. (2020) 'The COVID-19 pandemic has increased the care burden of women and families', *Sustainability: Science, Practice and Policy*, 16(1): 61–73.

Prasad, R. (2012) 'Social Security (Youth Support and Work Focus) Amendment Bill – In Committee, *Parliament of New Zealand*, [online] 18 July, Available from: https://www.parliament.nz/en/pb/hansard-debates/rhr/document/50HansD_20120718_00000012/social-security-youth-support-and-work-focus-amendment [Accessed 7 December 2020].

Prawitz, A. and Cohart, J. (2016) 'Financial management competency, financial resources, locus of control and financial wellness', *Journal of Financial Counselling and Planning*, 27(2): 142–57.

Preston, A. (2020) *Financial Literacy in Australia: Insights from HILDA Data*, Perth: University of Western Australia.

Ramia, G. (2020) *Governing Social Protection in the Long Term: Social Policy and Employment Relations in Australia and New Zealand*, London: Palgrave Macmillan.

Rantakeisu, U., Starrin, B. and Hagquist, C. (1999) 'Financial hardship and shame: a tentative model to understand the social and health effects of unemployment', *British Journal of Social Work*, 29(6): 877–901.

RNZ (2020) New Service to help Jobseekers Opens, [online] Available from: https://www.rnz.co.nz/news/business/423233/new-service-to-help-jobseekers-opens [Accessed 20 March 2021].

Roberts, M. (2020) *Hansard of the Northern Australia Agenda Select Committee, 15 December*, Canberra: Parliament of Australia.

Robson, S. (2021) Budget 2021: Benefits to increase by up to $55 per week, [online] Available from: https://www.rnz.co.nz/news/budget-2021/442987/budget-2021-benefits-to-increase-by-up-to-55-a-week [Accessed 10 November 2021].

Roche, S., Mendes, P., Marston, G., Bielefeld, S., Peterie, M., Staines, Z. and Humpage, L. (2021) 'Examining the consequences of welfare conditionality: a case study of compulsory income management in the regional community of Ceduna, Australia', *Social Policy and Society*, doi:10.1017/S1474746421000063.

Rohde, N., Tang, K., Osberg, L. and Rao, P. (2015) 'Economic insecurity in Australia: who is feeling the pinch and how?', *Economic Record*, 91(292): 1–15.

Rohde, N., Tang, K., Osberg, L. and Rao, P. (2016) 'The effect of economic insecurity on mental health: recent evidence from Australian panel data', *Social Science & Medicine*, 151: 250–8.

Rose, N. (1991) 'Governing by numbers: figuring out democracy', *Accounting, Organisations and Society*, 16(7): 673–92.

Rose, N. (1999) *Powers of Freedom: Reframing Political Thought*, Cambridge: Cambridge University Press.

Rotter, J. (1966) 'Generalized expectancies for internal versus external control of reinforcement', *Psychological Monographs: General and Applied*, 80(1): 1–28.

Roy, A. (2020) 'Arundhati Roy: the pandemic is a portal', *Financial Times*, [online] Available from: https://www.ft.com/content/10d8f5e8-74eb-11ea-95fe-fcd274e920ca [Accessed 14 March 2021].

Rush, M. and Keenan, M. (2014) 'The social politics of social work: anti-oppressive social work dilemmas in twenty-first century welfare regimes', *The British Journal of Social Work*, 44: 1436–53.

Ruston, A. (2019) 'Joint media release: expanding the cashless welfare in Hervey Bay and Bundaberg', *Anne Ruston*, [online] 11 September, Available from: https://www.anneruston.com.au/joint_media_release_expanding_the_cashless_welfare_in_hervey_bay_and_bundaberg [Accessed 8 March 2021].

Ruston, A. (2020) 'Cashless Debit Card update', *Department of Social Services*, [online] 5 May, Available from: https://ministers.dss.gov.au/media-releases/5801 [Accessed 23 March 2021].

Ryon, H. and Gleason, M. (2013) 'The role of locus of control in daily life', *Personality and Social Psychology Bulletin*, 40(1): 121–31.

Sabin, M. (2012) 'Social Security (Youth Support and Work Focus) Amendment Bill, second reading', *Parliament of New Zealand*, [online] 12 June, Available from: https://www.parliament.nz/en/pb/hansard-debates/rhr/document/50HansD_20120612/volume-680-week-13-tuesday-12-june-2012 [Accessed 10 Month 2020].

St Vincent de Paul Society (2013) *Two Australias: A Report on Poverty in the Land of Plenty*, [online], Available from: https://www.vinnies.org.au/icms_docs/257154_169073_Two_Australias_Report_on_Poverty.pdf [Accessed 17 August 2020].

Sanders, W. (2012) 'Coombs' bastard child: the troubled life of CDEP', *Australian Journal of Public Administration*, 71(4): 371–91.

Sandler, I. and Lakey, B. (1982) 'Locus of control as a stress moderator: the role of control perceptions and social support', *American Journal of Community Psychology*, 10: 65–80.

Schmitt, C. and Starke, P. (2011) 'Explaining convergence of OECD welfare states: a conditional approach', *Journal of European Social Policy*, 21(2): 120–35.

Schnitzlein, D. and Stephani, J. (2016) 'Locus of control and low-wage mobility', *Journal of Economic Psychology*, 53: 164–77.

Schram, S., Soss, S. and Fording, R. (eds) (2003) *Race and the Politics of Welfare Reform*, Michigan: University of Michigan Press.

Scott, J.C. (1985) *Weapons of the Weak: Everyday Forms of Peasant Resistance*, New Haven and London: Yale University Press.

Scott, J.C. (1986) 'Everyday forms of peasant resistance', *The Journal of Peasant Studies*, 13(2): 5–35.

Scott, J.C. (1989) 'Everyday forms of resistance', *The Copenhagen Journal of Asian Studies*, 4(1): 33–62.

Scott, J.C. (1990) *Domination and the Arts of Resistance: Hidden Transcripts*, New Haven: Yale University Press.

Scott, J.C., Higginson, A., Staines, Z., Zhen, L., Ryan, V. and Lauchs, M. (2018) *Strategic Review of Cape York Income Management*, Canberra: Department of Social Services.

Secretariat of National Aboriginal and Islander Child Care (2008) *Submission to Northern Territory Emergency Response Review Board*, Melbourne: Secretariat of National Aboriginal and Islander Child Care.

Sennett, R. (2003) *Respect in a World of Inequality*, New York: WW Norton.

Sepuloni, C. (2015a) 'Social Security (Extension of Young Persons Services and Remedial Matters) Amendment Bill – First Reading', *Parliament of New Zealand*, [online] 23 July, Available from: https://www.parliament.nz/en/pb/hansard-debates/rhr/document/51HansD_20150723_00000024/social-security-extension-of-young-persons-services-and [Accessed 10 December 2020].

Sepuloni, C. (2015b) 'Social Security (Extension of Young Persons Services and Remedial Matters) Amendment Bill – In Committee', *Parliament of New Zealand*, [online] 14 June, Available from: https://www.parliament.nz/en/pb/hansard-debates/rhr/combined/HansDeb_20160614_20160614_28 [Accessed 12 December 2020].

Shirky, C. (2008) *Here Comes Everybody: The Power of Organizing without Organizations*, London: Allen Lane.

Siewert, R. (2010) 'Speech to Senate', *Hansard*, 21 June: 3831–4.

Smith, R. (1985) '"Bitterness, shame, emptiness, waste": an introduction to unemployment and health', *British Medical Journal*, 291(6501): 1024–7.

Social Care Institute for Excellence (2015) *Co-production in Social Care: What It Is and How to Do It*, London: SCIE.

Social Prosperity Network (2017) *Social Prosperity for the Future: A Proposal for Universal Basic Services*, London: Institute for Global Prosperity.

Social Services Committee (2012) 'Social Security (Youth Support and Work Focus) Amendment Bill Government Bill', *New Zealand Parliament*, [online] Available from: https://www.parliament.nz/resource/en-NZ/50DBSCH_SCR5479_1/2912baf137477ef26e8d205f344132c13a34584f [Accessed 7 December 2020].

Soss, S. Fording, R. and Schram, S. (2011) *Disciplining the Poor: Neoliberal Paternalism and the Persistent Power of Race*, Chicago: Chicago University Press.

Sourdin, T. and Burstyner, N. (2014) 'Justice delayed is justice denied', *Victoria University Law and Justice Journal*, 4: 46–60.

Spies-Butcher, B. and Chester, L. (2014) 'Marketisation and the dual welfare state: neoliberalism and inequality in Australia', *The Economic and Labour Relations Review*, 25(2): 185–201.

Staines, Z., Marston, G., Bielefeld, S., Humpage, L., Mendes, P. and Peterie, M. (2020a) 'Governing poverty: Compulsory Income Management and Crime in Australia', *Critical Criminology*, [online first] https://doi.org/10.1007/s10612-020-09532-2

Staines, Z., Moore, C., Marston, G. and Humpage, L. (2020b) 'Big data and poverty governance under Australia and Aotearoa/New Zealand's "social investment" policies', *Australian Journal of Social Issues*, [online first] https://doi.org/10.1002/ajs4.129

Staines, Z. and Zahnow, R. (2021) 'Exploring the politics of strain: crime and welfare in remote Indigenous Australia', *Social Policy & Administration*, doi:10.1111/spol.12778.

Stam, K., Sieben, I., Verbakel, E. and de Graaf, P.M. (2016) 'Employment status and subjective well-being: the role of the social norm to work', *Work, Employment and Society*, 30(2): 309–33.

Standing, G. (2011) *The Precariat: The New Dangerous Class*, London: Bloomsbury Academic.

Statistics New Zealand (2019) '2018 Census Population and Dwelling Counts', *Statistics New Zealand*, [online] 23 September, Available from: https://www.stats.govt.nz/information-releases/2018-census-population-and-dwelling-counts [Accessed 15 January 2021].

Stephens, M. (2015) 'To work out their own salvation': Māori constitutionalism and the quest for welfare', *Victoria University of Wellington Law Review* 46(3): 907–93.

Stiglitz, J., Sen, A. and Fitoussi, J.P. (2009) *Report by the Commission on the Measurement of Economic Performance and Social Progress*, Paris: Commission on the Measurement of Economic Performance and Social Progress.

Stone, D. (2001) *Policy Paradox: The Art of Political Decision Making*, New York: W.W. Norton.

Stone, D. (2017) 'Understanding the transfer of policy failure: bricolage, experimentalism and translation', *Policy & Politics,* 45(1): 55–70.

Strategic Pay (2020) 'Understanding pay equity and analysing the gender pay gap in New Zealand', [online] Available from: https://www.hcamag.com/nz/news/general/overall-gender-pay-gap-is-17.7-in-nz/232375 [Accessed 18 December 2020].

Sullivan, J. (2013) *Media Audiences: Effects, Users, Institutions, and Power*, California: SAGE.

Sutton, E., Pemberton, S., Fahmy, E. and Tamiya, Y. (2014) 'Stigma, shame and experience of poverty in Japan and the United Kingdom', *Social Policy & Society*, 13(1): 143–54.

Taskforce on Whānau-centred Initiatives (2010) *Whānau Ora: Report of the Taskforce on Whānau-centred Initiatives*, Wellington: Ministry of Social Development.

Taylor-Gooby, P. (2013) 'Why do people stigmatise the poor at a time of rapidly increasing inequality, and what can be done about it?', *The Political Quarterly*, 84(1): 31–42.

Taylor, P. (2020) 'Covid money buying 'grog chaos and gambling'. *The Australian*, 26 August.

Te Arawhiti (nd) 'Building closer partnerships with Māori', *Te Arawhiti: The Office for Māori Crown Relations*, [online] Available from: https://www.tearawhiti.govt.nz/assets/Tools-and-Resources/Building-closer-partnerships-with-Maori-Principles.pdf [Accessed 10 February 2021].

Te Morenga, L., Pekepo, C., Corrigan, C., Matoe, L., Mules, R., Goodwin, D., Dymus, J., Tunks, M., Grey, J., Humphrey, G., Jull, A., Whittaker, R., Verbiest, M., Firestone, R. and Ni Mhurchu, C. (2018) 'Co-designing an mHealth tool in the Aotearoa New Zealand Māori community with a "Kaupapa Māori" approach', *AlterNative*, 14(1), 90–9.

Tennant, D. (2012) 'How place fares in place-based solutions', *Insight*, 7: 34–5.

Thaler, R. and Sunstein, C. (2008) *Nudge: Improving Decisions About Health, Wealth and Happiness* , Yale: Yale University Press.

Thomas, M. and Buckmaster, T. (2010) 'Paternalism in social policy: when is it justifiable?', *Parliament of Australia*, [online] Available from: https://www.aph.gov.au/About_Parliament/Parliamentary_Departments/Parliamentary_Library/pubs/rp/rp1011/11rp08 [Accessed 22 December 2020].

Tilly, C. (ed) (1999) *Citizenship, Identity and Social History*, Cambridge: Cambridge University Press.

Tolley, A. (2015) 'Social Security (Extension of Young Persons Services and Remedial Matters) Amendment Bill – First Reading', *Parliament of New Zealand*, [online] 23 July, Available from: https://www.parliament.nz/en/pb/hansard-debates/rhr/document/51HansD_20150723_00000024/social-security-extension-of-young-persons-services-and [Accessed 9 December 2020].

Torrie, R. and Baillie, R. (2017) *Frameworks and Approaches for Building the Financial Capability of New Zealanders Experiencing Hardship: What the Literature Says*, Wellington: Ministry of Social Development.

Tudge, A. (2015) 'Interview with Leon Compton', *ABC Radio Hobart*, 23 March.

Tufekci, Z. and Wilson, C. (2012) 'Social media and the decision to participate in political protest: observations from Tahrir Square', *Journal of Communication*, 62: 363–79.

Turnbull, M. (2017a) *A Bigger Picture*, Melbourne: Hardie Grant Books.

Turnbull, M. (2017b) 'Cashless welfare card for WA Goldfields', *Australian Government, Department of the Prime Minister and Cabinet, PM Transcripts, Transcripts from the Prime Ministers of Australia*, [Media Release] 1 September, Available from: https://pmtranscripts.pmc.gov.au/release/transcript-41153 [Accessed 21 October 2020].

Tyler, T. (2006) *Why People Obey the Law*, Princeton: Princeton University Press.

Uluru Statement from the Heart (2017) 'The Uluru Statement', *Uluru Statement from the Heart*, [online] Available from https://ulurustatement.org/ [Accessed 15 December 2020].

van Dijk, T.A. (1993) *Elite Discourse and Racism*, Thousand Oaks: Sage Publications.

Van Parijs, P. (1997) *Real Freedom for All: What (if Anything) Can Justify Capitalism?*, Oxford: Oxford University Press.

Vetter, S., Endrass, J., Schweizer, I., Hsun-Mei, T., Rossler, W. and Gallo, W.T. (2006) 'The effects of economic deprivation on psychological well-being among the working population of Switzerland', *BMC Public Health*, 6(223): 1–10.

Vinokur, A.D. and Schul, Y. (2002) 'The web of coping resources and pathways to reemployment following a job loss', *Journal of Occupational Health Psychology*, 7(1): 68–83.

von Sturmer, J. and Le Marseny, S. (2012) *Living Under the Family Responsibilities Commission: Experience and Testimony – 'Speaking Straight, Speaking from the Heart'*, Canberra: Department of Social Services.

Wacquant, L. (2009) *Punishing the Poor: The Neoliberal Government of Social Insecurity*, Durham: Duke University Press.

Walker, R. (2014) *The Shame of Poverty*, Oxford: Oxford University Press.

Walker, R., Bantebya Kyomuhendo, G., Chase, E., Choudhry, S., Gubrium, E.K., Yongmie, J., Lødemel, N.I., Mathew, L., Mwiine, A., Pellissery, S. and Ming, Y. (2013) 'Poverty in global perspective: is shame a common denominator?' *Journal of Social Policy*, 42(2): 215–33.

Wanberg, C.R. (2012) 'The individual experience of unemployment', *Annual Review of Psychology* 63: 369–96.

Waters, C. (2020) 'It's not money for jam': staff refusing to come to work but demanding JobKeeper payments', *Sydney Morning Herald*, 27 April: 7.

Watts, B. and Fitzpatrick, S. (2018) *Welfare Conditionality*, London: Routledge.

Wehipeihana, N., Were, L., Goodwin, D. and Pipi., K. (2018) *Addressing the Challenges of Young Māori Women Who Smoke: A Developmental Evaluation of the Phase Two Demonstration Project – Evaluation Report*, Wellington: Ministry of Health.

Weinstein, N. and Stone, D.N. (2018) 'Need depriving effects of financial insecurity: implications for well-being and financial behaviors', *Journal of Experimental Psychology*, 147(10): 1503–20.

Weeks, K. (2011) *The Problem with Work: Feminims, Marxism, Antiwork Politics and Postwork Imaginaries*, Durham: Duke University Press.

Welfare Expert Advisory Group (2019) *Whakamana Tāngata – Restoring Dignity to Social Security in New Zealand*, Wellington: Welfare Expert Advisory Group.

Welfare Working Group (2010a) *Reducing Long-term Benefit Dependency: The Issues – Detailed Paper*, Wellington: Welfare Working Group.

Welfare Working Group (2010b) *Reducing Long-term Benefit Dependency: The Options*, Wellington: Welfare Working Group.

Welfare Working Group (2011) *Reducing Long-term Benefit Dependency: Recommendations*, Wellington: Welfare Working Group.

Whiteford, P. (2019) 'Is Newstart really the pacesetter Scott Morrison says it is', *Inside Story*, [online] Available from: https://insidestory.org.au/is-newstart-the-pace-setter-scott-morrison-says-it-is/?fbclid=IwAR0B2Z9OJfQQ3gVKh1IsLxgGfqSbsV5uf3XwhgZ_5LqvOeEWgp1T7LE-szc [Accessed 15 March 2021].

Whiteford, P. and Bradbury, B. (2021) 'The $50 boost to JobSeeker will take Australia's payment from the lowest in the OECD to the second lowest after Greece', *The Conversation*, [online] Available from: https://theconversation.com/the-50-boost-to-jobseeker-will-take-australias-payment-from-the-lowest-in-the-oecd-to-the-second-lowest-after-greece-155739 [Accessed 14 March 2021].

Wilcock, S. (2017) 'Social security administration: producing poverty and punishment', in A. Durbach, B. Edgeworth and V. Sentas (eds), *Law and Poverty in Australia*. Sydney, NSW: The Federation Press, pp 199–213.

Williams, F. (1999) 'Good enough principles for welfare', *Journal of Social Policy*, 28(4): 667–87.

Williams, T. (2007) 'Empowerment of whom and for what? Financial literacy education and the new regulation of consumer financial services', *Law & Policy*, 29(2): 226–56.

Willis, L. (2008) 'Against financial-literacy education', *Iowa Law Review*, 94(1): 197–286.

Willis, L. (2009) 'Evidence and ideology in assessing the effectiveness of financial literacy education', *San Diego Law Review*, 46(2): 415–58.

Wilson, L. (2015) 'Workplace links needed to get young people into jobs: Dale Williams', *Stuff*, [online] 30 July, Available from: https://www.stuff.co.nz/waikato-times/news/70685766/workplace-links-needed-to-get-young-people-into-jobs-dale-williams [Accessed 10 March 2021].

Wood, P. (2016) 'Spending habits of Maori women', *Westpac Massey Fin-Ed Centre*, [online] Available from: https://www.massey.ac.nz/massey/fms/Colleges/College%20of%20Business/School%20of%20Economics%20&%20Finance/FinEd/Research/188803_A4_Copy.pdf [Accessed 12 February 2021].

Woodward, K. (2004) 'Calculating compassion', in L. Berlant (ed) *Compassion: The Culture and Politics of an Emotion*, New York: Routledge, pp 34–49.

Work and Income (2020a) 'Money management for youth clients', *New Zealand Government*, [online] Available from: https://www.workandincome.govt.nz/on-a-benefit/payments/money-management-youth.html [Accessed 3 February 2021].

Work and Income (2020b) 'Payment cards', *New Zealand Government*, [online] Available from: https://www.workandincome.govt.nz/on-a-benefit/payments/payment-cards.html [Accessed 4 February 2021].

Work and Income (2020c) 'Using your payment card', *New Zealand Government*, [online] Available from: https://www.workandincome.govt.nz/on-a-benefit/payments/using-your-payment-card.html#null [Accessed 4 February 2021].

Work and Income (2020d) 'Covid 19 income relief: payment or a benefit', *New Zealand Government*, [online] Available from: https://www.workandincome.govt.nz/covid-19/income-relief-payment/better-off.html [Accessed 22 March 2021].

Wright, S. (2016) 'Conceptualising the active welfare subject: welfare reform in discourse, policy and lived experience', *Policy and Politics*, 44(2): 323–44.

Yeates, N. and Amaya, A. (2018) 'Making social policy internationally: a participatory research perspective', in P. Beresford and S. Carr (eds) *Social Policy First Hand: An International Introduction to Participatory Welfare*, Bristol: Policy Press, pp 147–60.

Young, I.M. (2011) *Justice and the Politics of Difference*, Princeton and Oxford: Princeton University Press.

Index

D